"Friction with the Market"

Northampton, October 28th 1864

Dear T. S. — I rec'd. your two letters with great pleasure. The news contained in the first was very welcome altho' as you say, "not unmingled with misfortune." But I suppose I ought to be thankful for so much and not grumble that it is so little. One of these days we shall have certain persons *on* their *knees*, imploring for contributions. Thus:

It was very kind altho' not more so than I had a right to expect, of you, to write me a 2d time. The weather is dreadful — a

A proud author whose work cannot be bought cheaply by the *Atlantic Monthly:* a youthful sketch (1864) by Henry James illustrates the professional author's stance in the literary marketplace. "One of these days," he wrote to T. S. Perry, "we shall have certain persons *on their knees,* imploring for contributions."

"Friction with the Market"

HENRY JAMES AND THE PROFESSION OF AUTHORSHIP

MICHAEL ANESKO

New York Oxford
OXFORD UNIVERSITY PRESS
1986

Oxford University Press

Oxford New York Toronto
Dehli Bombay Calcutta Madras Karachi
Petaling Jaya Singapore Hong Kong Tokyo
Nairobi Dar es Salaam Cape Town
Melbourne Auckland

and associated companies in
Beirut Berlin Ibadan Nicosia

Published by Oxford University Press, Inc.,
200 Madison Avenue, New York, New York 10016

Library of Congress Cataloging-in-Publication Data
Anesko, Michael.
"Friction with the market."
Bibliography: p. Includes index.
1. James, Henry, 1843–1916—Authorship.
2. James, Henry, 1843–1916—Criticism and interpretation.
3. Authorship—Social aspects. 4. Authorship— Economic aspects. 5. Authors and publishers.
6. Authors and readers. I. Title. II. Title: Henry James
and the profession of authorship.
PS2127.A9A5 1986813'.4 85-31041
ISBN 0-19-504034-1

Frontispiece: Reproduced by permission of
the William R. Perkins Library, Duke University

Following page 39: Reproduced by permission of Macmillan Publishers Ltd. and the British Library
(Add. MS. 54931, ff. 37 & 37v).

Following page 83: Reproduced by permission of Houghton Mifflin Company
and the Houghton Library, Harvard University

2 4 6 8 10 9 7 5 3 1

Printed in the United States of America
on acid-free paper

This book is for
Margaret

Preface

Ever since the New Criticism began to explore the "poetics" of fiction, we have been in danger of ignoring the fact that novelists write to be purchased and read. This has been particularly true in the case of Henry James, whose twentieth-century revival largely coincided with the evolution of modernist sensibility. The Master's great and often difficult works have often seemed to align him with "art" rather than "the world," and most of James's autobiographical writings, as well as the testimony of his acolytes, reinforce the impression that he wrote exclusively from within the ivory tower (the title, incidentally, of his last, unfinished novel). Given the limited nature of his audience, James had every reason to subscribe to this romantic archetype of the artist's existence; but literary historians have fewer excuses for doing so. For too long we have taken James at his word, accepted uncritically his idealized (and, occasionally, melodramatic) portrait of the artist. Abundant evidence exists to show that James was continually engaged in an active, if ambivalent, dialogue with "the world," and that his finished works were shaped not merely by the imagination alone, but by a constant and lively "friction with the market."

The study that follows attempts to present this evidence, much of which is drawn from sources that have previously gone unexamined—publishers' records, correspondence between James and his editors, and documents pertaining to the novelist's literary income. A reconsideration of the fiction in tandem with this new material reveals many suggestive links between the operation of the marketplace and the working of James's "grasping imagination." What emerges is an essay in the sociology of literature, an attempt to reconstruct the social and economic context of the production of fiction, and to bring that reconstruction to bear upon the interpretation of one author's work. As such, this book cannot easily be classified either as literary criticism or literary history, and I have deliberately resisted the advice of some readers to make it look more like one or the other. Given the nature of the sources upon which my interpretation depends, such a distinction strikes me as artificial and perhaps even a little misleading.

One easily can be misled by other distinctions, however, especially the subtle kinds that multiply when one tries to state explicitly what is meant by "the profession of authorship" or literary "success." Both these ideas can be used in a number of shifting senses (not all of them laudable), and James himself did not always stand in a consistent relation to them. A "professional" writer lives, of course, by selling his wares; but the term also carries with it the suggestion that such a writer views his craft predominantly as a product of technical expertise rather than inspiration and is willing to accept the market as the primary arbiter of literary value. "Success" (on these terms) can be measured quite simply in proportion to readership and revenue. For Henry James, however, professionalism went beyond "the too-iterated money question," which tended, he felt, to obscure (if not obliterate) the other aspects of authorship. "The fact is," he forthrightly warned,

> that authorship is guilty of a great mistake, a gross want of tact, in formulating & publishing its claim to be a "profession." Let other trades call it so—& let it take no notice. That's enough. It ought to have of the professions only a professional thoroughness. But *never* to have that, & to cry on the housetops instead that it *is* the grocer & the shoemaker is to bring on itself a ridicule of which it will simply die.[1]

How to maintain that "professional thoroughness" in the face of a debased reading public was a burden that James shouldered throughout his writing career. "Success" on *these* terms was not merely a question of money, but of freedom.

As most of James's characters discover, freedom too can have a pecuniary basis. (Almost from the start, readers of James have been struck by the role that money plays in his fiction—as metaphor and material fact.) Far from being limited to matters of artistry, "professional thoroughness" for James extended to relations with his publishers. Almost always pressed by the need to "realize" (as he often said) on his work, James was uniquely situated, as a transatlantic author, to explore both English and American markets for his fiction. In an age when authors routinely took refuge in one house, assured there of publication, though often on only modest terms, James preferred the open thoroughfare of competition and

1. Henry James to Edmund Gosse, [10 May 1895] (Brotherton Collection, Univ. of Leeds).

offered his manuscripts to an unusual variety of publishers and periodicals throughout his long career. Indeed, James's story is worth reconstructing precisely because he dealt so widely in the marketplace of letters. Implicit in his own publishing history is the sum of its exclusions, the more typical arrangements by which his contemporaries worked the writer's trade.

The story of James's relation to the marketplace (and its impact on his imagination) is really twofold, because it involves not only the writer's search for a public audience, but also his calculated maneuvering in the more private confines of publishers' offices. The two aspects are, of course, related, but their implications for James's creative life are noticeably different. James anxiously desired to reach a mass audience at the same time that he remained suspicious of it; the hopes—and fears—that he associated with the fate of his literary commodity in the public sphere become translated into fictional parables of exposure (especially in the work of his middle years). But the episodes of James's private dealings with his publishers read more like parables of discretion. James actively manipulated his position as a transatlantic writer in his negotiations with rival sets of literary businessmen. Masquerading as the helpless victim of "publishing scoundrels," he often turned their genteel pretensions to account.

Such games of power and knowledge pervade James's fiction (the later novels, particularly), but I am not sure we need another book-length study of them. While it is true that two distinct literary situations are implicit in James's career—the public market of magazines, bookstores, and libraries (where his work was a consumer commodity), and the private market of the publisher's office (where his work was, in effect, a capital commodity)—we know so little about his public market that a slant in that direction seems desirable. This preference will explain the omission, here, of detailed treatment of the so-called major phase. Because James was wholly dependent on his income from writing only until 1893 (when his share of the family inheritance, previously set aside for his sister Alice, reverted to him after her death), a study of James's relation to the literary marketplace naturally should focus on his middle years. The unanticipated legacy certainly prolonged James's ill-fated dalliance with the theatre, but it also buffered him later from the more violent repercussions of the marketplace. James took more daring risks in his subsequent work, at least in part, because he could better afford them.

James's status as a transatlantic author gave him peculiar and prophetic insight into the evolution of an Anglo-American market for literary work, and he actively pressed this advantage in his dealings with publishers in both countries. By combining aspects of English and American trade practices in negotiating his contracts, James anticipated the professional standards that we recognize today in the literary marketplace. Historians have recently directed their attention to the "culture of professionalism" that emerged in the late nineteenth century as a response to increasingly complex systems of social and economic organization; but they have largely ignored the fact that literature, too, was affected by these trends. In a role he himself defined for the novelist, Henry James was both a contemporary witness and unofficial historian of the development of literary professionalism.

Cambridge, Massachusetts
June 1986

M.A.

Acknowledgments

Even though its specific tasks are often solitary, all true scholarship is a collective endeavor. The graduate program in the History of American Civilization at Harvard University generously provided me with the intellectual stimulation and financial support that made my research possible. In the final year of my graduate career, a Whiting Fellowship in the Humanities allowed me to substitute the rigors of composition for the rigors of the classroom. A grant from the Rollins Fund, administered by the Department of English and American Literature and Language at Harvard, has enabled me to embellish this book with visual evidence of the sources upon which it is based.

A special word of gratitude is due to the executor of the James estate, Mr. Alexander R. James, whose permission to quote from the family archives has enabled me to draw upon a much more extensive collection of relevant documents than otherwise would have been possible. The recently completed edition of *Henry James Letters,* while useful, remains frustratingly selective.

For their prompt and generous courtesy, I would also like to thank the many other individuals and institutions who have allowed me to quote from manuscript archives: the American Academy and Institute of Arts and Letters, New York; the British Library, London; CBS Educational and Professional Publishing, New York; Chatto & Windus/The Hogarth Press, London; the William R. Perkins Library, Duke University; the Houghton Library, Harvard University; Houghton Mifflin Company, Boston; the Brotherton Collection, University of Leeds; the Library of Congress, Washington, D.C.; Macmillan Publishing Company, New York; Macmillan Publishers Ltd., London; the Pierpont Morgan Library, New York; the Henry W. and Albert A. Berg Collection, The New York

Public Library, Astor, Lenox and Tilden Foundations, New York; the Firestone Library, Princeton University; The Library, University of Reading; Charles Scribner's Sons, New York; the Alderman Library, University of Virginia; and the Collection of American Literature, Beinecke Rare Book and Manuscript Library, Yale University. An early version of the book's concluding chapter first appeared as "'Friction with the Market': The Publication of Henry James's New York Edition" in *The New England Quarterly,* 56 (1983), 354–81; it is reprinted here with the permission of the editors. The list of debts is long (the list of omissions, I'm afraid, probably longer), but it cheerfully reminds me that the vitality of academic life is largely dependent on the goodwill of others.

Contents

"Friction with the Market"

I
Introduction

With the completion of Leon Edel's five-volume biography in 1972, it seems fair to say that the critical historiography of Henry James has entered a new phase. Whatever the shortcomings of Edel's work,[1] his labors as biographer and editor of James's letters, fiction, and plays have at last made accessible a remarkable wealth of documentation about the writer's life and art. Many questions remain to be answered, but the avenues of investigation are now more clearly mapped and illuminated.

Since a comprehensive overview of Jamesian criticism would fill many volumes,[2] no brief sketch can do full justice to the evolution of his treatment by modern critics. But if we borrow some terms from more conventional historiography, a figure in the carpet becomes discernible. Herbert Butterfield once identified three phases of historical interpretation through which the study of a particular event often passes. In the earliest or heroic phase, the narrative is written by participants in the event or their descendants. The stakes of personal involvement are such that the aims of objective interpretation are superseded by a kind of moral justification: what happened is interpreted to say that it should have happened. Forces or circumstances external to the primary actors are ignored or discounted and, instead, the morality of their decisions is key. Despite the limitations of this view, its necessary immediacy is important because it can capture the emotional texture of the event, an advantage available only to a contemporary witness. In the next phase, the event becomes locked into subsequent history and is interpreted with an eye to the resolution of issues in the historian's own time. The "Whig" historian (Butterfield's label has stuck)[3] is searching for antecedents to validate his convictions about contemporary problems. The context of the event is sacrificed to a felt demand for relevance.

The third or contextual interpretation can only be written when a wealth of information about the event is available and the limits of its historical context can be discerned. The historian can look at the event with greater objectivity, because, unlike its first recorders, he is not personally involved with its consequences. Moreover, his detachment implies a point of view in which the latent circumstances surrounding the event can finally be identified. The full context of the event, distorted by the Whig historian's preoccupation with current issues, is restored. Each phase, of course, has a distinctive value; little is gained by making invidious comparisons among them. The best history will employ the special insights available to each mode of inquiry. Truly to recapture the sense of the past, as one Jamesian protagonist observes, requires "evidence of a sort for which there [have] never been documents enough, or for which documents mainly, however multiplied, [will] never *be* enough."[4]

If we use Butterfield's synopsis and consider the artistic career of Henry James as a kind of historical event, certain phases of critical assessment suggest themselves. Needless to say, James himself supplied the heroic narrative in his Olympian prefaces to the New York Edition. At best obliquely personal, and concerned above all with the craft of fiction, James's prefaces were, as he told Howells, "a sort of plea for Criticism, for Discrimination, for Appreciation on other than infantile lines—as against the so almost universal Anglo-Saxon absence of these things; which tends so, in our general trade, it seems to me, to break the heart."[5] In writing his prefaces James had one of the rarest opportunities ever afforded to an artist: the chance to supply the king of intelligent criticism his work deserved, but which it had failed to elicit from contemporary readers or men of letters. As one critic of the time observed, the prefaces represented "the first serious attempt ever made in English to call upon [the] bewildered art [of fiction] to pause and give a conscious account of itself; to present its credentials and justify its existence."[6] The master had spoken, even if few were ready to listen.

It is surely no coincidence that a famous book of Jamesian anecdotes was later called *The Legend of the Master,*[7] for this was the biographical image that James actively wished to perpetuate. After James's death the tributes of his friends immediately began to appear, commemorating his sublime indifference to an uncaring (if not callously stupid) reading public. This defensive attitude permeated the writings of Percy Lubbock and Theodora Bosanquet, two of James's closest and most ardent disciples. When Lubbock was collecting and editing the novelist's letters, for example, he succumbed to the understandable temptation of taking the master's complaints about his unpopularity a bit too literally. The writer's nephew offered Lubbock a mild corrective:

> You speak in one of the introductions of the "blank silence with which his books were received." That seems to me too strong. Very early he had even

> in America a most devoted though small public. He also had a very considerable fame in the States, although it is true that it went little farther than an ignorant sort of supposition that he was a "distinguished American author." So that the words "blank silence" don't seem to me as happy as most of your other characterizations. Uncle Henry, in talking, always exaggerated his unpopularity. It undoubtedly gave him good cause for complaint, but he was morbidly self-conscious and sensitive about his work, and that state of mind inevitably results in exaggeration of speech.[8]

The younger James's advice was well taken, and Lubbock altered his phrasing;[9] but the acolyte's editorial interest (reinforced by keen familial discretion) was not in exploring the work-a-day realities of Henry James's career. Despite his choice of a homelier title for a subsequent study of James's methods (Lubbock called his book *The Craft of Fiction* rather than *The Art of Fiction*), he saw "no true working distinction to be drawn between them": *craft* in this sense carried no connotation of a trade or profession by which a livelihood is earned.[10] Bosanquet, too, exaggerated James's artistic isolation by portraying him as a "writer who had fasted for forty years in the wilderness of British and American misconceptions without yielding a scrap of intellectual integrity to editorial or publishing tempers."[11]

This passionate conviction, again seemingly relevant to James's later years, does not wholly square with the novelist's own words of advice to another struggling artist, whose fixation on an aesthetic ideal prevented him from maintaining a relation "to the *possible* possibilities." To the youthful sculptor, Hendrik Andersen, James wrote

> *Make the pot boil, at any price, as the only real basis* of freedom & sanity. Stop building in the air for a while & build on the ground. *Earn* the money that will give you the right to conceptions (& still more to executions,) like your fountain—though I am still wondering *what* American community is going to want to pay for 30 [or] 40 stark naked men & women, of whatever beauty, lifted into the raw light of one of their public places.

When his earnest warning seemed to fall on deaf ears, as Andersen continued to produce a"vast stripped stark sublime Family . . . of penises & bottoms & other private ornaments" on which he would never realize a penny, James reiterated his plea:

> You are attempting what no young artist *ever* did—to live on air indefinitely, by what I can make out, putting all your eggs into one extremely precarious & perforated basket, & declining the aid of the thing done meanwhile *to live,* to bring in its assistance from month to month: the potboiler call it if you like, the potboiler which represents, in the lives of all artists, some of the most beautiful things ever done by them. Stop your multiplication of unsaleable nakedness for a while & hurl yourself, by every cunning art you can command, into the production of the interesting, the charming, the vendible, the *placeable* small thing.

James did not write these words from atop an ivory tower. His admonishing letters were animated by a lifelong appreciation of "that benefit of *friction with the market* which is so true a one for solitary artists too much steeped in their mere personal dreams."[12]

Despite this unsuspected side of James's character, the image of him as a writer who practiced his trade from a necessity other than that of earning a living carried over into the next phase of interpretation—the great revival years of the 1930s and 1940s when R. P. Blackmur, F. O. Matthiessen, Lionel Trilling, and others wrote their seminal studies of James's achievement. However much this generation of critics can be credited with rescuing James from the oblivion to which Van Wyck Brooks and Vernon Louis Parrington would have consigned him,[13] it should also be recognized that their interest in him coincided with a larger ideological motive that lay behind the modernist movement generally. In the drive to legitimate their preference for detailed scrutiny of texts, the high priests of modernism were quick to impress James into their ranks, claiming his critical premises as their own and deriving their conviction from the magnificently isolated heroism of his example. While some of these commentators recognized the danger of excessively abstracting James from his immediate historical context, the remarkable zeal that they brought to the study of James's work was not matched by a complementary interest in the relevant circumstances of his career.

With characteristic shrewdness, Edmund Wilson noticed that this rather one-sided predisposition extended even to the publication of the basic source materials about James that were made available after the family papers were deposited at Harvard. In a review of James's *Notebooks* and Matthiessen's compendium volume, *The James Family,* Wilson observed that the editors had omitted many facts of historical and biographical significance and substituted—in the *Notebooks,* for example—"wordy and pedestrian and sometimes rather inept" summaries of James's stories and interpretations of them. Yet, Wilson continued, "we discover that the editors have excised certain entries in the notebooks themselves—dates that James wanted to record and figurings of his expenses—though they would probably have taken up less space than has been used to explain their omission." Why, for instance, should the reader find it more interesting to discover the editors' relief in James's substitution of *The Spoils of Poynton* for his original title *(The House Beautiful)* than to know "what Henry James spent in staying at clubs and hotels?"[14] Why indeed? And what of the other facts and figures relating to James's professional life? Like the "Whig" historians of their sister discipline, the modernist critics exaggerated the distinctiveness of James at the same time that they evaded some of the key questions his example ought finally to have raised.

Among these unanswered questions was the primary paradox of James's dedication to his calling. As Leon Edel has observed, the somewhat limited biographical data available before the appearance of his own volumes "offered the Henry James of the drawing-room and the week-end visits, rather than the James who wrote assiduously and sought in the market place of letters, to sell his precious wares." Edel rightly emphasized that, for all the published criticism about the novelist, the "'working' Henry James" was either "utterly lost from sight" or simply dismissed as "a kind of disembodied Mind [or] writing machine riveted to a desk creating characters without flesh and stories without passion."[15] Edel immediately revealed that, contrary to the received wisdom about the magnificence of the family fortune,[16] James had earned his way by literary labor until he was past fifty. Here was a professional side of James's character that previously had been eclipsed.

Even though Edel amplified this theme in subsequent volumes, the recently satisfied demand for an updated edition of *A Bibliography of Henry James* indicates that curiosity about this author's publishing history is still active. When the *Bibliography* first appeared in 1957, the editors legitimately restricted its scope to "the story of what happened to the writings of Henry James after they left his busy work-table to be set up in type and published in magazine and book." The story of their inception was to be found in James's *Notebooks* and the prefaces that he wrote for the New York Edition. "The chronicle of the intermediate stage—the author's descent into the market-place, manuscript in hand, to drive his bargains with editors and publishers—belong[ed] elsewhere."[17] The natural place for that chronicle, presumably, was Edel's narrative of James's life, then still appearing and now, of course, complete.

Yet for all its appearance of definitiveness, the Edel biography does not supply a comprehensive account of this intermediate stage. James's relations with his editors, publishers, and audience occasionally provide Edel with particular opportunities for treating his subject in large and sometimes lurid strokes: the revelation of James's chronic incapacity for making sows' ears out of silk purses; the quotation of his "farewell" letter to Frederick Macmillan when bargaining for *The Tragic Muse* apparently broke down; the pathetic tableau of the novelist's humiliation at the premiere of *Guy Domville*.[18] In filling in so large a canvas, however, Edel necessarily omitted much significant detail, at least insofar as James's professional career is concerned. The biography occasionally catches the drift of an insistent undercurrent in James's life—the need to sell literature as well as to create it—but Edel's final preoccupation is more explicitly psychological. This other preoccupation—of James's—remains largely unexplored.

The gap here in critical understanding is not peculiar to James scholarship. Although the reciprocal relation between the writer and society has long been recognized by students in the field, very little research has been done in America to demonstrate the dynamics of the writer's literary situation. Many years ago William Charvat advocated more careful study of the vital exchange between creators and consumers of literature; yet, too often, critics have assumed that the outline of literary history can be traced from a supposedly linear connection between writers and readers. "Actually," Charvat argued, "instead of being merely linear, the pattern is triangular. Opposite both the writer and the reader stands the whole complex organism of the book and magazine trade—a trade which for the last two centuries, at least, has had a positive and dynamic function in the world of literature."

Charvat also recognized that determining the full meaning of the publisher's function necessarily would involve a thorough reexamination of current critical methodology. "A writer's success in communing with society cannot be determined by guesswork," he insisted. "The critic and historian both need instruments: publishers' records; the correspondence of authors and editors (much of it still unpublished); facts about the circulation of magazines and sales of books; and—most difficult of all to find—reliable evidence of reader response." But which readers? And from what sources? The prolific "reception" and "reputation" studies of recent years have focused almost invariably upon published reviews of an author's work, but Charvat warned that in the book trade "it is not criticism that matters but publicity." Occasionally useful to the historian "as a clue to the thinking of the segment of society that produced it," past criticism "is almost valueless as a guide to reader taste."[19]

In spite of Charvat's shrewd admonition, the unfortunate limitations of this approach have distorted our view of Henry James for many years. Workmanlike dissertations have appeared,[20] and much of the periodical criticism of James's fiction has been resuscitated,[21] but we still know surprisingly little about the novelist's relations with his audience. Much of the most recent scholarship in the field, such as Henry Nash Smith's two chapters on James in *Democracy and the Novel* (1978), depends entirely on the slender (and by now familiar) evidence of periodical reviews and results (in Smith's case) in a conclusion that is curiously reminiscent of Van Wyck Brooks's deprecation of James's presumed alienation from his American public. From Smith's point of view, not one of America's major writers of the nineteenth century—Hawthorne, Melville, Howells, Twain, or James—"was able to establish a durable rapport with an audience that allowed him to develop his full potentialities."[22] But, at least with respect to James, this sweeping assertion ignores the persuasiveness of the evidence at hand. Any analysis that offers *The Golden Bowl* as an example of failed potential should be viewed with skepticism. In fact, a more convincing argument results if Smith's basic premise is reversed: that an artist's antagonisms with his audience can engender imaginative work at least comparable if not vastly superior to that produced by a more comfortably engaged sensibility. Are there simply no alternatives between "the roar of the market place and the silence of the tomb"? James recognized the dangers of these extremes and strove to find a middle way: to attain, as he once remarked, "an affluence of favor, yet without the taint of popularity!"[23]

II

Stuff as Dreams Are Made On: Henry James and His Audience

James's calculated attempt to avoid both the din of commercialism and the silence of oblivion betrays a characteristic tension between his honest desire for success and a fear of appearing too clamorous for the tangible rewards that the marketplace could confer. Stephen Spender once suggested that, "like most writers of great integrity," James "secretly yearned for success, even in the most vulgar and public sense."[1] Spender's intuitive understanding of this latent aspect of James's character was corroborated simultaneously by Edith Wharton, who had known James for years. In speaking of James's sensitiveness to criticism, Wharton observed that this trait "had nothing to do with vanity," but rather "was caused by the great artist's deep consciousness of his own powers, combined with a bitter, a life-long disappointment at the lack of his popular recognition." She often wondered whether James "had not secretly dreamed of being a 'best-seller' in the days when that odd form of literary fame was at its height."[2] Anxious for the public's approval, yet fearful of its disdain, James knew that by "the cruel crookedness of human conditions" he was destined "to affront a publicity" it was ever his "weakness to loathe."[3]

Those words were written after the humiliating premiere of *Guy Domville,* but their phrasing echoes loudly in James's fiction. The conception of "a certain young woman affronting her destiny" was the novelist's remembered point of departure in writing *The Portrait of a Lady,* but it was a subject so dear to his imagination that he was "resigned to keeping the precious object locked up indefinitely rather than commit it, at no matter what price, to vulgar hands."[4] James's price and publishing conditions eventually were met, however, and *The Portrait* was released to affront its destiny with the reading public just as Isabel is fated to affront hers with Gilbert Osmond. The similarity is not merely semantic. Richard Poirier has noticed that Isabel exemplifies the same ideals that James wants to see represented in the art of the novel; and that James's vocabulary when talking about fiction—such as the testament on "the great form" that he delivered in 1889 to the Deerfield Summer School—corresponds with that used to describe Isabel's hopes and ambitions.[5] Poirier uses this similarity to emphasize the depth of feeling that the novelist has for his protagonist, but the relation between James and Isabel becomes even more complex if we think of her as an embodiment of *his* ambitions and hopes.

In an early chapter of *The Portrait,* James directs our attention to the Albany house in which Isabel Archer largely has been raised and educated. James confessed in his autobiography that the scene was drawn from a childhood memory, "when the attempt to drag [him] crying and kicking to the first hour of [his] education failed on the threshold of the Dutch House in Albany."[6] Having rejected the opportunity to attend a public school across the street, Isabel, like James, spends a good deal of her time browsing in the family library:

> The foundation of her knowledge was really laid in the idleness of her grandmother's house, where, as most of the other inmates were not reading people, she had uncontrolled use of a library full of books with frontispieces, which she used to climb upon a chair to take down. When she had found one to her taste—she was guided in her selection chiefly by the frontispiece—she carried it into a mysterious apartment which lay beyond the library and which was called, traditionally, no one knew why, the office. Whose office it had been and at what period it had flourished, she never learned; it was enough for her that it contained an echo and a pleasant musty smell and that it was a chamber of disgrace for old pieces of furniture whose infirmities were not always apparent (so that the disgrace seemed unmerited and rendered them victims of injustice) and with which, in the manner of children, she had established relations almost human, or dramatic. There was an old haircloth sofa in especial, to which she had confided a hundred childish sorrows. The place owed much of its mysterious melancholy to the fact that it was properly entered from the second door of the house, the door that had been condemned, and that it was fastened by bolts which a particularly slender girl found it impossible to slide. She knew that this silent, motionless portal opened into the street; if the sidelights had not been filled with green paper she might have looked out upon the little brown stoop and the well-worn brick pavement. But she had no wish to look out, for this would have interfered with her theory that there was a strange, unseen place on the other side—a place which became to the child's imagination, according to its different moods, a region of delight or terror. . . . She had never opened the bolted door nor removed the green paper (renewed by other hands) from its side-lights; she had never assured herself that the vulgar street lay beyond it.[7]

At one level of significance, this architectural plan is intended as a blueprint of Isabel's innocent consciousness, a physical representation of her sheltered experience. But at another level, James has constructed a model of his own professional situation. The "mysterious" link between works of literature and their potential audience, between the sanctuary of culture (the library) and the vulgar street, is the marketplace (the office), a businesslike domain where values are filtered through a sole medium of exchange: windows papered in bank-note green.

The tone and structure of the passage reflect James's ambivalence toward the nature of this arrangment and his status within it. On the one hand, it seems clear that the office serves as a refuge or sanctuary, especially since Isabel has little desire to move or see beyond its confines. Privacy, rather than publicity, is essential to her youthful sense of self. But James's description oddly subverts this apparent intention. The novelist employs the indicative mood to inform us that this "particularly slender little girl found it impossible to slide" the bolts of the office door, suggesting that she has, in fact, applied her strength to the task, has been tempted to go beyond the "silent, motionless portal" into the street outside. Why does James eschew the conditional—"bolts which a particularly slender girl *would have found* it impossible to slide"—a construction that would have reinforced his otherwise unambiguous suggestion that Isabel is content to remain in her world of books? Having glanced at Isabel's latent desire to open the bolted door and enter the "vulgar street," James insists throughout the rest of the passage that she has no wish to look out. But the very emphasis of his retraction should give us pause. What gives this passage dramatic impact is the strange interruption of movement from the library to the street beyond the office door. Isabel carries her books away from the library to the office, but some defensive mechanism of her imagination is touched, like a spring, when she confronts the bolted door. Isabel's personal dilemma, analogous to James's professional one, is how to open an intercourse with the world.

Hawthorne, of course, had pondered that question before—a question that added a certain material gravity to his transcendental generation's simultaneous desire to establish, in Emerson's phrase, "an original relation to the universe."[8] Emerson's formulation voiced a concern for the integrity of the creative mind, for maintaining the deviation from the norm that constitutes style. Though surely no less a stylist, Hawthorne addressed more directly his anxiety about the writer's survival in a democratic culture and his need to find acceptance among the reading public. James inherited both impulses, which he internalized and transformed into an almost Gallic ideal of glory—a seductive, and elusive, synthesis of artistic integrity, popular acclaim, and its attendant riches.[9] We should take Edith Wharton at her word when she asserts that James entered the theatre, "apart from the creative joy the writing of his plays gave him," because "he longed intensely, incurably, for the shouting and the garlands so persistently refused to his great novels, and which, had he succeeded in his theatrical venture, would have come to him in a grosser and more susbstantial form." Wharton once remarked that Anglo-Saxons had no notion of what the French mean when they speak of *la gloire;* but in this respect she felt that James was a Latin, for "the last infirmity of noble minds was never renounced by his."[10]

At this early point in *The Portrait,* Isabel dreams more of romance than of glory; but the contradiction of motives implied in the passage is emblematic of a divided nature shared by the protagonist and her creator. The "vulgar street" is alternately "a region of delight or terror," and therein lies its fascination for both Isabel and James. That Isabel's slender hands cannot slide the bolts is both physically and psychologically appropriate to her character. As one critic has noticed, the recurrent image of a bolted door epitomizes the theme of *The Portrait,* insofar as this symbol is James's deliberate metaphor for the nature of Isabel's inner life.[11] But the office doorway and public thoroughfare beyond it were a more direct challenge to the novelist himself. The door to the publisher's office was the portal through which James had to pass, as a novelist, to affront a publicity it was his confessed weakness to loathe.

How deeply these images were fixed in James's consciousness is suggested by an early letter to Charles Eliot Norton, consoling the master of Shady Hill in the loss of his wife. "The human soul is mighty," James wrote, "and it seems to me we hardly know what it may achieve (as well as suffer) until it has been plunged deeply into trouble. Then indeed, there seems something infinite in pain and it opens out before us, door within door, and we seem doomed to tread its whole infinitude; but there seems also something infinite in effort and something supremely strong by its own right in the grim residuum of conscious manhood with which we stand face to face to the hard reality of things."[12] The metaphor of affliction extending "door within door" is an appropriate vehicle for James's stoicism, because it contains within itself the antidote to suffering—the restorative act of standing "face to face" with "the hard reality of things" in the unseen region beyond each successive doorway.

Isabel learns a similar lesson after following Osmond "into the mansion of his own habitation," only then seeing where she really is: "Between those four walls she had lived ever since; they were to surround her for the rest of her life. It was the house of darkness, the house of dumbness, the house of suffocation." In her long vigil before the dying fire, Isabel takes the full measure of her dwelling in a state of "incredulous terror."[13] Behind every door, one might say, lurks another aspect of Osmond's malignity; from a small high window he peeps down and mocks at her. But with the fortitude the James recommended to Norton, she also determines to face her problems. As the novelist said in his preface to the book, the whole episode was an attempted "representation simply of her motionlessly *seeing,* and an attempt withal to make the mere still lucidity of her act as 'interesting' as the surprise of a caravan or the identification of a pirate."[14]

James exploited the inherent melodrama of this metaphor of consciousness even more vividly in *A Small Boy and Others* (1913) to record "the most appalling yet most admirable nightmare" of his life.[15] James's account of his "dream-adventure" in the Galerie d'Apollon of the Louvre is familiar territory to modern scholars, who have seized upon it for a variety of critical uses;[16] but by narrowing their focus on the reported events of the dream itself, most critics have overlooked its relation to the clusters of images that come before it and act as subconscious stimuli to provoke a complex process of symbolic association in James's mind. When James turns the tables on his mysterious adversary in the Louvre, thrusting open the door he "had a moment before been desperately, and all the more abjectly, defending by the push of [his] shoulder against hard pressure on lock and bar from the other side" (pp. 196–97), he is re-experiencing the felt tension between the opposites of art and vulgarity explored earlier in the same chapter of his memoir.

The dense texture of James's autobiographical volumes has seldom been an aid to their appreciation, but we should recognize that the dream of the Louvre bridges two distinct episodes in the history of James's consciousness. The first is his recognition of art as an abstract ideal and the second his discovery of a practical vocation in literature. Prior to his recollection of the dream-adventure, James remembers the long walks he took with his brother William through the streets of Paris and hears again the chorus that seemed to rise up from the pavements and reverberate from the Palace itself:

> Art, art, art, don't you see? Learn, little gaping pilgrims, what *that* is! . . . Yes, small staring jeune homme, we are dignity and memory and measure, we are conscience and proportion and taste, not to mention strong sense too: for all of which good things take us—you won't find one of them when you find (as you're going soon to begin to at such a rate) vulgarity.

With the benefit of hindsight, James remarks that these youthful impressions "somehow held the secret of our future" (p. 191)—a future in which artistic ideals would always be shadowed by the compromises of the marketplace.

Vulgarity is left behind—or so James thinks—when he crosses

> that bridge over to Style constituted by the wondrous Galerie d'Apollon, drawn out for me as a long but assured initiation and seeming to form with its supreme coved ceiling and inordinately shining parquet a prodigious tube or tunnel through which I inhaled little by little, that is again and again, a general sense of *glory.* The glory meant ever so many things at once, not only

> beauty and art and supreme design, but history and fame and power, the world in fine raised to the richest and noblest expression. (p. 196)

But even here, in the palace of art, James is threatened by something other, and the account of the dream-adventure follows. As noted earlier, Edith Wharton provides the best gloss on James's conception of *la gloire,* and her observations of his concomitant longing for success with the public offer a clue to interpreting the meaning of James's nightmare. If the glory that James desired was no mere private virtue, but a matter of public record ("history and fame and power"), he could only attain it by confronting the public and claiming its withheld crown of laurels as his own. According to Isabel's frame of mind, the "vulgar street" beyond the office door is "a region of delight or terror," emotions equivalent to James's experience here: the effect of the dream adventure on the writer's "intense young fancy" is that of "a love-philtre or fear-philtre which fixes for the senses their supreme symbol of the fair or the strange." At first terrified by the appalling presence of his unseen visitant, James suddenly throws open the bolted door and dashes at his opponent with "straight aggression and dire intention" (p. 196). It is an "act indeed of life-saving energy" (p. 197); but even more wonderful is his immediate possession and recognition of the Galerie d'Apollon, the citadel of glory remembered from his childhood and the chamber in which the imperial crown of France is kept.

Appropriately enough, James repeats this symbolic rendering of self-discovered power when he concludes *A Small Boy and Others* with the disclosure of his newly perceived destiny in letters. As the stream of association rolls on, James recounts the "exposure" of his "small scared consciousness" to the mysteries of painting, sculpture, and above all the theatre (p. 198), but he closes his volume with a discovery of another kind. Art could not only be "other," but might of himself, originating even in the small scared consciousness of an American boy. Repeating the stimulus from his dream, James's recognition again is sparked by felt danger—in this case the threat of grave illness—and his vocabulary reverts to the scene in the Louvre. While recovering from a nearly fatal attack of typhoid, James takes on

> the sense of being a boy of other dimensions somehow altogether, and even with a new dimension introduced and acquired; a dimension that I was eventually to think of as a stretch in the direction of essential change or of living straight into a part of myself previously quite unvisited and now made accessible as by the sharp forcing of a closed door. (p. 224)

If the language of James's dream-adventure invites multiple interpretation, the same imagery here conveys more explicitly the internal operations of consciousness. A small boy is becoming an adult (though in a way, as we have seen that Isabel Archer never equally achieves: she cannot force the closed door). Even more important, however, is the perceived cause of James's new maturity; for what propels him into an "unvisited" region of being is the attraction of a literary form and the life-saving preoccupation, in his months of illness, of reading:

> The blest novel in three volumes exercised through its form, to my sense, on grounds lying deeper for me to-day than my deepest sounding, an appeal that fairly made it do with me what it would. Possibly a drivelling confession, and the more drivelling perhaps the more development I should attempt for it; from which, however, the very difficulty of the case saves me. Too many associations, too much of the ferment of memory and fancy, are somehow stirred; they beset me again, they hover and whirl about me while I stand, as I used to stand, within the positively sanctified walls of the [book]shop (so of the *vieux temps* now their aspect and fashion and worked system: by which I mean again of the frumpiest and civillest mid-Victorian), and surrender to the vision of the shelves packed with their rich individual trinities. (p. 233)

When James recalled the evenings spent with his tutor poring over the "blest novel in three volumes," he recognized the latent meaning of his labor: "How can I allow then that we hadn't planted together, with a loose felicity, some of the seed of work?—even though the sprouting was so long put off" (p. 236).

And so we come full circle. The book-lined shelves, the shop, the forcing of a closed door, the discovery of latent power and personal destiny—the setting from *The Portrait,* the significance symbolized in the dream of the Louvre—James's discovery of vocation concludes the first volume of his memoirs and figures elsewhere in his fiction. The drama of confrontation thus occurs on two levels. Privately the artist must quell the demon of self-doubt to become the master of his talents. Publicly he must launch himself before an audience if the prospect of glory is to be achieved. In no sense is this pattern of confrontation peculiar to James, but its pervasiveness and centrality to the working of his imagination are remarkable.

If the body of James's writing did not supply the evidence in support of this claim, the facts of his biography would. The best single illustration of James's creatively adversarial relation to his audience is his ill-fated assault on the theatre, an episode in his career that demonstrates with uncanny vividness the latent meaning of his dream-adventure in the Louvre. From earliest childhood James associated the stage with both triumph and humiliation; as an avenue of publicity it too could be a region of delight or terror. When the youthful James heard Adelina Patti sing before the footlights in New York, he learned "what 'acclamation' might mean" and remembered the sound of "the vast high-piled auditory thundering applause at the beautiful pink lady's clear bird-notes" as "a thrilling, a tremendous experience."[17] But this memory is immediately contrasted in the autobiography to a tormenting recollection of a more vulnerable moment, when his brother William and a childhood companion

> practised on my innocence to seduce me to the stage and there plunge me into the shame of my sad failure to account arithmetically for [a magician's] bewilderingly subtracted or added or divided pocket handkerchiefs and playing-cards; a paralysis of wit as to which I once more, and with the same wan despair, feel my companions' shy telegraphy of relief, their snickerings and mouthings and raised numerical fingers, reach me from the benches. (pp. 66–67)

Clearly the stage had its dangers as well as its glories.

Even more revealing, however, is a later episode from *Notes of a Son and Brother,* in which James describes another scene of humiliation that was profoundly important to his ultimate choice of vocation. In a fragment called "The Turning Point of My Life" (which Howells had invited James to contribute to a similarly titled series by other writers), James recalled the hour when, "in the cold shade of queer old Dane Hall" at the Harvard Law School, he "stood at the parting of [his] ways, recognised the false steps, even though few enough, already taken," and consciously committed himself to his literary calling. If James stood at the crossroads, he assuredly did not feel like Hercules, so little confidence did he then have in his powers. In fact, the heroic phrasing was actually Howells's, whose discourse James was recording; the novelist himself doubted whether his youth "*had* in fact enjoyed that amount of drama."[18] But the theatricality of another episode at Harvard could not be denied, and James preserved it in his autobiography:

> I have kept to this hour a black little memory of my having attempted to argue one afternoon, by way of exercise and under what seemed to me a perfect glare of publicity, the fierce light of a "moot-court," some case proposed to me by a fellow-student—who can only have been one of the most benign of men unless he was darkly the designingest, and to whom I was at any rate to owe it that I figured my shame for years much in the image of my having stood forth before an audience with a fiddle and bow and trusted myself to rub them together desperately enough (after the fashion of Rousseau in a passage of the Confessions,) to make some appearance of music. My music, I recall, before the look on the faces around me, quavered away into mere collapse and cessation, a void now engulfing memory itself, so that I liken it all to a merciful fall of the curtain on some actor stricken and stammering. (p. 438)

Like his bewildering boyhood experience with the stage magician, the lurid "glare of publicity" in Dane Hall again exposed James to humiliation and defeat. The closing phrases of this recollection had even more poignant significance for a man who had been "hooted at . . . by a brutal mob" as he stood before the curtain after the first performance of *Guy*

Domville. The heroic confrontation James imagined in his dream never materialized at the St. James Theatre on the evening of 5 January 1895: routed, dismayed, the tables turned on him by an audience so surpassing him for straight aggression and dire intention, he stood amid "jeers and catcalls" waiting vainly for the merciful fall of the curtain. When it failed to descend, James fled from the stage, his face "green with dismay."[19]

Most critics have followed Leon Edel in treating James's dramatic years as an anomalous interlude in his professional career. By asserting that the writing of fiction was, to James, a kind of private religion in which the public played no part (hadn't he, after all, written to his brother, "One has always a 'public' enough if one has an audible vibration—even if it should only come from one's self"?),[20] Edel claimed that when James ventured into the theatre he was suddenly forced to obtain approval of his work "from men with a greater concern for the pocketbook than for 'audible vibration'—except as the vibration meant box office returns." "For the first time in his life," Edel wrote, James "was seeking to vend his wares in a competitive market."[21] But this analysis of James's literary situation seriously distorts the historical realities of the publishing world as he experienced them. Publishers no less than producers clamored for cash returns on their investments; and as for competitiveness, witnessing "the desire and the demand for [his] productions [reduced] to zero" was one of James's primary motives for entering the theatre in the first place.[22] James's plays may indeed be literary curiosities, but his professional experiment with the theatre epitomizes the concern for fame, art, and fortune that affected the entire range of his career.

From his earliest days James equated the theatre with money-making, a fact that helps to explain both its attraction and his occasionally squeamish remarks about entering it. After William James had seen a play by Howells in the spring of 1878 and told his brother that it "seemed very charming in representation," Henry immediately expressed his hope to the author that Howells "felt the charm in the region of [his] purse-strings."[23] Desiring to cash in on the vogue of "Daisy Miller," James dramatized his short story in 1882, rewriting the ending so that Daisy survives her bout with malaria and marries Winterbourne. The cleverly revised script failed to arouse the interest of stage managers in New York or London, however, and James prudently committed it to the channels of publicity he knew best—magazine and book.

Edel claims that "Henry seems to have been naive enough to think that in the world of the theatre managers were like magazine editors; he was a master of the latter, he knew exactly how to deal with them. In the theatre, however, where direct business negotiation was involved wholly without the amenities and courtesies of the publishing world, he was usually baffled—and defeated."[24] But the publication history of *Daisy Miller: A Comedy* would seem to require a modification of this view. What crippled James in his dealings with the theatre was not his naiveté but a conscientious professionalism that could tolerate few compromises with the conditions of the English or American stage. His handling of *Daisy Miller* demonstrates how refined his instinct for "business negotiation" truly was.

That James was fully aware of the theatre's limitations can be gauged by an article that he published in the *Atlantic* while bargaining for his play was still in progress. The portion of this article, "London Pictures and London Plays," devoted to the theatre is a remarkable attack on the appalling dilettantism of the dramatic profession in England. Proposals to establish a dramatic conservatory were being talked of in London, but James concluded that "even the hottest histrionic forcing-house" would fail to make an English school of actors that could rival the French; the "consummate want of study" was too deeply ingrained in the English character.[25] Knowing that such comments would jeopardize his relations with English managers and actors, James insisted to Thomas Bailey Aldrich, the *Atlantic* editor, that his article "*must*—oh MUST!—be rigidly anonymous."[26] Shrewdly covering all his bases, James offered *Daisy Miller* to the *Century Magazine* for serial publication at the end of July, even before his play's chances for stage production were exhausted. Both prospects, however, fell through: in a meeting with yet another producer on 22 August James failed to make an acceptable arrangement for the play;[27] and his extraordinary demand of $1500 for the serial rights (for 38 pages of text) made the experiment too risky for the *Century*.[28] In the meantime Aldrich appealed to James for use of the play in the *Atlantic*, "where it seems," James told his publishers, "they are in a bad way for fiction." Aldrich was willing to pay $1000 for the serial rights, considerably more than the *Century*'s top offer of $20 per page ($760), and James closed the deal when his last theatrical avenue was blocked.[29]

This setback revealed to him "the baseness of the English-speaking stage," the proprietors of which "behaved like asses and sharpers combined"; but in spite of *Daisy Miller*'s rejection, James vowed to continue his experiments with dramatic form. "[T]hough I am disgusted," he confided to his journal, "I do not think I am discouraged. The reason of this latter is that I simply can't afford to be."[30] Even though artistic scruples forced him to decline an invitation to dramatize *The Portrait of a Lady* in 1884, James told the actor Lawrence Barrett, who suggested it, that he would "be glad to try something next year. . . . I should probably be prepared to write a play, to take or to leave, as you should like it or not, on the chance that if you *should* like it, it would open the door to my acquiring a goodish sum of money.[31] The open door might imply prosperity to James, but it also threatened to expose him to the vulgar street beyond. Just two years later he confided to Julian Sturgis that his interest in the theatre had waned because of "the whole general disillusionment that has come over me. . . . When I was younger that was really a very dear dream with me—but it has faded away with the mere increase of observation—observation, I mean, of the deadly vulgarity and illiteracy of the world one enters, practically, in knocking at a manager's door."[32] Unlike Isabel Archer, however, James could not resist the temptation to lift the green paper from the windows. If she had her doubts as to the reality of the world outside, James had few illusions about the nature of the marketplace in which he worked.

Even such knowledge, however, could not extinguish his burning desire for popular acclaim. By 1889 he had resolved to try the theatre again. To his friends he excused his embrace of the playwright's "sordid profession" as a gesture of necessity. "It isn't the love of art and the pursuit of truth that have goaded me into such miry ways," he told Howells; "it is the definite necessity of making, for my palsied old age, more money than literature ever consented or evidently *will* ever consent to yield me."[33] At more vulnerable moments, though, James unmasked desires of a different order. When a provincial audience greeted his dramatized version of *The American* with outbursts of applause, James's response struck deeper than his pocketbook, as he exclaimed to his sister:

> It was really *beautiful*—the splendid success of the whole thing, reflected as large as the surface presented by a Southport audience (and the audience was very big indeed) could permit. The attention, the interest, the outbursts of applause and appreciation hushed quickly for fear of losing . . . what was to follow, the final outbreak at the end for "author, *author,* AUTHOR!" in duly *delayed* response to which, with the whole company grinning delight and sympathy (behind the curtain) I was led before . . . to receive the first "ovation," but I trust not the last of my life.[34]

Edith Wharton never saw this letter, but it confirms exactly her impression of James's hunger for *la gloire.*

A later critic, Walter Isle, has asserted that James's strongest motive for entering the theatre was a complementary desire for success and communication with some kind of audience, the drama being the medium which provides the closest personal contact an author can have with his public.[35] While this view substantially modifies Edel's suggestion that James's attraction to the stage was wholly passive,[36] Isle does not fully explore the ramifications of his remark. Since his primary interest is the dramatic form of the novels that followed James's theatrical years, he casually observes that the personal rejection that James suffered on the opening night of *Guy Domville* gave him the excuse he needed to return to fiction: "It is almost as if James's sole interest had been personal acceptance and when that became impossible he returned to the art of the novel."[37] In fact, the suggestiveness of Isle's observation deserves careful examination, because it provides a clue to a more complete interpretation of James's dramatic years.

When James entered the theatre to confront his audience in the most personal way, he was reenacting the dream of the Louvre and unconsciously providing us with concrete referents for the highly charged symbols of that imaginative encounter. On the day of *The American*'s premiere at Southport, James wrote to his brother William and pondered the meaning of his suspenseful anticipation of "the verdict that I am so oddly (till my complicated but valid material reasons are explained) seeking of this Philistine provincial public." After reviewing the unpromising circumstances in which the play was to be performed, James lapsed into an imaginary dialogue with himself (so thoroughly was he saturated with the instinct for drama), as if to illustrate the conflict between the side of his nature that hungered for popular success and the other side that remained committed to a more private artistic religion:

> The omens and auspices are good. . . . God grant that tonight—between 8 and 11 (spend *you* the terrible hours in fasting, silence and supplication!) I don't get the lie in my teeth. Still, I *am,* at present, in a state of abject, lonely fear—sufficient to make me say in retort to my purpose of trying again, again and yet again,—"What, a repetition of *this* horrid and quite peculiar preliminary?"[38]

As we have seen from James's letter to his sister, posted the following day, his triumph over the Southport audience triggered an exuberant outpouring of his most deeply felt desires. To his other correspondents James assumed an almost martial air, describing his success in unusually aggressive language. When he feasted with the cast after the opening performance, James felt "as if we were carousing among the slain."[39] The play's continued run only intensified his fierce ambitions; after a month he told William:

> Now that I have tasted blood, *c'est une rage* (of determination to *do,* and triumph, on my part), for I feel at last as if I had found my *real* form, which I am capable of carrying far, and for which the pale little art of fiction, as I have practised it, has been, for me, but a limited and restricted substitute. The strange thing is that I always, innermostly, knew *this* was my more characteristic form—but was kept away from it by a half-modest half-exaggerated sense of the difficulty (that is, I mean the practical odiousness) of the conditions. But now that I have accepted them and met them, I see that one isn't at all, needfully, their victim, but is, from the moment one *is* anything, one's self, worth speaking of, their *master;* and may use them, command them, squeeze them, lift them up and better them.[40]

Having accepted and met the vulgar conditions of the theatre,[41] James recognized that he need not be their "victim," but might turn the tables and be their "master," a revelation that encapsulates perfectly the meaning of his dream-adventure in the Louvre.

Unfortunately, James was never to match even the modest success of *The American* in the difficult years to come. On the eve of his provincial debut he had written to a friend, advising prayer the following night at eight o'clock and drawn breath till eleven: "if it appears at that hour that I have made a fool of myself *I* shall cease to draw it forever; unless I survive to make a bigger one still."[42] The unconscious irony of James's remark would literally come to haunt him four years later, when, in a single dreadful moment, he became a fool of embarrassing magnitude before the curtain at the St. James Theatre. His anxiety on the day that *Guy Domville* opened was intense. With virtually the same words he had used when *The American* began its run, James told his brother that he felt "plucky, but, all the same, lonely and terrified."[43] His adjectives were worthy of his imagined self in the Galerie d'Apollon, but the outcome of his ordeal at the St. James was assuredly less triumphant. In the wake of his humiliating exposure, James confided to a friend, "Deep and dark is the theatre. Even in the full consciousness of the purity and lucidity of one's motives (mine are worthy of Benjamin Franklin) one asks one's self what one is doing in that *galère*."[44] The tables were turned; vulgarity had triumphed; and the glorious *Galerie* degenerated into a self-mocking *galère*.

Some time later when James was reminded of his experience in the theatre, he suggestively told Howells that his dramatic years were buried "beneath fifty layers of dead nightmares." His remark was touched off by Howells's report of seeing a successful New York performance of *Disengaged,* the play (originally called *Mrs. Jasper*) over which James had quarreled bitterly with the manager Augustin Daly and the actress Ada Rehan in 1892–93, and which later found its way into *Theatricals* (1894), without the benefit of a stage career.[45] If only for one rather wistful epistolary moment, the news from New York rekindled in James the flame of a long-extinguished desire. How he wished he had been there to greet the company of actors!

> The dear young ingenuous benighted things! I could kiss them all with tears. But the present case to me is that there is so much, so ridiculously much more I could tell you about the poor little old ugly tragic joke of the original [*Mrs. Jasper*], & her squalid Daly-Rehan history (of 10 years ago,) than your very sweetest impression of her, even, could prompt you to tell *me.* But don't be afraid—now. . . . And yet you divinely tell me that the thing you *saw* was, or could pass for, lively; & that is enough, & I swoon away, on it, into sublimities of universal acceptance. It "went," it "went," and as *you* went, my cup sufficiently overflows from it! It isn't that I couldn't drink down oceans more; but one can't be more than gloriously drunk; & such now is my everlasting doom.[46]

Beneath all the dead nightmares was the memory of a living vision of triumph.

By 1902 Henry James could only dream of a "universal acceptance" approaching the sublime; reality was closer to its ridiculous neighbor. Though hardly consigned to "everlasting doom," James had come to accept the fate of a writer whose success is more of esteem than of dollars. But the imagery and meaning of the dream-adventure never wholly left him. When Howells wrote again later in the year to congratulate James on the beauty of *The Wings of the Dove* and to remark on its success with the periodical press, the novelist responded in, by now, a familiar voice:

> I haven't known anything about the American "notices," heaven save the mark! any more than about those here (which I am told, however, have been remarkably genial;) so that I have *not* had the sense of confrontation with a public more than usually childish—I mean had it in any special way. I confess, however, that that is my chronic sense—the more than usual childishness of publics: and it is (has been,) in my mind, long since discounted, and my work definitely insists upon being independent of such phantasms and on unfolding itself wholly from its own "innards." Of course, in our conditions, doing anything decent is pure disinterested, unsupported, unrewarded heroism; but that's in the day's work.[47]

Even while professing his indifference to the market, James returned to the archetype of his dream-adventure: "confrontation"—"public"—"phantasms"—"heroism." After his disastrous confrontation with the public at the premiere of *Guy Domville,* James reconsecrated his vows to literary labor by saying, "I have only to *face* my problems." His solution, wholly self-prescribed, was to convert the material of failure into the stuff of imagination, a process in which his allegiance to art could offer the interest, the support, and the rewards that the public had denied him. "It is now indeed," James wrote, "that I may do the work of my life. And I will."[48]

III
Henry James and the Profession of Authorship

THE PROBLEM OF VOCATION

When Henry James suffered rejection by the public, he did not retreat into a wholly private universe. Between the artist's sanctuary and the vulgar street lay the intermediary domain of publishing, symbolized by the "office" in *The Portrait of a Lady*. Even with its implications of commercialism, the literary marketplace offered certain consolations to James, especially in comparison with the theatre. In the security of the "office," Isabel can confide her sorrows to an old haircloth sofa; James often found a similar kind of sympathy among the human furniture of editorial rooms in England and America. Even if a book received adverse reviews and stubbornly refused to sell, its career did not involve the public exposure that went with a play. A magazine's rejection of a story was a private matter between editor and writer. But success at the box office typically required advance promotion to stimulate the public's curiosity, a commercial reality of which Henry James was only too well aware. As Leon Edel has suggested, "when a play was announced, publicized, promised to the public, and then not produced, or failed in production, the author was, in the process, publicly rejected. This was what Henry James feared more than anything else."[1]

The triangular configuration of the publishing world, by which the artist is at least partially shielded from contact with his audience, was a distinct advantage to James, particularly during the early years of his development as a writer. Although he had determined to become a man of letters during his short stint at Harvard (1862–63), the problem of vocation continued to plague him for an unusually long time. Nearly two years elapsed before anything from his pen reached publication and, for the rest of the decade, James struggled to achieve and maintain the professional writer's necessary discipline. One of his earliest protagonists discovers that "to learn to live is to learn to work."[2] For James himself the equation was reversed: to learn to work was to learn to live.

While many of the writer's earliest tales are populated by young men in search of their proper callings, a famous epistolary tribute to William Dean Howells, who had begun his literary career with the *Atlantic Monthly* after the Civil War, contains the most suggestive testimony about James's vocational problem.

> My debt to you [James wrote in 1912] began well-nigh half a century ago, in the most personal way possible, and then kept growing and growing with your own admirable growth—but always rooted in the early intimate benefit. This benefit was that you held out your open editorial hand to me at the time I began to write—and I allude especially to the summer of 1866—with a frankness and sweetness of hospitality that was really the making of me, the making of the confidence that required help and sympathy and that I should otherwise, I think, have strayed and stumbled about a long time without acquiring. You showed me the way and opened me the door; you wrote to me, and confessed yourself struck with me—I have never forgotten the beautiful thrill of *that.* You published me at once—and paid me, above all, with a dazzling promptitude; magnificently, I felt, and so that nothing since has ever quite come up to it. More than this even, you cheered me on with a sympathy that was in itself an inspiration. I mean that you talked genially and suggestively conversed and consorted with me. This won me to you irresistibly and made you the most interesting person I knew—lost as I was in the charming sense that my best friend was an editor, and an almost insatiable editor, and that such a delicious being as that was a kind of property of my own.[3]

Written at a time when James's imagination worked at a feverishly retrospective pitch, his letter to Howells is akin to the autobiographical volumes and in some ways represents a modest extension of them. The symbolic treatment of the marketplace appears here in familiar guise—"You showed me the way and opened me the door"—although the commemorative function of the letter necessarily suppresses any ambiguity about the author's actual sense of relation to his public.

Interesting, too, is the frank confession about the significance of compensation ("You published me at once—and paid me, above all, with a dazzling promptitude"), for in *Notes of a Son and Brother* the author's consecration to letters is confirmed by the receipt of twelve greenbacks for his first published piece:

> I see before me, in the rich, the many-hued light of my room . . . the very greenbacks, to the total value of twelve dollars, into which I had changed the cheque representing my first earned wage. I had earned it, I couldn't but feel, with fabulous felicity: a circumstance so strangely mixed with the fact that

> literary composition of a high order had, at that very table where the greenbacks were spread out, quite viciously declined, and with the air of its being also once for all, to "come" on any save its own essential terms, which it seemed to distinguish in the most invidious manner conceivable from mine. It was to insist through all my course on this distinction, and sordid gain thereby never again to seem so easy as in that prime handling of my fee.[4]

Donald Mull has claimed that this passage presents a complex of attitude and meaning central to the whole canon of Henry James,[5] an assertion made credible by the felt tension evidenced here between "literary composition of a high order" and its cash equivalent in the marketplace. In strange succession the author's writing table is covered first by sheets of manuscript and then by dollar bills, distinguished somewhat uncomfortably by their "queer . . . rather greasy complexion" (p. 476).

If the passage emphasizes James's difficulty in reconciling his art with "sordid gain," the remainder of the paragraph, as Mull suggests, indicates a sense in which the two can be rendered compatible. Recalling the hospitality shown him by Charles Eliot Norton, the editor of the *North American Review* who paid the young author his fee, James remembered his afternoon appointment in the library at Norton's home as "a positive consecration to letters":

> the winter sunshine touched serene bookshelves and arrayed pictures, the whole embrowned composition of objects in my view, with I knew not what golden light of promise, what assurance of things to come: there was to be nothing exactly like it later on—the conditions of perfect rightness for a certain fresh felicity, certain decisive pressures of the spring, *can* occur, it would seem, but once. This was on the other hand the beginning of so many intentions that it mattered little if the particular occasion was not repeated; for what did I do again and again, though all the years, but handle in plenty what I might have called the small change of it? (p. 477)

Mull shrewdly notices that the "golden light of promise" James sees at Shady Hill relates directly to the "rich, the many-hued light" that falls upon the greenbacks in his room at Ashburton Place; with James's formal admisssion into the world of literature, the "highly connotative terms associated with money ('rich' and 'golden') are taken out of the context of 'wage' and 'gain' to symbolize, as the light bathing the scene in which the young writer realizes them, the ambiguous potentialities of the imagination."[6] Money thus modulates between the poles of commerce and imagination for James, a distinction that Mull employs quite deftly in his analysis of the novels and tales. But we should also recognize that money alone is not the primary vehicle for reconciling James's attitudes toward art and the marketplace. What renders "literary composition of a high order" compatible with "sordid gain" is precisely the "positive consecration to letters" James experienced on that golden afternoon—his signal commitment to the literary vocation.

The significance of James's choice takes on a certain psychological urgency when we remember that "the note of [his] own house was the absence of any profession" whatsoever (p. 146). The conspicuous absence of vocation in the James household was deliberately fostered by the novelist's father, whose

> prime uneasiness in presence of any particular form of success we might, according to our lights as then glimmering, propose to invoke was that it bravely, or with such inward assurance, dispensed with any suggestion of an alternative. What we were to do instead was just to *be* something, something unconnected with specific doing, something free and uncommitted, something finer than being *that,* whatever it was, might consist of. (p. 268)

Austin Warren once claimed that the James children benefited greatly from their father's refusal to take up a more exacting career, because he was thereby able to devote his fine intelligence to their education.[7] This confident assertion must be qualified, however, by the testimony of the children themselves.

In his autobiography, Henry explicitly recorded his discomfort with the paternal philosophy of mere being; but even more revealing in some ways are the implicit consequences of that philosophy, suggested by Isabel Archer's fate in *The Portrait of a Lady.* Immediately following the description of the "office" that we have already examined, Isabel is discovered by her aunt, Lydia Touchett, who had quarreled years before with Isabel's father over the cavalier manner in which his children have been raised. The similarity to the James's upbringing is conspicuous:

> They had had no regular education and no permanent home; they had been at once spoiled and neglected; they had lived with nursemaids and governesses (usually very bad ones), or had been sent to strange schools, kept by foreigners, from which, at the end of a month, they had been removed in tears.[8]

To Isabel, of course, this view of the matter excites "indignation, for to her own sense her opportunities had been large." But filial sympathy cannot obscure the facts of circumstance. With Mr. Archer's death the family's resources run dry, Isabel is taken in by her relatives, and the Albany house is put on the market:

> "How much money do you expect to get for it?" Mrs. Touchett asked [Isabel], who had brought her to sit in the front-parlour, which she had inspected without enthusiasm.
>
> "I haven't the least idea," said the girl.
>
> "That's the second time you have said that to me," her aunt rejoined. "And yet you don't look at all stupid."
>
> "I'm not stupid; but I don't know anything about money."
>
> "Yes, that's the way you were brought up—as if you were to inherit a million."[9]

Ironically, Isabel shall inherit a sizable fortune from Lydia Touchett's husband and thus be liberated to follow freely the dictates of her idiosyncratically educated imagination.

The parallel between James's situation and his protagonist's becomes even more striking when we recall that Isabel's family has been so far removed from business that no one can remember how the "office" earned its peculiar designation. Similarly, in the James family, "our consciousness was positively disfurnished, as that of young Americans went, of the actualities of 'business' in a world of business. As to that we all formed together quite a monstrous exception; business in a world of business was the thing we most agreed . . . in knowing nothing about" (p. 35). From the time his paternal grandfather had bequeathed one of the largest American fortunes of its day, his descendants, James recalled, "were never in a single case, I think, for two generations, guilty of a stroke of business":

> the word had been passed, all round, that we didn't, that we couldn't and shouldn't, understand these things, questions of arithmetic and of fond calculation, questions of the counting-house and the market; and we appear to have held to our agreement as loyally and to have accepted our doom as serenely as if our faith had been mutually pledged. (p. 109)

The money they received from their inheritance, like the green paper at the office windows, was "renewed by other hands"; no member of the James family would be tainted by familiarity with "an office or a 'store,' places in which people sat close and made money" (p. 30).

Even to Isabel's innocent consciousness, the office is a "chamber of disgrace," though she feels a certain sympathy for its cast-off occupants, even if they are pieces of furniture. In his youth James had witnessed much rearrangement of the human furniture, as various foredoomed and vocationless uncles made their hapless way toward premature death, leaving nothing but a vast impoverished cousinage in their wake. To be immersed in business seemed fatal to character, but to be leisured in a commercial culture was almost equally regrettable. The only alternative to the pursuit of money, apparently, was the pursuit of pleasure, "sought, and sought only in places in which people got tipsy. There was clearly no mean," James recalled, "least of all the golden one, for it was just the ready, even when the moderate, possession of gold that determined, that hurried on disaster. . . . The field was strictly covered, to my young eyes, by three classes, the busy, the tipsy, and Daniel Webster" (p. 30).

The zeal with which James's father sought to avert these grim alternatives for his sons is legendary, but no less revealing is the novelist's ambiguous appreciation of his parent's effort. Surrounded by other American children who could boast of their fathers' worldly accomplishments, James remembered well "how when we were all young together we had, under pressure of the American ideal in the matter, then so rigid, felt it tasteless and even humiliating that the head of our little family was *not* in business, and that even among our relatives on each side couldn't so much as name anyone who was" (pp. 278–79). The conspicuous absence of vocation in the James household was matched by an equal disregard for an established religious affiliation, and in both instances James felt profoundly embarrassed by the disjunction between his father's values and society's cultural norms. "What shall we tell them you *are*?" the children would ask. But the parent's response—"Say I'm a philosopher, say I'm a seeker for truth, say I'm a lover of my kind, say I'm an author of books if you like; or, best of all, just say I'm a Student"—struck James as abject (pp. 337–38). His father, to paraphrase Hawthorne, might as well have been a fiddler![10]

The question of social identity looms large in *The Portrait* as a determining factor in Isabel's decision to marry Gilbert Osmond. Donald Mull has observed that when Madame Merle first mentions Osmond to Isabel she "denigrates him in such a fashion that he is sure to be of interest to her," baiting the trap first by questioning the identity of Ralph Touchett, Isabel's consumptive cousin, and then by producing Osmond as the ultimate extension of Ralph's case, the man who exists outside the matrix of conventional social roles:

> "Look at poor Ralph Touchett; what sort of a figure do you call that? Fortunately he has got a consumption; I say fortunately, because it gives him something to do. His consumption is his career; it's a kind of position. . . . But without that, who would he be, what would he represent? 'Mr. Ralph Touchett, an American who lives in Europe.' That signifies absolutely nothing—it's impossible that anything should signify less. . . . With the poor old father it's different; he has his identity, and it is rather a massive one. He represents a great financial house, and that, in our day, is as good as anything else. . . . The worst case, I think, is a friend of mine, a countryman of ours, who lives in Italy (where he also was brought before he knew better), and who is one of the most delightful men I know. . . . I'll bring you together, and then you will see what I mean. He is Gilbert Osmond—he lives in Italy; that is all one can say about him. He is exceedingly clever, a man made to be distinguished; but, as I say, you exhaust the description when you say that he is Mr. Osmond, who lives in Italy. No career, no name, no position, no fortune, no past, no future, no anything."[11]

According to Madame Merle's description, Osmond virtually epitomizes the individualist ideal of the elder Henry James, for more than any other character in the novel he remains "unconnected with specific doing." To introduce him here, as Mull writes, is

> a masterstroke on Madame Merle's part, since he becomes associated [to Isabel] with the autonomous individual. . . . His lack of external determination and definition—the fact that he lacks career, name, position, fortune,

past, future, anything, that he is, in short, the antithesis of everything that Lord Warburton is—is what will appeal to Isabel, what will make him figure for her the free individual unconstrained by externals.[12]

Despite her illusion of freedom, Isabel is destined to be "ground in the very mill of the conventional" through her marriage to Osmond—hardly the end Henry James, Sr. would have anticipated for one of his brood.[13] Nevertheless, Osmond curiously represents the fate to which James himself might have been drawn, if he had not positively resisted his father's benign indifference to any choice of vocation for his sons.

How intensely James reacted against his parent's vocational amorphousness can be read in the tender condescension with which he treats his father's literary career in the autobiography. Despite the fact that his father applied himself at his writing table with daily "regularity" and "piety" ("as if he had been working under pressure for his bread and ours"), the exercise of the elder James's "remarkable genius brought him in fact throughout the long years no ghost of a reward in the form of pence, and could proceed to publicity, as it repeatedly did, not only by the copious and resigned sacrifice of such calculations, but by his meeting in every single case all the expenses of the process" (p. 330). While James can admire the purity of his father's motives, he also feels a kind of professional embarrassment over the circumstances by which the paternal philosophy found its way into print. For not one of a dozen books by the senior Henry James would a publisher assume the risk of plates and paper—hardly an auspicious precedent for his son's literary ambitions.

The difference between the publishing experiences of father and son reflects, in part, the maturation of the American book trade in the nineteenth century. Asking authors to underwrite the cost of production was a standard practice among journeyman printers before the Civil War; later, as publishers began to assume this risk as part of their professional function, many firms demanded that a certain number of copies of a book's first printing be exempted from royalty.[14] Such practices were familiar to the elder Henry James, who in turn recommended them to his son. Almost a decade after James had begun to publish reviews, travel sketches, and stories in American magazines, his father and other literary advisers urged him to collect some of his work for issue in book form. In the spring of 1873 James's father went to see James R. Osgood, a Boston publisher, about the prospects for a volume by his son. Osgood repeated the offer he had earlier mentioned to the younger Henry: a royalty of 10 percent on every copy sold after the first thousand if the publisher assumed all risks; 15 percent if James paid for the stereotype plates. Henry James, Sr. preferred the latter course. "I shall be willing," he wrote to his son, who was in Europe at this time, "(in case you would like to publish, and I think it is time for you to do so) to bear the expense of stereotyping, and if you will pick out what you would like to be included, we shall set to work at once, and have the book ready by next Autumn."[15]

But his son looked at Osgood's proposal with a colder eye. Rather than hurrying into print a mere hodge-podge of his stories—most of which, moreover, were "full of thin spots in the writing"—James preferred to wait until he had enough material for a thematically coherent volume as his first entry into the field. As this response to his parents demonstrates, he showed from the first a deliberate awareness of the marketplace:

> What I desire is this: to make a volume, a short time hence, of tales on the theme of American adventurers in Europe, leading off with the *Passionate Pilgrim*. I have three or four more to write: one I have lately sent to Howells and have half finished another. They will all have been the work of the last three years and be much better and maturer than their predecessors. . . . The money I should get would not (probably) be enough to make a sacrifice for—so long as (as I properly) I can keep making enough to get on with comfortably.—I should loathe, too, to have you spending money on my plates—though it's noble to offer it.[16]

James's modest estimate of his income from such a book was absolutely correct; and when he deprecated the investment of his own (or the family's) money in stereotype plates, he was openly repudiating his father's confirmed manner of dealing with publishers.

When James returned to America the following year "to start [him]self on a remunerative and perfectly practical literary basis," he came with plans for two books in mind.[17] The collection of tales was now possible, but James also hoped to assemble his recent travel articles and letters about Europe in a complementary volume of nonfiction. For a beginning writer, here was a unique chance to experiment with publishing arrangements; and James promptly negotiated contracts with Osgood that would clarify his work's market value. Both *A Passionate Pilgrim* and *Transatlantic Sketches* appeared early in 1875, were priced at $2, and printed in identical quantities (1500 copies each). Both works were also published by Osgood, who paid for the plates of *A Passionate Pilgrim* and gave James a 10 percent royalty on every copy sold (including the first 1000); but for *Transatlantic Sketches* James assumed the cost of stereotyping in exchange for a royalty of 15 percent. With his first two forays into the literary marketplace, James had an unusual (if serendipitous) opportunity to determine which arrangement was more advantageous.

The results were not long in coming. By the time Osgood tallied his semiannual accounts in the autumn of 1875, he had sold 441 copies of *A Passionate Pilgrim* and 656 of *Transatlantic Sketches,* yielding respective royalties of $88.20 and $196.80, payable in December.[18] The modest returns from *A Passionate Pilgrim* were at least clear profit; but the larger royalty from *Transatlantic Sketches* had to be balanced against James's investment in stereotype plates. These had cost him $555,[19] and to recover this sum *Transatlantic Sketches* would have to sell 1850 copies at a royalty of 15 percent of the retail price ($2). In fact, James did not break even on the book until 1906.[20] James's first lesson in literary economics was not forgotten: *Transatlantic Sketches* was the only book in his long career for which he agreed to purchase the stereotype plates.

The contrast with his father's publishing experience could not have been more complete. Years later, when James looked back at his father's first communication from Osgood, he smiled, recognizing "the admirable anxiety with which thought could be taken, even though 'amateurishly,' in my professional interest" (p. 401). The son's tenderly deprecating words speak volumes.[21] Despite the idiosyncrasies of his father's "amateurishly" literary efforts—his style "too philosophic for life, and at the same time too living . . . for thought," his career "so destitute of every worldly or literary ambition"—James wanted to believe he "was yet a great writer."[22] But the son was determined to become a greater one still, even if that meant shrugging off the mantle of his father's disinterested philosophy.

AN INTERNATIONAL EPISODE: THE MAN OF LETTERS IN ENGLAND AND AMERICA

James's slowly emerging professionalism answered to both social and psychological necessities. If within the family circle the young man felt a need to be "just literary" (p. 413), thus distinguishing himself from his more technically trained elder brother, his career as a writer was also shaped by economic forces that were transforming the Anglo-American literary marketplace in the latter half of the nineteenth century. The rapid rise and expansion of the reading public, the proliferation of periodicals, and the development of the modern publishing firm all contributed to the making of Henry James; the shape of his career parallels (and, in some respects, anticipates) the transformation of literature's status in the culture at large. Even though James was among the first observers to recognize the commercialization of literature that, by the end of the century, was so widely deplored,[23] his own behavior in the marketplace effectively demonstrates the changing nature of the literary vocation. Although the business of authorship had long since ceased to be the exclusive domain of gentlemen of taste and leisure, its ranks were swelled in James's lifetime by men and women who approached their calling with an increasingly professional self-consciousness, writers for whom the written—better still, the published—word was not merely an intellectual diversion but primarily a source of income and status. When James described one of his contemporaries as a member of the "modern class of trained men of letters . . . not an occasional or a desultory poet [but] a novelist to his fingertips—a soldier in the great army of constant producers,"[24] he was defining a role to which he himself had declared allegiance.

Membership in James's army was not for the tender-minded; and he was flanked by thousands of other professional writers at the end of the century who wrote books, edited an ever-increasing number of periodicals, and filled their pages with print. In 1881 the English census tabulated 3400 respondents who had identified themselves as authors, editors, or journalists; in ten years the number had grown to 6000, and almost doubled again by 1901 to reach 11,000.[25] Such surging statistics were easily matched, if not exceeded, by developments in America, where, as Carl Bode has noted, the advent of the industrial revolution in the publishing business occurred simultaneously with the advent of popular literacy.[26] What the union of those two forces produced was not always attractive to James,[27] but his insights into the sociological underpinnings of the literary life have rarely been matched in forcefulness or prophetic awareness. Even though an expanding literary marketplace created new opportunities for the discovery and promotion of artistic talent, the conditions by which such phenomenal growth was achieved carried with them new threats to the writer's integrity and to the very habits of mind that made possible the creation of a lasting and significant literature.

Despite important differences between the nineteenth-century English and American book trades, their common experience was expansion—the discovery of new reading publics and the proliferation of titles and marketing mechanisms to attract and serve them. The volume of book production in the United States not only showed a constant absolute increase throughout the century, but outran population growth as well. In the 1830's American publishers issued about 1000 new titles annually; by the 1870s the number had grown to 3000; and at the beginning of the twentieth century 6000 new books were coming from the presses every year. Such promising figures were not without their attendant anxieties to publishers, because each new title involved not only the labor of making arrangements with an author and obtaining a satisfactory manuscript, but also the even more difficult task of marketing a new product. The evidence of growth was only superficially encouraging, for the distribution mechanisms of the book trade in England and America were woefully inadequate to handle the mushrooming of books in print, creating problems that industry executives still ponder.[28]

If leaders of modern publishing firms, equipped with computers and sophisticated marketing strategies, find conditions of the book trade difficult to understand, their counterparts in the nineteenth century were even more bewildered by the contemporary transformation of the industry. Most of them failed to recognize the fundamental causes of their problems (chronic overproduction and an inability to control the retail distribution and pricing of books), and they sought instead to explain them away by occasional sermonizing on the commercialization of literature and the short-sighted rapacity of authors who were disrupting an older and presumably more agreeable pattern of cooperation between producers and publishers.

Like most myths of the golden age, their vision of a loving-cup era in publishing had its convenient uses, for it allowed literary businessmen to fashion a genteel pedigree for themselves, going back to a time when their profession was not sullied by the crass requirements of the marketplace. And like most myths it also embodied a certain measure of truth, for in contrast to many other business enterprises in the nineteenth century, publishing firms largely resisted the monopolistic impulse to integrate manufacturing and distribution capacities and expand vertically. Even though publishers were not wholly innocent of the more notorious aspects of capitalism in the Gilded Age (occasionally bribing school boards to secure the adoption of particular textbooks, perpetrating inflated publicity schemes, and pirating foreign books), what seems remarkable to modern historians is that the larger and more successful firms succumbed least to these practices. Among the leaders in the industry there existed a code of etiquette that was honored far more often than it was ignored. Gentility had its uses, of course, as a means of restraining competition; but the fact remains that the regular trade publishers were among the industry's most scrupulous men rather than its most grasping.[29] Much like the authors they served, publishers were "poised between trade and profession, with the rewards of the first, the dignity of the second, and the anxieties of both."[30]

Not surprisingly, the common problems of authors and publishers were less conspicuous at the time than their perceived antagonisms. The documentary evidence of the quarrel between these two groups is unusually revealing, and from it we can understand better the social and economic factors that influenced Henry James's emergence as a well-disciplined soldier in the "great army" of literary producers. The martial imagery and tone James often adopted to describe the working man of letters were themselves representative of the verbal hostility between authors and publishers that occasionally erupted in the literary journalism of the period. But to interpret such outbursts properly (and publishers' responses to them) we must read between the lines of both offensive and defensive arguments; for while writers often characterized the publisher as a vulgar businessman "moved by no enthusiasms for literature, but simply by the consideration of what will pay,"[31] publishers casually dismissed authorial criticism as irrelevant sniping from members of "a *genus irritable,* whose perceptions of the facts and equities of business transactions [had to] be taken with much allowance."[32] A more disinterested narrative emerges only after a comparative evaluation of these sources.

Michael Sadlier has claimed that "the most vital relationship in the whole tragi-comedy of bookdom is the relationship between author and publisher";[33] and the case of Henry James certainly validates his assertion. What distinguishes James's career and gives it such documentary significance is the fact that he was among the first men of letters to deal effectively with publishers in both England and America. Of course, books had crossed the sea in both directions before James established himself in London in 1876, but they were typically victims of piracy and usually of no financial significance to their authors in either country. An American book could be registered for copyright in England, but the legal basis on which such claims were founded was often subject to question and occasionally disallowed by the English courts. If the English issue anticipated American publication and an American author was residing in an English jurisdiction when his book appeared, the law seemed to offer some protection. If the stakes were high enough, some Americans (Mark Twain, for example) made it a point to vacation in Canada while their English publishers rushed books through the press. For James, of course, the matter was simpler: London was his home, and England, at last, his declared country. While English custom afforded Americans at least some prospect of legal protection, no reciprocal guarantees were possible under the American statute, which reserved copyright in the United States to American citizens. What payments Englishmen occasionally received from their American publishers were gestures of courtesy, and even these were rarely forthcoming. Not until 1891 was this embarrassingly lopsided situation corrected, when the United States finally signed its first international copyright agreement with Great Britain.[34]

In the meantime, James effectively established himself as a writer under conditions by which he profited from both the security of American law and the ambiguity of the English. He suffered the penalty of piracy in volume form only twice[35] and promptly learned from his mistakes to safeguard his interests in both countries by timing his publications carefully and registering pre-publication copyright editions of his work with the Library of Congress when material that was to appear first in England anticipated the American issue by more than a few weeks. Almost continuous residence abroad was undoubtedly congenial to James's artistic imagination, but it may also have been necessary for the more worldly requirements of his pocketbook. By securing English copyright for his wares and often selling them to English as well as American periodicals for serial use, James effectively doubled his income as a writer. Doubtful that he would ever have truly mass appeal, James wisely settled on a course that offered him at least the modest comforts of a discerning audience in two countries, when one market probably would have proved insufficient to his needs.

As early as 1872 James supposedly had given up "the ambition of ever being a free-going and light-paced enough writer to please the multitude." "The multitude," he told his brother William, "has absolutely no taste—none at least that a thinking man is bound to defer to. To write for the few who have is doubtless to lose money—but I am not afraid of starving."[36] James was not afraid of starving—and not just because he would eventually accept 107 dinner invitations in a single London season. Far from being condescending, James's rather patrician tone here implies a flattering confidence in the public's potential appetite for serious literature (or at least for books whose virtues were not exhausted by the adjectives "free-going" and "light-paced"). In 1867 Howells had shrewdly predicted that, because of James's penchant for irony and subtle psychology, he would have to "in a very great degree create his audience."[37] James was not afraid of starving because he had accepted that challenge and intended to meet it head on.

In his professional capacity as a writer, Henry James conducted a siege of London that was worthy of one of his fictional characters. When he arrived in the Anglo-Saxon literary capital, almost no Englishmen had ever signed royalty contracts with their publishers; few had ever received any payment in advance of publication; and many were content simply to part with their copyrights forever in exchange for a fixed, if modest, sum.[38] Yet within twenty years, the literary world would be transformed along recognizably modern lines. By the late 1890s English authors routinely signed royalty contracts for their books and often received healthy sums for them in advance of publication; they hired literary agents to market their wares competitively; and they freely explored the vast opportunities of the American market. In no sense was James singly responsible for all these changes, but his special status as a transatlantic author placed him squarely between the forces of innovation and tradition and made him an ideal exponent for the professionalization of the literary vocation.

Surely no one would have predicted this from James's first adult residence in England (1869–70, 1872–74), years in which his vocational dilemma was aggravated by the practical problem of where to set up his literary workshop. Recalling the modest figure the young American cut when he arrived in London in 1870, Edmund Gosse noted that, while James carried letters of introduction to John Ruskin, William Morris, and other spokesmen of eminent artistic and literary circles, he plainly "made no impression whatever upon them":

> The time for Henry James to "make an impression" on others was not come yet; he was simply the well-bred, rather shy, young American invalid, with excellent introductions, who crossed the path of English activities, almost without casting a shadow. He had published no book; he had no distinct call-

> ing; he was a deprecating and punctilious young stranger from somewhere in Massachusetts, immature-looking for all his seven-and-twenty years.[39]

In the eyes of literary London only the tangible symbol of a book in print could give substance to a young man's vaguely literary aspirations, and James approached the question of his first deliberate appearance before the English public with the kind of diplomacy only a foreigner would feel compelled to exhibit.

When his mother urged him in 1872 to "find a brisker market" for his wares than the *Atlantic* and the *Nation* afforded, James begged for patience; if traveling had been more propitious to writing, he might have ceased to depend on those magazines. "Yet," he wondered, "with the shabby American periodicals & the inaccessible English ones—what is one to do?"[40] James rightly felt that the travel sketches he was writing could be of interest only to a more provincial American audience;[41] his early stories were disqualified by their equally limited appeal. "One must approach English organs on some other basis than American subjects," he told his parents, "unless they are 'racy' & of the Bret Harte & Joaquin Miller type."[42] James had no Wild West stories up his sleeve (though the melodramatic story of one Californian, Christopher Newman, was promptly pirated by an English reprint house a few years later), and he wisely chose to defer his entry into the British market until a more appropriate hour.

When that hour arrived, after James took up residence in London during the winter of 1876, he moved with deliberate caution, ever conscious of his peculiar status as an alien in the citadel of literature. "I don't mean to try to 'collaborate' on the London magazines," he confided to his old Newport friend Thomas Sergeant Perry, "tho' surely a novelist, among them is greatly wanted. Someday, if I pile up my fame, I may be less easy; but meanwhile I make shift with our own vulgar organs." Another stimulus to "make shift" with American periodicals was the fact that they paid better. "I am told it is the deuce to get money out of the London Mags.," he added to Perry. "Half the work is done by rich dilletanti [*sic*] gratis."[43] Even though the marketplace, glutted with amateurs, was not altogether promising, James's professional ambition was quietly waiting for the right opportunity to unmask itself.

Ironically, James's first run before the British public was a hare over which he had no control—Ward, Lock's pirated edition of *The American,* issued in December 1877. In one sense it was the most auspicious start he could have hoped for. Piracy implied a felt demand in the marketplace; if James himself was unsure about the suitability of his fiction for English readers, at least one literary hustler with an eye on the cash register had no such qualms. A quiet awareness of that fact may have softened James's reaction to the unanticipated appearance of the book, which, he told his mother, was reprinted (and vilely *mis*printed) in a cheap railway library, "with a wonderful picture on the cover[.] But this of course is a piracy, & I get no profit from it."[44] If he made no money from this edition, he might still hope to make a name by it; in time he would act to shore up his growing reputation with legitimate publications.

In fact, James's first authorized English book (*French Poets and Novelists,* 1878) was in press at the time of Ward, Lock's piracy, though it is worth noting that the author's legitimate publisher, Macmillan, was first attracted to him after seeing J. R. Osgood's edition of *The American* in the summer of the preceding year. When James got wind of Macmillan's interest, he anxiously awaited their proposal for republication; but when no offer for the book arrived, he took the initiative to send the firm a more sober alternative, a collection of his essays on contemporary French literature.[45] Macmillan agreed to publish the book, even though the firm's previous experience with volumes of reprinted essays had "not been such as to make us very sanguine about the success of the venture"; nevertheless, they were willing "to take the risk of printing the book, sharing with [James] any profit that [might] result from its publication." In selecting the table of contents from the long list he had first submitted, James was advised, however, "to retain those papers most likely to be interesting to that strange creature the 'general reader.'"[46]

Macmillan's initial overture to James is worthy of remark on several counts. As a first gesture toward a writer of considerable promise, its tone is shrewdly conservative, almost calculated to keep ambitious expectations at bay. The offer of half-profits is made to seem a concession, especially in light of the book's assuredly limited appeal. James's response is equally interesting, because while he was glad that the firm would publish the volume, he preferred to discuss the terms of the arrangement face to face when he returned to London from the country.[47] What transpired at this meeting we can probably surmise, for James had never dealt with an English publisher before and in all likelihood knew very little about the details of a half-profits contract. If Macmillan's terms seemed imprecise to James, they were only consistent with many other aspects of English life, in which social behavior was governed by customs and traditions so deeply ingrained that, in contrast with America, no one felt a need to articulate or define them. Of infinitely greater importance to the American was the fact that the process of his literary assimilation had at last begun; a London publisher had opened the door in response to his knock, and a volume was in the works.

James spent the autumn on the continent, correcting proof for his book in Paris. On his return to England at Christmastime, he dined almost immediately with Frederick Macmillan, the junior partner of the firm, who had lived in New York, married an American wife, and, James reported to his sister, was "a nice young fellow and very friendly."[48] The

Memorandum of Agreement

Dated Jan 20 · 1879.

BETWEEN

Henry James Esq

AND

MACMILLAN AND CO.

FOR THE PUBLICATION OF

'Daisy Miller', 'The Europeans,'

'The American', & 'French Poets'

½ Profits.

Henry James's first contract with Macmillan, dated 20 January 1879, for *Daisy Miller and Other Stories, French Poets and Novelists, The Europeans,* and *The American*: a customary "half-profits" agreement, typical of Victorian publishing practice.

Memorandum of Agreement made this *20th*

day of *January* 18*79*, between *Henry James Junr. Esq.*

on the one part, and Messrs. Macmillan and Co. on the other part.

It is Agreed that the said Messrs. Macmillan and Co. shall publish at their own risk and expense *"Daisy Miller" and other stories*

the copyright of which shall be the joint property of *Henry James Junr. Esq.* and Messrs. Macmillan and Co. in the proportions stated below, and after deducting from the produce of the sale thereof all the expenses of printing, paper, boarding, advertising, trade allowances, and other incidental expenses, the profits remaining of every edition that may be printed of the work during the term of legal copyright are to be divided into *two equal* parts, *one part* to be paid to the said *Henry James Junr. Esq.*

and the other to belong to Messrs. Macmillan and Co.

The books to be accounted for at the trade-sale price, twenty-five as twenty-four, unless it be thought advisable to dispose of copies or of the remainder at a lower price, which is left to the discretion of Messrs. Macmillan and Co.

Accounts to be made up annually to Midsummer, delivered on or before October 1, and settled by cash in the ensuing January.

It is further agreed that "French Poets & Novelists" "The Europeans" and "The American" shall be published on the above terms

Macmillan & Co.

Henry James jr

American soon became a frequent guest at the Macmillans' home in St. John's Wood, a development that underscores the importance of informal social contact in the nineteenth-century publishing world. Perhaps even more revealing, however, is the informality with which Macmillan and James conducted their business. No contract was signed for *French Poets and Novelists* until 20 January 1879—almost a year after publication—by which time Macmillan had also issued *Daisy Miller, The Europeans,* and the authorized edition of *The American.*[49] English publishing, as James first encountered it, was clearly dominated by the gentleman's agreement; and he was willing, at least initially, to accommodate himself to a custom not entirely his own. Unlike so many of his American characters who are baffled or frustrated by European society, James knew precisely how to balance his personal ambition with political decorum. He would try the English publishers on their accustomed terms, for only time would provide the hard financial evidence with which to gauge the merit of the half-profits arrangement he had concluded.

In the meantime, James dined regularly with Macmillan and arranged for the publication of the stories that were flowing from his pen with quickened regularity. The path to fame and fortune seemed clearly marked, as the writer confided to his brother in January 1878:

> If I keep along here patiently for a certain time I rather think I shall become a (sufficiently) great man. I have got back to work with great zest after my autumnal loafings, and mean to do some this year which will make a mark. I am, as you suppose, weary of writing articles about places, and mere potboilers of all kinds; but shall probably, after the next six months, be able to forswear it altogether, and give myself up seriously to "creative" writing. Then, and not till then, my real career will begin. After that *gare à vous!*

After meeting with Macmillan two weeks later, James was even more emphatic: "It is time I should rend the veil from the ferocious ambition which has always *couvé* beneath a tranquil exterior; which enabled me to support unrecorded physical misery in my younger years; and which is perfectly confident of accomplishing considerable things!"[50] Ward, Lock's piracy of *The American* demonstrated that James's fiction did indeed have an audience in England, and Macmillan invited James to serialize his next novel in *Macmillan's Magazine* simultaneously with the *Atlantic.* The publisher's encouragement clearly stimulated James's appetite for glory, and throughout the ensuing year, as one volume followed another under the Macmillan imprint, his faith in his creative abilities grew.

Despite Macmillan's enthusiasm for his American friend, the firm's adoption of James was by no means automatic. John Morley, a respected reader for Macmillan, had registered complaints about his critical essays; and when James expressed his desire that the company combat Ward,

Lock's piracy, by issuing *The American* themselves, another Macmillan editor, George Grove, apparently could not even finish reading the novel. This setback did not dissuade James from continuing his modest assault, for he knew that in the long run his influence with one of the firm's partners would probably transcend the conservative, if not benighted, taste of its editors. When Macmillan hinted to James that Grove had reservations about the book, the novelist shot back, "You might tell Mr. Grove—to impress the editorial imagination—that the book has been twice translated into German."[51] Henceforth James knew that his best strategy in dealing with the house would be to discuss his plans directly with Frederick Macmillan, a man with whom his professional relationship was reinforced by social bonds.

Besides giving James his much-needed entry into the English literary world, Macmillan's advocacy also emboldened the novelist in his dealings with American publishing firms. With the quantity of material he was capable of producing, James had already learned that he could not afford to be "too fastidious" in his relations with magazine editors; compromises with the market were inevitable if he wanted to dispose of his wares. Steering his friend away from New York periodicals like the *Galaxy* and *Scribner's Monthly,* William Dean Howells had urged James in 1874 to keep back his fiction for the *Atlantic,* a magazine with a finer literary pedigree. James appreciated his editor's flattering praises, but said, "I *can't* really get on without exacting tribute" from other sources. "It's a mere money question," James continued. "The *Atlantic* can't publish as many stories as I ought and expect to be writing. . . . I need more strings to my bow and more irons always on the fire." When James was ready to embark upon *Roderick Hudson* later that year, he turned his rising fame to account by informing Howells of an offer he had received from *Scribner's* for a serial, waiting for a counterproposal from the *Atlantic.* "Sentimentally, I should prefer the *A[tlantic]*," he confessed, "but as things stand with me, I have no right to let it be anything but a pure money question." Howells was able to top Scribner's offer of $1000 (boosting the price to $1200 for twelve monthly installments), and he got James's novel. A similar competition between the *Atlantic* and the *Galaxy* netted James $1350 for *The American,* which he had planned originally in nine installments at $150 each. When the *Galaxy*'s editors could not meet James's demand that the serial begin its run immediately, they forfeited the manuscript to the *Atlantic.* Howells paid James his asking price; but the magazine could not accommodate *The American*'s longer installments, and the novelist divided the book into twelve monthly segments.[52]

While James had become rather adept in disposing of the serial rights to his work, he had also come to rely on the more conservative publishers of Boston when he collected his material in book form. As we have seen, his earliest contracts with James R. Osgood actually were better than average for a new author, because James never sacrificed royalties on his first editions. But the returns on books were slow in coming: publishers made up their accounts at best twice a year, and then disbursed royalties only after an additional delay of four to six months. Like most authors, James preferred to receive money as soon as a book was completed, thus making it easier for him to move on to new work. As James gained confidence in his bargaining power, he began to venture into different publishers' offices, seeking offers to compete with the modest standards of Boston.

Late in life James remembered his youthful fascination with literature and "what would seem a precocious interest in title-pages, and above all . . . the mysterious or behind-the-scenes world suggested by publishers' names—which in their various collocations, had a color and a character beyond even those of authors, even those of books themselves."[53] As a newly prosperous author (albeit no longer youthful), he gave fuller rein to his curiosity and began to explore new avenues of publicity for his work. From his dealings with magazine editors, James quickly realized that competition was inspiring to his purse; and he logically concluded that publishers too might be tempted to bid against each other for the privilege of issuing his work in volume form.

James's marketing instinct seems natural enough, but in the context of nineteenth-century publishing, he was violating one of the industry's most venerable (though legally unenforceable) customs—courtesy of the trade. Defended at the time as the code of honor by which all gentleman-publishers did business, trade courtesy actually originated as a method of controlling competition in the sale of pirated British books. By common consent, an American publisher established his claim to the books of a productive English author by printing them first. Other firms agreed to respect this priority and voluntarily relinquished their legal right to reprint uncopyrighted material, thus giving the original publisher monopoly control over the market for a particular author's work.[54] This practice also extended to relations with American authors. As Henry Holt recalled, "From about 1870 to 1890, no American publisher, among the first dozen, would have been more apt to think of approaching an author identified with another publisher, than men in other professions would be to think of approaching one another's clients."[55] An appropriate symbol for this era in American publishing was the huge loving cup commissioned in 1880 by Holt and three other trade leaders to toast the wedding of George haven Putnam, and from which all of them drank in turn. Well they could celebrate, for rarely in the annals of American business was the mere appearance of virtue so highly profitable. "Nowhere that I know of does intelligent selfishness so much consist in altruism as in American publishing," Holt boasted to Putnam.[56] Benjamin Franklin could not have improved on his formula.

Unfortunately for Henry Holt, some of his amiable friends did not always practice what they collectively preached. When Henry James approached Holt in 1878 with the manuscript of "Daisy Miller," the publisher bowed him out of the office and told him to keep the book in Osgood's hands. But James had taken his phenomenally popular story elsewhere to demonstrate to his Boston publishers that he was producing distinctly vendible merchandise. The Harpers' scruples were less refined than Holt's, and James was welcomed into the growing fold of native writers whose books were issued from Franklin Square.[57] The Harpers obeyed the letter of publishing's unwritten law—*they* didn't lure James away from Osgood—but they violated the spirit of its intention by signing a contract with a writer to whom Osgood had given his start. In the absence of more restrictive copyright legislation, the custom of trade courtesy was always vulnerable to the pressure of the market; and James knew that with the proven appeal of "Daisy Miller" he had an undeniable bargaining edge.

As often happens in James's fiction, his knowledge was purchased at a price. The popularity of "Daisy Miller" was demonstrated only when it was pirated in America before James could find a buyer for the serial rights. After the editor of *Lippincott's* in Philadelphia had returned the manuscript without comment, James turned it over in April 1879 to Leslie Stephen of the prestigious *Cornhill,* who accepted it effusively. When he received a printed copy of the story, James intended to sell the advance sheets for simultaneous publication in America—probably to *Harper's*—but Stephen rushed the first half of the story into the June number, without leaving James sufficient margin to arrange for an authorized magazine appearance in America.[58] Leon Edel has claimed that his lapse meant that James lost the American copyright on "Daisy Miller,"[59] but, in fact, James lost only what the serial market would have brought him. On 28 August 1878 he signed a contract with the Harpers for the book rights to "Daisy Miller," and he received a royalty of 10 percent of the retail price on every copy sold.[60] Hoping to cash in on the story's immediate vogue, the Harpers published "Daisy Miller" in the cheapest possible format (in paper wrappers at twenty cents, thirty-five cents in cloth), and 20,000 copies were sold in weeks. Such a large circulation, unprecedented for James, was some consolation for the sobering lesson of the publisher's arithmetic: because the book was so inexpensive, 10 percent of the immediate returns yielded the novelist only $200, even though it was destined to become the "most prosperous child" of his invention.[61]

More important to James at the time was the catalytic effect of sudden publicity. "I am very glad indeed," he told his brother, "that you were pleased with 'Daisy Miller,'"

> who appears (*literally*) to have made a great hit here. "Everyone is talking about it" etc., and it has been much noticed in the papers. Its success has encouraged me as regards the faculty of appreciation of the English public; for the thing is sufficiently subtle, yet people appear to have comprehended it. It has given me a capital start here, and in future I shall publish all my things in English magazines (at least all the *good* ones) and sell advance sheets in America; thereby doubling my profits.[62]

As James's first strategically important entry into the British literary marketplace, so much anticipated and so long deferred, "Daisy Miller" was an extraordinary publishing event. His fame—and hers—spread quickly in both countries, confirming James's faith in his powers and whetting his appetite for greatness. Henceforth he would bargain for simultaneous publication (at least for his "good" work) and monitor his arrangements carefully to protect his rights in the American market. The success of "Daisy Miller" was a turning point in James's career. From this point on he would work as a professional man of letters in both England and America.

While "Daisy Miller" was entertaining readers of the *Cornhill,* Macmillan moved quickly to strengthen James's attachment to his firm. In July he offered a half-profits arrangement for *The Europeans,* expressing the hope that "the British public may take to the book in such a way as to make these same profits enormous."[63] James was flattered, but not altogether convinced of the book's appeal; he considered his "sketch" too meager to excite much enthusiasm among English readers, whose thirst for fiction was best slaked by the voluminous Victorian triple-decker.[64] Still, James was very glad that Macmillan wanted the book. "As regards the profits," he rejoined, "I am afraid there is not much danger of their being 'enormous,' exactly: but even if they are only moderate, it will be a beginning of my appearance before the British Public as a novelist—as *the* novelist of the future, destined to extract from the B. P. eventually (both for himself and his publishers) a colossal fortune!"[65] Whatever the magnitude of his private doubts, James had not yet entirely given up the hope of pleasing the multitude.

Before James properly could assume his role as "*the* novelist of the future" (by writing *The Portrait of a Lady*), he was obliged to complete a series of less substantial novels and tales for editors on both sides of the Atlantic who eagerly desired material from the newest literary celebrity. Simply by turning the tables of his plot, James conceived "An International Episode" as "a *pendant* or counterpart" to "Daisy Miller," and he quickly sold it to the *Cornhill* and *Harper's* for simultaneous publication in December.[66] Between both sources James received £95 ($460)—"more money," he told his mother, "than I have ever got for so little labor." Immediately after "Daisy Miller" began to take the public by storm, Leslie Stephen asked the jubilant American for the serial rights to his next novel, but James had the advantage of replying to him that his next book was promised to Macmillan. "So you see," James boasted confidentially to his family in Quincy Street, "I am in a superior position, being able to work the 2 leading magazines against each other. But don't breathe a word of this: I do nothing save discreetly."[67]

James's discretion soon paid him some handsome dividends. Macmillan brought out *The Europeans* in September and tripled the number of copies in print within two months. At the end of October James happily conveyed news of its success to his family. The flattering reviews and notices, all of which he clipped and sent to America, reaffirmed his professional self-confidence. "I have only to keep quietly working," he told his family, "to arrive at fame & fortune. As I have an excellent, healthy appetite for work the inference is obvious."[68] Obvious, too, was the growing demand for his work, a fact that prompted James to renew his bid for an authorized English edition of *The American.* Despite George Grove's unpromising experience with it, James felt that the time for the book had come. "Even if it should not sell very largely," he told Macmillan, "a small profit would be welcome; & I cannot but think it would have a tolerable sale." With *The Europeans* going into a third edition, Macmillan was inclined to agree, and the book was published in March of the following year.[69] The month before, the firm brought out "An International Episode," which had just completed its run in the *Cornhill,* together with "Daisy Miller" and another international tale ("Four Meetings") in two volumes. When the novelist received his copies he found them "extremely pretty. I don't see how all the world can keep from reading them."[70] Some portion of the world did read them, but sales of the first edition did not match those for *The Europeans.*[71] Nevertheless, with four books published in the span of a year, James had finally launched himself before the venerable "B.P."

Fully to appreciate the magnitude (and the limits) of James's transatlantic success, we must be acquainted with the customs of the book trade in each country during this phase of his career. After mid-century the proliferation of periodicals in England and America created new outlets for literature, and novels often were first published serially in magazines. First book editions appeared soon after a serial completed its run, but here trade practices diverged. The novel in America typically appeared in one volume, printed from stereotype plates, and was priced at $1.50 to $2.00. Cheaper, paper-bound reprints occasionally were issued to satisfy the needs of summer travelers and to compete with the flood of inexpensive pirated fiction that poured from the less reputable American presses, but the ordinary issue of an American book, uniformly bound, was designed to appeal to a fairly broad spectrum of book buyers.

In England the marketing of books was aligned more directly with the stratifications of social class. First editions of novels were aimed at the circulating library market of middle and upper-middle class readers. Almost without exception, the novel appeared in three volumes, printed from standing type, and was priced at 31 shillings and 6 pence (three to four times the price of an American first edition). As one critic has observed, the triple-decker, "[o]verlong, overpriced and almost from the first overdue for extinction," nevertheless survived from the time of Scott to the end of Thomas Hardy's novel-writing career. Remarkably enough, in England "the new novel, that most speculative of commercial ventures, was the most stably priced and sized commodity in the whole nineteenth-century market place."[72] Because the libraries had such powerful control over the market for new fiction, they successfully demanded that publishers refrain from issuing cheaper, one-volume reprints of novels until at least a year after their first publication. Designed for individual buyers rather than borrowers, these reprints, typically priced at 6 shillings (about $1.50), were analogous to American first editions. When demand for this kind of book was exhausted, a publisher might issue a 3 shilling and 6 pence or 2 shilling "yellowback" reprint for the railway bookstalls. But before a book could appear in a form inexpensive enough to allow for anything like mass distribution, it had to pass the litmus test of library circulation.[73]

Because of an artificially high price mechanism, the novelty of an English book was inversely proportional to the number of copies in print, although the relatively small printings of expensive first editions (issues of only 500 copies were not uncommon) achieved much wider circulation than mere numbers would indicate. First editions of novels continued to appear in three volumes until the end of the century, because the libraries could more easily meet the demand for a new title by circulating individual volumes of the same novel in succession, thus tripling the number of subscribers who would be serviced by each set purchased. In 1890, Mudie's, the most popular and influential circulating library, had 25,000 subscribers. Despite its higher cost, an Englist first edition probably had more readers (if not buyers) than its American counterpart, owing to the ingenuity with which Englishmen had circumvented the price mechanism in publishing. While the cost of English books remained high, the cost of reading them was low, because of the devices of corporate buying—proprietary libraries, book clubs, and especially circulating libraries—that gave the Victorian literary marketplace its peculiar stability throughout the nineteenth century. As early as 1879 Henry James advised an American friend to find a British publisher for his books, because they "would have more readers in England than with us. . . . [I]t is a patriotic fallacy that we read more than they. *We don't!*"[74]

Although to some English novelists (notably Gissing), the long reign of the triple-decker became synonymous with a kind of publishers' tyranny, fatal to artistic endeavor, J. A. Sutherland has recently reminded us that the three-volume system was in fact a boon to English fiction, because it provided to publishers "a kind of built-in insurance against loss." Since the high price of books meant that publishers were able to make ends meet on even very small editions, they could offer encouragement to a wider range of literary talents. Sutherland clinches his argument by comparing the situation in America, where publishers were less likely to sustain an author who did not promise to yield substantial and immediate returns. Because the publishing industry in the United States had stabilized on a low-price equilibrium, it was under more consistent pressure to achieve large-volume sales. Such a market was favorable to manufacturers and retailers of books, but less so to the men and women who wrote them. Sutherland sums up the situation neatly: "Copy for copy American publishers vastly outproduced English; title for title English novelists vastly outproduced American. In America the nineteenth century may have been a 'gilded age' of publishing, but it was certainly not a golden age of fiction."[75]

One important advantage that English publishers did enjoy was the lower cost of labor, and this, too, had a subtle bearing on the market's clemency for artistic endeavor. Because American compositors and pressmen were paid higher wages than English laborers, publishers in the United States pioneered the development of stereo- and electrotype plates for printing, which were manufactured as soon as an author's proof was corrected and the type readjusted. In England publishers could afford to keep type standing for months at a time, reprinting editions directly from type if the market demanded them. Only if a book seemed likely to go through long runs or frequent reprintings would the sizable investment for plates be made. These differences help to explain the American publisher's constant need for rapid and consistent sellers, as well as the pressure that was sometimes exerted on authors to exempt a first edition from royalties, conditions that were not especially favorable to the development of an indigenous literature.[76]

Even though the English first editions of James's work seldom exceeded 500 copies, Macmillan continued to support his American friend and encourage his literary efforts by serializing his work in the firm's magazines and publishing his earlier novels under its imprint. No single American publisher lavished such attention on James, beyond the steadfast editorial encouragement he received at this time from William Dean Howells. Indeed, what struck James was "the most absurd facility" of his success in England. "Here are fifteen years that I have been addressing the American public," he wrote Howells from London, "and at the end of a few months I appear to have gone as far with this one as I ever got at home."[77] Fame and fortune, however, were not necessarily coterminous. Even though *Daisy Miller* had entered the vernacular as a synonym for an innocent American girl, James easily recognized the disparity between his literary reputation, "expanding between two hemispheres," and a "pecuniary equivalent almost grotesquely small." The account he received from Howells of the popularity of his two little Harper tales in America was particularly disturbing, because of the modest profit he made by them. Harpers thus far had paid him $200 for the whole American career of "Daisy Miller" and $200 more for all rights to "An International Episode." "The truth is," he told Howells, "I am a very bad bargainer and I was born to be victimized by the pitiless race of publishers."[78] This much-quoted confession must be read in proper context, however, for Howells was an influential editor whom James frequently enlisted in his negotiations with American publishers. If they were pitiless, Howells was a merciful agent whose professional connections with the businessmen of American letters proved invaluable to his expatriated friend. By emphasizing, if not exaggerating, his own need of assistance, James affirmed the value of Howells's continued advocacy; in return, he used his own influence in London to secure commitments from editors for the serialization of Howells's work in England.

In striking contrast to James's self-deprecating letter to Howells is a much more confident communiqué posted to Quincy Street only two days before. Responding to his mother's hopeful inquiry about the profits from the large sale of his two Harper stories, James had to confess that his returns were modest. This was largely due to factors that were beyond the writer's control: Harpers' editors, not James, had decided on an extremely cheap format for the tales. More important to him, professionally, was the fact that the Harpers (one of Osgood's chief competitors) were publishing him at all. Even if he had accepted the usual 10 percent royalty, he had at last made a strategic move outside the comparatively restrictive publishing circle of Boston. James also explained that he could not have anticipated his sudden popularity: an American editor had, after all, rejected "Daisy Miller" without comment; and James disposed of "An International Episode" quickly to avoid another profitless piracy of his work. The writer in him was not discouraged. He faced the future with thoroughly professional assurance:

> I am working along very quickly & steadily, & consider no reasonable show of fame & no decent literary competence out of my reach. À propos of such matters, mother expresses in her last night's letter the hope that I have derived much gold from the large sale (upwards of 20,000 copies) of my two little Harper stories. I am sorry to say I have done nothing of the sort. Having in advance no prevision of their success I made a very poor bargain. The *Episode* I sold outright (copyright & all!) for a very moderate sum of ready

> money—so I have had no percentage at all on the sale! For Daisy Miller I have rec'd simply the usual 10%—which, as it sells for twenty cents brings me but 2 cents a copy. This has a beggarly sound, but the Harpers sent me the other day a cheque for $200. This represents but meanly so great a vogue—but you may be sure that I shall clinch the Harpers in future; as having now taught them my value I shall be able to do. A man's 1*st* successes are those, always, by which he makes least. I am not a grasping business-man—on the contrary, and I sometimes—or rather, often—strike myself as gaining wofully less money than fame. My reputation in England seems (considering what it is based on) ludicrously larger than any cash payments that I have yet received for it. The Macmillans are everything that's friendly—caressing—old [Alexander] Macmillan physically *hugs* me; but the delicious ring of the sovereign is conspicuous in our intercourse by its absence. However, I am sure of the future—that is the great thing—& it is something to behave like a gentleman even when other people don't. I shall have made by the end of this year very much more money than I have ever made before; & next year I shall make as much as that again. As for the years after that—nous verrons bien.[79]

James was not alone in his dissatisfaction with the returns from his English sales—English authors generally were becoming restive with the conventional half-profits contract for their wares—but as an American he brought to his relations with Macmillan a different set of professional expectations. While James rose to fame on the ingenuity of his international theme and the transatlantic contrast of manners, he felt a similar tension of opposing values in the region of his pocketbook. Even though James R. Osgood was occasionally delinquent in making payments, his and most other American firms negotiated more straightforward royalty contracts, drew up accounts semiannually, and paid their authors twice a year. To receive such prompt remuneration in England, James was forced to beg favors. Six months after *French Poets and Novelists* appeared, *The Europeans* also having been on the market for some time, James wrote to Macmillan for a statement. "As you know," the publisher responded, "we only balance our books formally once a year"; but he sent James £50 ($240), "which represents as nearly as I can get it, what we should owe you if accounts between us were to be made up now."[80] Macmillan's vagueness is not surprising when we remember that at this point James had not yet signed a contract with the firm for any of his books. A month later Macmillan was reminded of this fact when arrangements were being made for the English edition of "Daisy Miller" and James's other international tales. Perhaps the most remarkable aspect of Macmillan's discovery is the casualness with which he remedied it. On the placid surface of Victorian social intercourse, concern for money had no legitimate expression. The absence of a contract was nothing more than an amusing oversight. "By the way," Macmillan wrote, "I find that although we settled between us the terms on which your books were to be published, we have no written memorandum of the arrangement. We find it convenient always to have something of the kind. I shall be much obliged therefore if you will sign the enclosed papers and return them to me."[81] Having received a sizable payment from the firm and eager to adapt himself to the customs of the English literary scene, James promptly signed the agreement and returned it to Macmillan.

Six months after receiving a partial settlement from his publisher, James again was forced to write for money. Although Macmillan had hinted that the proceeds from his books "were the reverse of copious," James retorted that "their being small would not prevent [him] from accepting them."[82] Once more the publisher emphasized that, while accounts were usually drawn up in June, authors were not notified of the year's sales until October, and then not paid until the following January. Clearly anxious to placate his American friend, however, Macmillan sent James £50 as an advance on the critical biography of Hawthorne that he had agreed to write for the firm's popular English Men of Letters series. James's response, ripe with the very American humor that, in *Hawthorne,* he would term the "national gift," gives new meaning to his famous respect for a truly grasping imagination:

> I didn't know how it would be about the accounts; I thought you might have mysterious ways of judging. But if they are being looked into, let it stand by all means till the results are known. Thank you meanwhile for the £50 for *Hawthorne.* I have as a general thing a lively aversion to receiving money in anticipation for work not delivered, & I think that if you had proposed this yesterday I should have said *NO,* for the present. But I should feel ungracious in returning the cheque—so I keep it, with many acknowledgements.[83]

Although the Macmillans were willing to meet his occasional demand for ready money, James was not entirely comfortable with the pattern of reluctant remuneration that was evolving. When Thomas Sergeant Perry told him in September that the firm was going to bring out a volume of critical essays, James warned, "don't nurse yourself in the fond illusion that [they] will give you a palpable sum of money in consequence. That is not the strong point of the good Macmillans."[84] As if to confirm this judgment, two weeks later Macmillan sent James his annual account of sales, the results of which were "not brilliant—on the contrary." "I grieve," James wrote, "that the books should not do better. It seems to me an anomaly that they don't, as they have been on the whole largely and favourably noticed, and apparently a good deal talked about."[85] Even less inspiring than his sales, however, was the apparent necessity of behaving (as James complained to his brother) like a "grasping business-man" in his relations with the firm. To get even what little cash he earned on his half-profits contract, James was forced to step beyond the conventions of decorum that still governed the literary marketplace and cloaked the question of money in silence and shame. Macmillan's accounts would not be settled until January, but James could not wait. "I should be greatly obliged to you," he wrote to his publisher,

> if you would send me a cheque, without further delay, for the remainder of the amount I was to receive for the Hawthorne. . . . Excuse my appearance of dunning you—but I am rather in want of the money. The same motive leads me to add that I shld. take it very kindly if you would include in the same cheque whatever money is owing me on the account of sales of my books, sent me the other day. This sum is apparently very small . . . but such as it is it will be a convenience to me to have it—& not an inconvenience to you, I hope, to send it, though I believe your regular way is not to settle those matters till somewhat later.[86]

Again Macmillan obliged him and sent a cheque, but James had come to a second turning point in his career as an Anglo-American man of letters.

"WHAT A SENTIMENTAL RACE PUBLISHERS ARE": THE EXAMPLE OF CONFIDENCE

James's dissatisfaction with Macmillan stemmed from the imprecise nature of the half-profits contract. These agreements were not unknown in America—an exemplary victim of them was Melville[87]—but by the time James was coming into his professional stride, the royalty contract was the industry standard. George Haven Putnam estimated that the trade's customary royalty of 10 percent would yield an author "about half the net profits" on a book, but he failed to elaborate on his method of calculation.[88] Indeed, his failure was characteristic, for the absence of accountability was the most pernicious feature of the half-profits system. Since publishers made no payments on such a contract until their manufacturing costs were recovered, they often yielded to the temptation of inflating the cost of production or adding surcharges to their expenses. Authors were virtually defenseless when confronted by publishers' accounts, because the trade houses had a monopoly on the technical information relating to book manufacture. All too often publishers would simply report that they had no profits to divide. As one British critic of the trade announced in 1867, the true explanation for the mystery of non-existent profits, and of the necessity of keeping it a mystery, was simply this—"that it is the custom of the trade to add to each item of expense some percentage, unknown to those out of the trade, by way of profit upon each transaction [in the process of manufacture], before the division of what are *called* the profits begins."[89] More than once in his long life, Henry James had occasion to confess his frailty with arithmetic, but when Macmillan's statements arrived, even he knew that his share of the profits was not truly half.

Just as he relished the opportunity to play one editor against another for serial rights to his work, James quickly entered into relations with other London publishers when payments from Macmillan seemed incommensurate with his labors. With appropriate irony, however, James embarked on his new course with a volume entitled *Confidence.* Critics have rightly dismissed this book as the least successful of James's novels,[90] but the complicated history of its publication illustrates perfectly the author's professional capacity in dealing with the Anglo-American literary marketplace.

Confidence was serialized in America by *Scribner's Monthly,* the only novel that James sold to the magazine. Even though Howells tried to steer his friend away from *Scribner's* columns,[91] James contributed five stories to the magazine between 1874 and 1878. More aggressively managed than other American literary periodicals, *Scribner's* was willing to pay higher prices to compete for the work of emerging talents like James; Dr. Josiah Holland, *Scribner's* editor, paid the young writer $150 a story compared to the *Atlantic*'s usual $100.[92] James's connection with *Scribner's* was probably reinforced by the fact that his father was a good friend of the editor as well as a frequent contributor; but the novelist seems to have shared Howells's opinion about the magazine's literary mediocrity, and he promised to send his best work to the *Atlantic.* As James's writing grew in volume, however, he soon fulfilled a youthful fantasy about "having certain persons *on their knees,* imploring for contributions," a caption that accompanied his 1864 drawing of a man representing the *Atlantic Monthly* supplicating before a disdainful author (see Frontispiece).[93]

After *The American* had started its run in the *Atlantic* for June 1876, James felt obliged to inform Howells that he was in correspondence with Dr. Holland about a serial to begin in *Scribner's* the following year. Nothing was yet settled, but the prospects were good. The vision of a serial in *Scribner's* did not, James confessed, "aesthetically delight" him; but it was the best thing he could do, under the circumstances. Having a "perpetual serial running" had defined itself as a "financial necessity."[94] For the time being, nothing came of Scribner's overture, but to secure James's next short novel, *The Europeans,* which appeared in 1878, Howells upped the ante and paid the author $250 a number for his four-part sketch.[95] But by then James's productivity had outstripped the *Atlantic*'s capacity to publish him, and the "syren song" of Dr. Holland proved irresistible. In the spring of 1879 James confided to his sister,

> I think I mentioned in writing last to William that I was getting on very well with a (short) novel which is to begin in the August *Scribner* and run through six numbers. You will probably lament its appearance in that periodical; but this won't matter on view of its immediate republication both at home and here. And after all in *Scribners,* one's things are read by the great American people—the circulation, I believe is enormous. Last, not least, I am to be very

> well paid—$1500 for a thing not much longer than *The Europeans. . . . Please speak to no living creature of this Scribner matter till the thing is announced by the magazine.*[96]

As always, James did nothing "save discreetly," especially when the rewards promised to be handsome.

A similar discretion guided the novelist when the time came to negotiate the volume rights for *Confidence.* James was increasingly dissatisfied with the scant income his books provided, even though he had found publishers for them in two countries. Already for "Daisy Miller" he had moved outside the conservative publishing circles of Boston, though the Harpers had not yet improved upon "the usual 10%" royalty. With *Confidence* he would try again.

Publishers who purchased serial rights in an author's work often sought—or demanded—the option of issuing such material in volume form, because, until the advent of commercial advertising for books much later in the century, serial publication was often the most effective means of promoting the sale of literature. Like the tradition of trade courtesy, the tie-in between publishing houses and the magazines they sponsored was generally respected as an unwritten law. Hence it was not unusual for Scribner's to approach James about the book rights for *Confidence:*

> We take the liberty of asking you whether you have in view any arrangement for the publication here, in book form, of your story of "Confidence," now appearing as a serial in our Magazine? Should you have made no definite plan in regard to it, it would give us much pleasure to submit to you an offer for its issue by our house; and we should be glad to know whether such a proposition on our part would be agreeable to you.[97]

More revealing, however, is an internal memorandum that one of Scribner's editors, Edward L. Burlingame, sent to the firm's president after James's response was received, for it exposes the vulnerability of trade courtesy to less genteel market forces:

> I enclose a personal letter just received—and also a copy of one that has just come from Henry James, & that seems to need immediate attention. Doesn't it seem to you—as it certainly does to me—that it is worth while to make him a decidedly good offer on this opportunity [to publish *Confidence* in book form]? He is (thus far) almost entirely unattached in the matter of publishing; and his future is certainly valuable enough to make an effort to connect him here. But of course all this "goes without saying," after all.[98]

Seeing the opportunity to foster a healthy competition for his book, James asked Scribner's to make him an offer—and they did:

> We shall be pleased to make either one of two arrangements for the publication of "Confidence": either to offer you the royalty of 12-½ per cent. on

> the retail price of all copies sold from the beginning—which is the highest rate of copyright we are accustomed to pay—or (should this method be more agreeable to you), to pay you $250 on the publication and a royalty of ten per cent, in addition, on all copies sold.
>
> We trust that our letter may find you still at liberty to take our proposition into consideration, and that it may prove satisfactory to you. Should it be impossible in this case, we shall be glad to have our offer before you, should you feel disposed to consider it, with others, in regard to any future work.[99]

The most interesting result of Scribner's eagerness to lure James away from the firm of Houghton, Osgood is his offer of a sizable advance independent of royalties, a gesture virtually unheard of at this time. The prospect of a sum down on publication was especially cheering to James, whose patience was sorely tried (and whose pocketbook was severely tested) by the long interval between a book's appearance and the publisher's first account of its sales. Even though the novelist eventually declined Scribner's offer (for very good reasons, as we shall see), the implication of their proposal did not escape him. In the future James demanded—and received—a sum down or an advance on royalties for almost every book he published, in England as well as in America. At least in James's case, the relations between author and publisher were rapidly approaching the pattern still followed in the literary marketplace today.

In the meantime, James received the disappointing account of his profits from Macmillan, and—with Scribner's proposal in mind—he wrote to another London publisher about *Confidence.* To Chatto & Windus he made this inquiry:

> I desire to publish in England about Jan. 1st a short novel which is running through (six numbers of) an American magazine (*Scribner's.*) The work in question is entitled *Confidence,* & might, I should say, appear in either 1 vol. or 2, as might be desired. Would it suit your convenience to let me know if you would be disposed to publish it, & what terms in this case you would offer? I should tell you that I ask this question rather tentatively. My own idea would be to receive a royalty & a certain sum of money down. The novel of course is to appear in America, but I should naturally make a point of securing copyright in England by slightly anticipating the American publication.[100]

James asked what terms Chatto & Windus might offer, but clearly stated his preference for a royalty contract and an advance. These terms were utterly foreign to English publishers at this time, and the firm responded with a more conventional proposal to lease the copyright from James for a period of three years, paying him £100 ($485) on publication, provided that *Confidence* could be made to fill two volumes of the usual novel size. After reflecting on these terms, which, in turn, were new to James, the novelist accepted Chatto's offer. He also told the firm not to worry about the length of the manuscript, since it was heftier than *The Europeans,* which had been issued by Macmillan a year ago as a two-volume novel.[101]

The publisher was concerned about the length of James's story, because the profits of an English first edition were directly proportional to the number of volumes a novel could fill. Students of James have sometimes wondered why the English edition of *Confidence* is divided into thirty-one chapters, while the American edition has only thirty. Chatto's anxiety about the size of their edition helps to explain this bibliographical curiosity. Every interruption of the text allowed for additional blank pages; and James clearly had no artistic objections to extra divisions. In fact, he probably was responsible for them. James supplied Chatto & Windus with proof sheets from *Scribner's,* considerably revised, as they were sent from America. The novelist also redivided the twelve original chapters, symmetrically balanced for the six-part serial but overly long for a book, "into XXXII (or there-abouts) smaller ones." With most of the manuscript in hand, Chatto & Windus were confident that they would have sufficient copy for two volumes "in rather displayed type"—almost an understatement, considering the liberal margins and generous typography of the English first edition. For the more compact American issue, James revised separate proof sheets and failed to retain the same chapter divisions.[102]

If James's editing of *Confidence* at times seems careless, his marketing of the book assuredly was not. By giving his book to one of Macmillan's chief competitors, James was following a strategy to which he had given considerable thought. He had no desire merely to become a "grasping business-man," but neither was he willing to part with his work cheaply. After closing the deal with Chatto & Windus, James detailed his plan for his family in America. For his next novel, at least, he would leave "the unremunerative Macmillans," who (at long last) had sent him their first account of sales. James's share in the profits of six books was so largely to the publisher's advantage, and so little to his, that he immediately resolved to take his new book elsewhere. Chatto & Windus had responded amiably to his overture and the affair was quickly settled. James knew he was taking a calculated risk—certainly breaching the unwritten code of literary gentility—but he hoped his move would operate as a "salubrious irritant" to Macmillan, "who want[ed his] books very much but [didn't] want to pay for them!"[103] James's letter conveys his growing sense of the inequities inherent in the half-profits arrangement with Macmillan. Now, with a statement finally in hand, he could see that his share of the proceeds from six books was diminished by expenses credited to the publisher.[104] The tactic of desertion might get him better terms on his future books.

For this strategy James had taken his cue from Scribner's bid for the American book rights. But when Osgood got wind of the writer's inclination to publish *Confidence* elsewhere, he sent James "such a plaintive letter" that the novelist relented. It was a "weak proceeding," he confessed wryly to Quincy Street, "natural to the son of my father."[105] In fact, it was a shrewd concession. With the firm of Houghton, Osgood James had to be more careful. The novelist's plans for *The Portrait of a Lady* were rapidly forming; James knew it would be his most important book to date. Because the sale of serial rights was almost always more lucrative than the money James received on published volumes, his dream and desire for the *Portrait* was simultaneous publication in both English and American magazines. Difficult negotiations for the novel were already in progress with the *Atlantic,* and James did not want to alienate the magazine's owners, Henry Oscar Houghton and James Ripley Osgood. The novelist's mother chastised him for not accepting Scribner's lucrative offer for *Confidence,* but James urged diplomacy in his defense:

> I winced (but very discreetly) under your comments upon my weakness of conduct with Houghton & Osgood. But this was not pure weakness—it was also diplomacy. I was just at that moment negotiating with them the terms of publication of my next year's novel in the *Atlantic,* & I thought that if I was disobliging in the matter of my little book this year, they might revenge themselves by being difficult with regard to that. I think it probable, by the event, that I was well-inspired. Between the *Atlantic* & *Macmillan* I am to receive for the production in question upwards of 700 £, (seven hundred pounds.)[106]

James instinctively knew that appropriate terms for his projected masterpiece were more important than any short-run gain on a confessed potboiler.

The immediate success of James's strategy revealed the shrewdness of his plan. Confirmed in the habit of doing nothing "save discreetly" in the publishing world, James remained silent to Macmillan on the subject of *Confidence.* As the serial neared the end of its run in *Scribner's,* Frederick Macmillan reminded James of the firm's interest in the book. "What about *Confidence?*" he inquired. "It ought to appear in England before it is all published in 'Scribner' so that there may be no question about copyright. Will you be able to get early proofs for us to print from?"[107] James could hold his tongue no longer: the book was to be published by Chatto & Windus, who had offered him better terms. Macmillan was clearly stung by James's defection. "I am sorry to hear," he told James,

> that "Confidence" is to appear under another imprint than ours, especially as I thought when you told me about the story in the summer it was understood that we were to publish it. We always hoped to have the whole of your books in a uniform edition, and it was rather for the sake of completeness than in the expectation of a remunerative sale that we undertook to print *The American* in the face of the two shilling piracy. If your going elsewhere was a

question of terms, if for instance you wished to sell the book outright, or to be paid something on publication on account of future profits, I wish you had mentioned it to me first for we have every wish to deal liberally with you and would have tried to meet your wishes with any matter of the kind.[108]

James's response has not survived, but from Macmillan's next letter, posted two days later, we can see that the novelist became much more explicit about money matters. In contrast to Macmillan's suspicious frugality, Chatto & Windus had offered a hundred pounds down on publication. Money was money—such a large sum seemed irresistible—but James hoped Macmillan was not seriously offended. The publisher confessed, however, that he "did feel hurt about 'Confidence'":

Of course we don't pretend to any claim over your work, but as we have been your publishers hitherto I am sorry you should have gone elsewhere merely because you wanted some ready money. If you had written to my uncle proposing that we should advance you £100 on account of future profits, you would undoubtedly have received a cheque by return of post.[109]

Taking Macmillan strictly at his word, James immediately wrote to the firm's business office to ask for an advance of £100 on his next year's sales—a request that Macmillan's secretary, George Lillie Craik, was happy to oblige! When Frederick Macmillan discovered James's clever subterfuge, he dashed off a letter to suggest that Craik's action was both hasty and highly irregular; but the house would be forgiving and more financially indulgent with James in the future if the novelist returned to Macmillan's fold.[110] For the time being, however, promises were less important to James than pounds, and he sounded the note of triumph in a letter to his mother:

You will perhaps be interested to hear that my going to Chatto & Windus has had a most salutary effect upon Macmillan, who have come down with a second cheque, much larger that the 1*st*, & an assurance that they are "*hurt*" by my conduct. That was Osgood's argument, too; I am rapidly learning what a sentimental race publishers are.[111]

If publishers were indeed a sentimental race, James quickly learned that some were less so than others. Without James's knowledge, Chatto & Windus offered to sell the foreign rights to *Confidence* to the German publishing mogul, Baron Christian Bernard von Tauchnitz, whose firm issued on average one volume a week for a hundred years and had a virtual monopoly on the continental market for English-language books designed for travelers. Tauchnitz secured the goodwill of English writers and publishers by offering them modest permissions fees, despite the absence of international copyright restrictions. The sums involved were never large—rarely more than £20—but even such small amounts were more attractive to writers than outright piracy. Relatively few authors, however, were even aware of the continental market. It was a common practice for English publishers to buy books outright or for a term of years without mention of overseas sales, sell the foreign rights to Tauchnitz, and then pocket the money.[112]

Such were Chatto's intentions when they wrote to the Baron on 3 February 1880: "We have the pleasure of forwarding you . . . a copy of a very charming new novel by Henry James junior entitled 'Confidence' which is making a great success in this country and which we think you will find most suitable for your collection of English Authors. We can offer you the continental rights for £30."[113] What Chatto & Windus could not have known, however, was that Tauchnitz had made a personal overture to James two years prior to arrange for continental republication of *The American* and virtually all of his other early volumes.[114] The honorable Baron rightly suspected that Chatto & Windus were dealing behind James's back, and he insisted that the novelist become a partner in the negotiations.

When Chatto informed James of their almost completed arrangement with Tauchnitz, the novelist was infuriated and demanded an immediate explanation and apology. Eager to publish James's future work, the firm responded with masterful diplomacy:

> When you assigned to us for three years the copyright and all your interest in the English edition of "*Confidence*" we concluded that as usual in such cases, no other edition except in America could be brought out without our consent. We were strengthened in this belief by the knowledge that any publisher either in England or on the continent may reprint an American author's works without acknowledgement, but no[t] so if they be copyrighted in England by first publication here, and that therefore any payment from Baron Tauchnitz would not in the present case be of so entirely and complimentary a nature as for books first issued in America.
>
> Should it have been your intention to reserve not only your American interest in "*Confidence*" but also the continental rights we shall have much pleasure in handing you the amount which Baron Tauchnitz has agreed to pay [£20] for the right of reproduction and (as our consent is certainly necessary as holders of the English copyright) in joining with you in the assignment he requires; as it is our desire that our transactions shall be most harmonious also, and that we may have the opportunity of publishing the English editions of your forthcoming work.[115]

James minced few words, however, in asking for his money and rebuking Chatto & Windus for their impudence:

> I shall be very happy to receive from you the sum that Baron Tauchnitz has agreed to pay you for *Confidence*, as I never had an idea of making over to you the foreign interest in the book. I should have as soon thought of making

> this dependent upon my English publishers as I should have expected Baron Tauchnitz (had I happened to make an arrangement with him in advance, while my book was coming out in America) to exact the asking of *his* assent to the issue of the book here. On these terms I shall be very happy to sign the agreement that you wrote me about the other day.[116]

The firm's lease on *Confidence* was never renewed.

Revealing as they are of James's professional development, the legal and financial aspects of this novel's publication history are matched in significance by the texts of *Confidence* itself. The plural is used advisedly, for the book survives in four surprisingly different forms: manuscript, serial, first English edition, and first American. At every stage of the publishing process, James's editorial hand was active. It is probable that he corrected serial proof before *Confidence* appeared in *Scribner's Monthly,*[117] and he definitely revised separate proofs for each publisher's edition. Comparison of the two editions further suggests that James deliberately chose certain textual variants to cater to the linguistic preferences of each national audience.[118] The different forms of the novel afford a rare glimpse of James's characteristic preoccupation with style.

A collation of all available texts reveals at least one interesting variation that occurs between the manuscript and serial, a change which is incorporated into the Osgood text but which receives yet another transformation in the English edition. In the sentence, "He [Gordon Wright] was not intending to stop in England; [his wife] Blanche desired to proceed immediately to the French capital, to confer with her ______," the last word was changed to satisfy different audiences. In the manuscript of *Confidence,* James used the appropriate French word, *couturière.* The serial text, however, reads *man-milliner*—a change retained in the American edition of the novel—but which becomes *tailor* in the English. In substituting the colloquial American *man-milliner* for the serial and Osgood text, James may have been responding to critics who disliked his frequent Gallicisms, but the change also implies a slight derogation of Blanche Wright, since she now confers with a man (according to Webster) "who is busied with trifling occupations or embellishments." On the other hand, *tailor* was currently preferred in English usage, and all available evidence suggests that James was concerned about getting his colloquial expressions right. Earlier in the same year that *Confidence* appeared, James had defended himself against a charge that the dialogue of the two Englishmen in "An International Episode" made them sound like two vulgar "'Arries." "[I]f it didn't sound too fatuous," James replied to his critic, "I should say that I had been congratulated by several people whom I suppose to be of an observing turn upon the verisimilitude of [their] conversation."[119]

The following list is a sampling of variants which conveys quite clearly

James's concern for "verisimilitude" and his awareness of two distinct markets for his work.[120]

Serial and American Edition	*English Edition*
awfully	fearfully
this loathesome gossip	this idiotic fiction
a couple of red-tiled roofs	a brace of red-tiled roofs
El Dorado	a hidden treasure
whence he had drawn the ability for so remarkable a feat	how the deuce he had managed it
I stuck it to the end	I saw it through

The painstaking revision of even so minor a work as *Confidence* reveals James at a vulnerable moment in his career as a self-conscious American writer trying to assimilate himself to the linguistic conventions of the English literary marketplace without alienating his native audience. In spite of the book's title, James was still rather insecure about addressing his readers in a consistent voice.

From a strictly professional point of view, however, James anticipated his artistic independence in the editorial room by asserting his freedom in the business office. A year later he could write to his sister,

> I am fast becoming a good enough Englishman to respect, inveterately, my own habits & do, wherever I may be, only exactly what I want. This is the secret of prosperity here—provided of course one has a certain number of sociable & conformable habits, & civil inclinations, as a starting-point. After that, the more positive your idiosyncrasies the more positive the convenience.[121]

The context was social ("But it is drawing toward lunch," he added, "& I can't carry my personality quite so far as to be late for that"), but the implications of James's remarks carried over into his career as a man of letters. By accommodating himself to English customs—accepting, at first, the conventional half-profits arrangement for his books—he eventually gained the confidence to deal idiosyncratically with his publishers, insisting upon foreign terms for his work and maintaining an upper hand in negotiations, despite the modest level of his sales. With the publication of *Confidence,* James discovered "the secret of prosperity" in the world of letters. As he told Howells at the start of the new year, "there are natural limits to one's sympathy with one's publishers."[122] Throughout the rest of his career, Henry James explored those limits with the delicacy and deliberation of a consummately professional man of letters.

IV
James's Hawthorne: The Last Primitive Man of Letters

Despite James's admirable discretion, the evidence of his emerging professionalism was not confined to his private correspondence. In fashioning a role for himself as a man of letters, James was not entirely bereft of American antecedents; of all his fellow countrymen who had dedicated themselves to the literary life, none was more important to him than Nathaniel Hawthorne. What James said of Balzac in 1905 is equally applicable to his American predecessor: he was conscious of so large a debt to repay Hawthorne that it had positively to be discharged in installments, as if one could never have at once all the required cash in hand. The biography of Hawthorne that James wrote in 1879 was not his first attempt at repayment, but it was surely the most important.[1] Written in the very years that James was coming to professional maturity, the Hawthorne biography announces a point of departure—not from Hawthorne's literary influence, which indeed grew even more pervasive in James's work over the years—but from the pattern of Hawthorne's career as a writer. Hawthorne was, to James, "the last specimen of the primitive type of the man of letters," an artist whose creative life, beautiful but brief, effectively closed a chapter in the history of the profession of authorship.[2]

Comparative criticism of these two writers has usually centered on questions of literary influence and their shared concern for moral and psychological problems. Robert Emmet Long's recent study, *The Great Succession: Henry James and the Legacy of Hawthorne,* is in some respects a consummation of this kind of inquiry. Backed by contemporary theoretical explorations of literary influence and the anxieties it generates, Long is well equipped to analyze the ways in which James absorbed Hawthorne's motifs and mythopoeic structures into realistic fiction while simultaneously repudiating Hawthorne's more romantic preferences. The implications of Long's approach, however, occasionally exceed the limits of his demonstration. Long claims, for example, that Hawthorne's characters proved of irreplaceable value to James, because they provided him with "prototype models of American experience."[3] But more so than any of his fictional characters, to James, Hawthorne himself was a prototype of the American artist, whose fate exemplified the possibilities—and the limits—of imaginative life in their native land. In the critical biography James explored not only the meaning of Hawthorne's fiction but also the significance of his career.

Virtually since the day it was published, *Hawthorne* has provoked strenuous (and, occasionally, rather bewildered) criticism. Readers past and present have been disturbed by James's apparent denigration of Hawthorne's artistic achievement. When, for example, James dismisses Hawthorne's metaphysical stories as, at best, "graceful and felicitous conceits" (p. 70), the products of Coleridgean fancy rather than imagination, resistance in the reader runs high. As Lionel Trilling once asked,

> What are we to do with a judgment of this sort—how are we to escape from its embarrassments? It is one of our great masters who speaks, and we hold him to be great not only in the practice of his art but also in its theory. From him many of us learned how high, even sacred, is the mission of the artist, and from him we derived many of the tenets by which we judge success in art. Yet it is he who makes this estimate of another of our masters, the one who, of all Americans, was the master of Henry James himself.[4]

To contemporary readers, of course, Henry James was not yet considered a "great master," and his book seemed ungracious, even brash. American reviewers largely missed the generous play of James's affection for his subject and were simply stung by the satire his sympathy was intended to mitigate. The outrageous catalogue of "the items of high civilization . . . absent from the texture of American life" (too famous now to quote, and which, James warned, "might, indeed, with a little ingenuity, be made almost ludicrous" [p. 55]) was ludicrous indeed, but it pricked the native consciousness of even his most sympathetic readers, including William Dean Howells. James clearly was not prepared for the ferocity his work inspired—*he* thought "the tone of the book gentle and good-natured enough to disarm reprobation"[5]—but the flood of abusive notices sent back from America simply confirmed him in the biography's final judgments. "The hubbub produced by my poor little *Hawthorne,*" he told Thomas Sergeant Perry, "is most ridiculous":

> The vulgarity, ignorance, rabid vanity and general idiocy of [the reviews] is truly incredible. But I hold it a great piece of good fortune to have stirred up such a clatter. The whole episode projects a lurid light upon the state of American "culture," and furnishes me with a hundred wonderful examples,

> where, before, I had only more or less vague impressions. Whatever might have been my own evidence for calling American taste "provincial," my successors at least will have no excuse for not doing it.[6]

The reactions of the press were not difficult to fathom; as James told an American friend, "We are surely the most-thin-skinned idiots in the world, & I blush for my compatriots."[7] More perplexing were James's motives for writing the kind of book he did. Most critics have recognized that James's condescending attitude toward Hawthorne was not altogether new; his 1872 review of Hawthorne's *French and Italian Notebooks* anticipated many of the biography's judgments.[8] What was new was the patronizing stance he took toward Hawthorne's whole career. Like *Roderick Hudson* before it, which reshaped the materials of *The Marble Faun,* the biography reveals James's assertion of his own narrative art, in contrast to his predecessor's. In it he seems practically to repudiate Hawthorne as the last of the provincials.

Perhaps because of the biography's inherent aggressiveness, writing it was not a happy task for James. On 9 October 1878 John Morley first invited the American to contribute a volume on Irving or Hawthorne to Macmillan's English Men of Letters series; two days later James had framed a reply, consenting, but he could not bring himself to mail it. Within a week he renounced the project altogether. To his father he wrote, "I have declined, on acct. of insufficient material for a Life. One can't write a volume about H[awthorne]. But the proposal will please you & attest my growing fame." Macmillan refused to let the offer lapse, however, and by the end of the year James relented.[9]

James finally signed an agreement for the book on 22 January 1879, although he did not begin work on it until the end of the summer. Once again, the contract for *Hawthorne* reveals the extent to which James was willing to accommodate himself to British publishing conventions at this stage of his career. For all the titles in the English Men of Letters series, the Macmillans paid authors a standard fee of £100 to purchase the copyright. Frederick Macmillan made a similar offer to James for *Hawthorne,* but shortly before the book was announced, Harper and Brothers of New York made an unusual appeal to Macmillan for distribution rights in the United States. To market the series the American firm was willing to pay a 10 percent royalty on every copy sold. Since James was an American citizen, and therefore the legal owner of his copyright in the United States, Macmillan gave the author a choice: he could sell all interest in the book outright for £100, or take £75 for the English copyright and the Harpers' 10 percent on the American sale. To make up the difference the Harpers would have had to sell at least 1200 copies at their usual retail price of $1; but from the first James seems to have been skeptical of the book's probable appeal in America. "The amount of the profit of my

'Hawthorne' being uncertain," he told Macmillan, "& the convenience to me of receiving a round sum, down, on the completion of the book, being considered, I prefer, of your two alternatives, the 1st: viz: the £100, covering everything. I shall content myselt with a disinterested observation of the sale, whatever it is, that the book may have in the Harpers' hands." A year later, however, after becoming increasingly dissatisfied with his arrangements at Macmillan, James bristled when the family informed him of the book's vogue and notoriety in Boston: "I hope indeed it *may* have some success in America—though I know not why I should, since I have none of the profit of it. The whole of this, by the pre-arranged conditions of the affair, is between the Macmillans & Harpers. So if you see it selling, don't glory, but repine, as the money will all flow into the over-gorged coffers of Bedford St."[10] James's querulous fib about "pre-arranged conditions" reveals the measure of his disenchantment with Macmillan as well as his tendency to portray himself to friends and family as the victim of publishing scoundrels. In fact, James's decision made good business sense. As they did with several other titles in the English Men of Letters Series, the Harpers initially printed 2500 copies of *Hawthorne,* but no pertinent figures have survived as to the book's actual sales.[11] Even if these exceeded James's break-even point of 1200, the author would have had to wait many months for his share of the returns. He needed money quickly (as we have seen, he would eventually take £50 as an advance from a publisher even before completing the manuscript), and Macmillan's first offer ensured a quick and sizable payment.

Want of money, however, was hardly James's chief motive in writing the book. If it had been, he would have completed the manuscript promptly. Instead James kept putting it off. Other publishing projects intervened, but he clearly was not eager to pursue the biography. In August James mentioned to his sister that he was writing his long-delayed *Hawthorne* "slowly and laboriously, for I don't interest myself in the task," though within a month he would claim (to his publisher) that the book was all the better for his having been long about it. This inspirational rose-color faded by the time the volume appeared. To Grace Norton, James confessed that he had written *Hawthorne* "sadly against my will. I wanted to let him alone."[12]

However much James wanted to distance himself from the alleged provinciality of his predecessor's genius, the novelist's sympathies were engaged by the implicit heroism of Hawthorne's choice of vocation. "He was poor, he was solitary, and he undertook to devote himself to literature in a community in which the interest in literature was as yet of the smallest," James wrote:

> he was one of, at most, some dozen Americans who had taken up literature as a profession. The profession in the United States is still very young, and

> of diminutive stature; but in the year 1830 its head could hardly have been seen above ground. It strikes the observer of to-day that Hawthorne showed great courage in entering a field in which the honours and emoluments were so scanty as the profits of authorship must have been at that time. (pp. 45–46)

James had little concrete evidence on which to base his conclusions, but modern research has only confirmed his intuitive impressions. For much of his early career Hawthorne was virtually enslaved to Samuel Griswold Goodrich, publisher of *The Token,* a gift-book annual in which many of the writer's early stories appeared. Goodrich exploited Hawthorne's natural reserve by encouraging him to publish anonymously, under a *nom de plume,* or merely by attribution (e.g., "By the Author of 'The Gentle Boy'"), so that he could fill *The Token*'s pages with Hawthorne's stories without revealing to the public that most of the volume's contents derived from a single pen. In the 1837 issue, for example, Hawthorne contributed no fewer than eight stories, for which he was paid $108, or just over $1 per page.[13] Even later, after the publication of *The Scarlet Letter,* when fame and fortune were somewhat more commensurate with Hawthorne's talent, his income, James carefully notes, "never exceeded very modest proportions" (p. 34). The risks of authorship were many and the rewards few, but Hawthorne took up his pen deliberately. In the record of Hawthorne's early manhood James found "nothing of those experiments in counting-houses or lawyers' offices, of which a permanent invocation to the Muse is often the inconsequent sequel" (pp. 46–47). Like James himself, Hawthorne aimed to be "just literary."

James was hardly indifferent to Hawthorne's intentions, but he judged them on a strictly professional basis—by their results. The signs were not altogether encouraging. In the absence of "larger openings," for example, "Hawthorne had, as the phrase is, to make himself small," doing thankless editorial work and ghost-writing for *Peter Parley's Universal History of the World,* a landmark in American juvenile literature fathered by the tyrannical Goodrich. "There is something pitiful in this episode," James remarks, "and something really touching in the sight of a delicate and superior genius obliged to concern himself with such paltry undertakings." The critic resisted any impulse of sentimentality, however; Hawthorne's demeaning employment probably "cost him less," James asserts, "than it would have cost a more copious and strenuous genius, for his modesty was evidently extreme." James doubted whether "he had any very ardent consciousness of rare talent" (p. 51). The provinciality of America's cultural environment notwithstanding, something in Hawthorne's temperament prevented him from committing himself wholly to the literary life. If for years Hawthorne remained the obscurest man of letters in America (as he famously lamented), James suggests that he had only himself to blame:

> The truth is, he cannot have been in any very high degree ambitious; he was not an abundant producer, and there was manifestly a strain of generous indolence in his composition. There was a loveable want of eagerness about him. Let the encouragement offered have been what it might, he had waited till he was lapsing from middle-life to strike his first noticeable blow [with *The Scarlet Letter*]; and during the last ten years of his career he put forth but two complete works, and the fragment of a third. (p. 49)

Such quantitative criteria are not often associated with James's critical judgments, and the novelist's insistence on them lends some credence to Lionel Trilling's unusual claim that *Hawthorne* is permeated by a Philistine sensibility.[14] Apart from the fact that James was primarily addressing an English audience, not an American one, or the definite possibility that he was attempting to justify the different path he had elected to follow as an artist, his patronizing attitude toward Hawthorne was intensified by an acute awareness of his predecessor's limited success in the marketplace. Hawthorne's professionalism was reluctant at best; he never ceased to avail himself of opportunities for patronage appointments, even though "the immediate effect of his ameliorated fortune was to make him stop writing" (p. 104); and he failed to adjust to the changing nature of the literary environment, when the rise of the monthly magazine threatened him with the necessity of maintaining a kind of professional discipline of which he was incapable.

Hawthorne's problems became acute, as James noted, when he returned to America in 1860. After leaving his consular post at Liverpool and spending two years in Italy, he had finally managed to complete *The Marble Faun.* With the Republican party in power, however, he was forced to support his family by his pen. His American publisher, James T. Fields, encouraged him to keep writing by offering lucrative payments for contributions to the *Atlantic,* but money alone could not court the muse. ("If you want me to write a good book," Hawthorne told his publisher, "send me a good pen; not a gold one, for they seldom suit me; but a pen flexible, and capacious of ink, and that will not grow stiff and rheumatic the moment I begin to get attached to it. I never met with a good pen in my life; so I don't suppose you can find one. The one I write with was made in H[ell] and it is d[amna]tion to write with.")[15] Only with great difficulty did he meet his publisher's deadlines for the serial installments of *Our Old Home* (1863); with *The Dolliver Romance,* which had been promised to the subscribers of the *Atlantic Monthly* for 1864, he broke down altogether. James quotes liberally from Hawthorne's confessions of failure—"I hardly know what to say to the public about this abortive romance, though I know pretty well what the case will be[:] I shall never finish it" (p. 164)—words that presaged the extinction of "the last specimen of the more primitive men of letters."

James's conclusion is only more remarkable for being intuitively arrived at. From the start he had confessed an inability to research his subject exhaustively, but its meaning did not escape him. Equipped with his own instincts as a writer, James felt the very pulse of Hawthorne's career, even when more formal documentation was lacking; he was perfectly justified in remarking on Hawthorne's diffident stance in the marketplace.

Even after *The Scarlet Letter* rescued him from obscurity, Hawthorne's doubts about his artistry persisted. "He blushes like a girl when he is praised," Fields told a friend, "and thinks himself the most over rated man in America."[16] During the most productive phase of his career, virtually coterminous with the critically claimed American Renaissance, Hawthorne scorned the symptoms of success. "I am glad you have got rid of so many of the new books," he told his publisher in 1852. "Sweep them off as fast as you can. Don't let your shelves be disgraced with such trash."[17] The writer's abundant sense of humor is much in evidence here, but his jocular tone does not altogether conceal a rather deprecating view of his own role as an artist.[18]

The same ambivalent attitude carried over into Hawthorne's fiction at numerous points, but its complex implications are best illustrated in *The House of the Seven Gables,* a novel patterned loosely on the writer's family history. In describing the curious "office" of the Albany house in *The Portrait of a Lady,* Henry James gave symbolic form to his anxieties about the marketplace; it seems remarkable, however, that Hawthorne should have designed a similarly suggestive blueprint for the Pyncheon mansion in his novel. Hawthorne devotes the entire first chapter of his book to a description of the house and a narrative of its blood-stained past, but before he can proceed with his tale, he feels compelled to add one final detail:

> There is one other feature, very essential to be noticed, but which, we greatly fear, may damage any picturesque and romantic impression, which we have been willing to throw over our sketch of this respectable edifice. In the front gable, under the impending brow of the second story, and contiguous to the street, was a shop-door, divided horizontally in the midst, and with a window of its upper segment, such as is often seen in dwellings of a somewhat ancient date. This same shop-door had been a subject of no slight mortification to the present occupant of the august Pyncheon-house [Hepzibah], as well as to some of her predecessors. The matter is disagreeably delicate to handle; but, since the reader must needs be let into the secret, he will please to understand, that, about a century ago, the head of the Pyncheons found himself involved in serious financial difficulties. The fellow (gentleman as he styled himself) can hardly have been other than a spurious interloper; for, instead of seeking office from the King or the royal Governor, or urging his hereditary claim to eastern lands, he bethought himself of no better avenue to wealth, than by

> cutting a shop-door through the side of his ancestral residence. It was the custom of the time, indeed, for merchants to store their goods, and transact business, in their own dwellings. But there was something pitifully small in this old Pyncheon's mode of setting about his commercial operations; it was whispered, that, with his own hands, all beruffled as they were, he used to give change for a shilling, and would turn a half-penny twice over, to make sure that it was a good one. Beyond all question, he had the blood of a petty huckster in his veins, through whatever channel it may have found its way there.
>
> Immediately on his death, the shop-door had been locked, bolted, and barred, and, down to the period of our story, had probably never once been opened. The old counter, shelves, and other fixtures of the little shop, remained just as he left them. It used to be affirmed, that the dead shop-keeper, in a white wig, a faded velvet coat, an apron at his waist, and his ruffles carefully turned back from his wrists, might be seen through the chinks of the shutters, any night of the year, ransacking his till, or poring over the dingy pages of his day-book. From the look of unutterable woe upon his face, it appeared to be his doom to spend eternity in a vain effort to make his accounts balance.[19]

The passage is long, but as Hawthorne himself observes, it must not be overlooked. For all their lordly pretensions, the "absurd delusion of family importance" (p. 19) which has always characterized the Pyncheons, they cannot escape the common doom in America of commercial activity. The shop-door is the vulnerable joint in the Pyncheon armor; as Richard Fogle once suggested, it reveals the true origins of the family's fortune and values, divested of their usual trappings.[20] The significance of the doorway was not lost on Henry James, who considered its reopening "the central incident of the tale, and, as Hawthorne relates it, . . . an incident of the most impressive magnitude and most touching interest" (*Hawthorne,* p. 120). Almost as if she were a superannuated Isabel Archer, Hepzibah Pyncheon must open the bolted door and establish a relation to the vulgar street beyond it.

Although Hawthorne ridicules Hepzibah's ordeal as "the final [throe][21] of what called itself old gentility" (p. 36), a certain sympathy mingles with his satire. For the first time in her life, Hepzibah must confront a problem that had plagued Hawthorne as well: after spending many years "in strict seclusion, taking no part in the business of life" (p. 31), she must open an intercourse with the world. Hepzibah's forced appearance before the public has penitential overtones; as a descendant of the stern-browed Puritan magistrate who wrongly sentenced Matthew Maule to death (for the convenience of seizing his land), she labors under a curse that has become part of the family's inheritance. She may not have blood to drink like her cousin Jaffrey, but her pride is bitter to the taste and swallow she must. As Hawthorne coolly observes, "in this republican country, amid the fluctuating waves of our social life, somebody is always at the drowning point":

> Let us behold in poor Hepzibah, the immemorial lady—two hundred years old, on this side of the water, and thrice as many, on the other—with her antique portraits, pedigrees, coats of arms, records, and traditions . . . born, too, in Pyncheon-street, under the Pyncheon-elm, and in the Pyncheon-house, where she has spent all her days—reduced now, in that very house, to be the hucksteress of a cent-shop! (p. 38)

Hawthorne, too, was conscious of a diminution in his family's fortunes, and in the Custom-House Introduction to *The Scarlet Letter* he traces its causes back to a similar case of Puritan injustice. Hawthorne fancies that a curse has descended on his lineage (because of an ancestor's role in prosecuting the Salem witchcraft trials), and he offers up a graceful appeal for a turn in its affairs; but the writer's situation mirrors Hepzibah's in that penance can be achieved only through unwanted publicity. To right the family's wrongs, Hepzibah must peddle gingerbread and Hawthorne must sell storybooks. Outwardly, Hepzibah's situation is absurd—as she "perplex[es] her stiff and somber intellect with the question of how to tempt little boys into her premises!" (p. 37)—but it bears curious resemblance to Hawthorne's problem of finding an audience for his work. At the end of his career, Hawthorne recognized that his "stiff and sombre intellect" infused his books with an "element of unpopularity which (as nobody knows better than myself) pervades them all." "I will try to write a more genial book," he promised his publisher, "but the Devil himself always seems to get into my inkstand, and I can only exorcise him by pensful at a time."[22]

The devil apparently had a hand in the composition of *The Scarlet Letter,* for in hearing its closing pages read from the manuscript, Sophia Hawthorne retired to bed with a fierce headache, which her husband looked upon as a sign of great success. Fearing, however, that few people would be tempted to read the novel because of its unmitigated gloom, Hawthorne recommended to his publisher that it be collected with a number of more cheerful New England sketches (including "The Custom House") and marketed like his previous volumes of stories. Because the novel kept "the same dark idea to the reader's eye," Hawthorne was afraid that it would "weary very many people and disgust some." Was it safe, he asked his publisher, to stake the fate of the book entirely on this one chance?

> A hunter loads his gun with a bullet and several buckshot; and, following his sagacious example, it was my purpose to conjoin the one long story with half a dozen shorter ones, so that, failing to kill the public outright with my biggest and heaviest lump of lead, I might have other chances with the smaller bits, individually and in the aggregate.

In the event that *The Scarlet Letter* should appear independently, Hawthorne recommended that the title page be printed in a lurid red ink. "I am not quite sure about the good taste of so doing," he confessed, "but it would certainly be piquant and appropriate, and, I think, attractive to the great gull whom we are endeavoring to circumvent."[23] Hawthorne's posture here is not much different from Hepzibah's, as she nervously arranges her wares in the window, hoping to entice potential customers into her shop. After pieces of musty gingerbread crumble in her hands and a tumbler of marbles spills its contents across the floor, the narrator apologizes for having stolen upon his beleaguered heroine "too irreverently, at the instant of time when the patrician lady is to be transformed into the plebeian woman" (p. 38); but Hawthorne's letters to his publisher disclose a similar transformation in the status of authorship in America. Only with great reluctance did Hawthorne abandon the attitude of a gentleman amateur, and like poor Hepzibah he often felt humiliated by the necessity of catering to the public's wants.

James T. Fields, the publisher who resurrected Hawthorne's career in 1850, was shrewd enough to recognize that in the literary marketplace an author's name was a commodity, but one that the public was likely to forget if not constantly reminded of its presence. After the modest successes of *The Scarlet Letter* (1850) and *The House of the Seven Gables* (1851), Fields eagerly encouraged his friend to "keep the pot a-boiling like a true Yankee." At the behest of his businesslike patron, Hawthorne pulled together almost all of his uncollected stories for publication in the autumn of 1851 *(The Snow Image),* and he also took up Field's suggestion that "a Book of Stories for children for next season would do wonderfully well."[24] Just as Hepzibah sacrificed her dignity by purveying penny gingerbread to a schoolboy ("The sordid stain of that copper-coin could never be washed away from her palm" [p. 51]), Hawthorne was forced to write storybooks for children as his publisher recommended.

Unfortunately, the rewards of Hawthorne's labor were hardly more profitable than Hepzibah's. Ticknor & Fields issued seven new books and two new editions of his work between 1850 and 1853, an astonishing average of one title every five months; nevertheless, Hawthorne's income from all these publications was only $1500 a year. This was better than he had ever done before, but who could keep up such a pace? Hawthorne could not and gratefully accepted the consulship at Liverpool. As we have seen, the same problems afflicted Hawthorne at the end of the decade when he took up his pen once more. Pressured by his publisher to produce another novel after *The Marble Faun,* Hawthorne tried repeatedly to fashion material from his notebooks into a coherent narrative. Largely oblivious to his author's desperate struggle, Fields promised readers of the *Atlantic* a serial from Hawthorne's pen. But the announcement was ultimately withdrawn, after Hawthorne told him that "too great an effort [to finish the book] will be my death. . . . I should smother myself in mud of my own making."[25] Hawthorne was buried three months later, and James T. Fields dutifully attended the ceremony.

William Charvat reminds us that to blame Hawthorne's death

> on his well-meaning publisher or on the appetites of readers would be false and sentimental. Fiction, after all, is one of the most public of literary arts; and though the truly creative novelist always has the private vision of the poet, he must, if he wants to be professional, find a surface formula acceptable to that middle-brow culture to which our literary publishing has been attuned every since it came to maturity in the middle of the last century.[26]

Hawthorne probably would have concurred with this assessment, especially since the middle-brow artists of his creation (Holgrave in *The House of the Seven Gables* and Kenyon in *The Marble Faun*) are consistently rewarded for their accommodation to the commonplace realities of American life. The novelist himself remained painfully on the fringe, retreating from public exposure (as Hepzibah runs in terror from the sound of the shop-door bell), yet longing for popular acceptance (like Clifford Pyncheon at the arched window, who must be "restrained from plunging into the surging stream of human sympathies" in the bustling street below [p. 165]).

Born to be apart from the world, Clifford can only blow soap bubbles and scatter them from his isolated perch:

> Little, impalpable worlds were those soap-bubbles, with the big world depicted, in hues bright as imagination, on the nothing of their surface. It was curious to see how the passers-by regarded these brilliant fantasies, as they came floating down, and made the dull atmosphere imaginative about them. Some stopt to gaze, and perhaps carried a pleasant recollection of the bubbles, onward, as far as the street-corner; some looked angrily upward, as if poor Clifford wronged them, by setting an image of beauty afloat so near their dusty pathway. A great many put out their fingers, or their walking-sticks, to touch withal, and were perversely gratified, no doubt, when the bubble, with all its pictured earth and sky scene, vanished as if it had never been. (p. 171)

Thus did Hawthorne scatter his romances, iridescent bubbles of imagination, to the world, warning the public not to expect gross reality in their "atmospherical medium" (p. 1). If his books were read in broad daylight, he famously remarked, they were apt to look exceedingly like volumes of blank pages. Virtually all of Hawthorne's charming prefaces were attempts at educating an audience to appreciate his intentions, but the "surface formula" of a soap bubble was too delicate and impalpable for a reading public that preferred the sentimental excesses of "a d[amne]d mob of scribbling women."[27]

Henry James shared Hawthorne's reluctance to advertise himself before an indifferent audience, but he better understood the necessities of survival in a democratic culture and eventually developed more effective strategies to cope with the frictions of the market. As we have seen, James's critical attitude toward his predecessor derived as much from professional impatience with Hawthorne's "generous indolence" and want of ambition as from the apparent provinciality of his milieu. The facts were suggested in Hawthorne's lifetime by his meager productivity, but the situation became a much more public embarrassment after the writer's death. Simply put, Hawthorne's widow and children could not survive on the income derived from the sales of his books. In his review of the posthumously published notebooks, James had wondered why such trivial (and trivializing) records had been committed to publicity. One possible explanation, he suggested, was "the general fondness for squeezing an orange dry."[28] Perhaps unwittingly James had seized upon the truth. Given the family's desperate circumstances, had it not been for Mrs. Hawthorne's editorial labors, there would have been hardly enough income for life's simplest necessities.[29]

When Hawthorne ridiculed Hepzibah Pyncheon's genteel pretensions and described her pitiable transformation into the "hucksteress of a cent shop," he probably never dreamed that the scowling old maid would be capable of exacting her revenge. After the writer's death, when family expenses continually exceeded the royalty income from his books, Sophia Hawthorne was obliged to follow Hepzibah's demeaning example by dismissing her servants, hiring out one of her daughters (Una) as a gymnastics instructor at a female seminary, and selling the amateur watercolors of the other daughter (Rose) at a local curiosity shop.[30] Sophia's desperate economies did not go unnoticed by her friends and neighbors, though most people found it hard to believe that the income from Hawthorne's universally acclaimed books could not provide for his widow's needs. News of Sophia's difficulties struck a particularly responsive chord in Mary Abigail Dodge, a shrewd New England authoress, whose acumen once led Hawthorne to exclaim to his publisher, "I had no idea there was such a sensible woman of letters in the world."[31] Dodge (who wrote under the pseudonym Gail Hamilton) was also having problems with Ticknor & Fields, and she came to Mrs. Hawthorne's aid.

The immediate cause for this discontent was an apparent discrepancy between sales figures reported by Ticknor & Fields and the earnings generated by them. Postwar inflation had driven up the retail price of fiction (typically from $1.25 or $1.50 to $2.00 a volume), but royalty payments had not increased proportionately; in fact, Ticknor & Fields had ignored their copyright contracts and paid, in Mrs. Hawthorne's case, a flat rate of twelve cents per copy for all books sold. Such remuneration was a far cry from 10 or 15 percent to which she felt entitled, and her publisher's rationalizations were hardly satisfactory. James T. Fields maintained that at the time of Hawthorne's death (1864), the estate's attorney, George Hillard, had agreed to a royalty of twelve cents per copy on all of Hawthorne's books, regardless of the retail price. The economic effects of the war had severely disrupted the publishing industry, and most firms were unsure whether consumers would tolerate higher prices for books. Even though manufacturing costs had almost doubled, the firm simply could not have anticipated that retail prices would stabilize at a higher level. Moreover, Fields warned, no one could guarantee that prices would not eventually come down. In that case, a fixed rate of return was preferable to a variable one.

Mrs. Hawthorne was confident, however, that her husband had negotiated better terms for his books with William D. Ticknor (who had died only months before Hawthorne). With the formidable Mary Abigail Dodge behind her, she began a systematic inquiry into Hawthorne's business dealings with Ticknor & Fields. Her letters bristled with rage ("You see how fiercely sharp I am getting—as a lioness over her cubs—when their lives are in danger"),[32] and she insisted on seeing her husband's original contracts. To her chagrin, Fields informed her that none had ever existed: "The arrangements for copyr[igh]t on the volumes consisted simply of mutual agreements made by Mr. Hawthorne or his attorney, at the various times of publication of the various works."[33]

As details of the earlier arrangements gradually surfaced, Mrs. Hawthorne realized that, over the years, her husband had become almost completely dependent on his publisher's goodwill. Ticknor & Fields were justifiably proud of their reputation for integrity, a word that had become firmly associated with their imprint in the antebellum period. They paid Hawthorne generous royalties and published everything he wrote, but they never signed a contract or drew up a complete statement of sales for any of his books. William D. Ticknor managed Hawthorne's investments and had virtually complete control over his bank account. In short, Hawthorne's unblinking confidence in Ticknor epitomized the relationship between authors and publishers that prevailed in a pre-professional era.[34]

Times changed, however, and so did trade practices. As the publishing business was transformed in the latter half of the nineteenth century, the industry's leaders tried desperately to preserve their reputation for being culturally enlightened gentlemen whose liberal assistance to authors was largely responsible for the flowering of a native American literature. James T. Fields himself contributed significantly to this public relations campaign by assembling an ever-so-slightly patronizing memoir, *Yesterdays with Authors* (1871), in which he told the famous story of (and took sufficient credit for) convincing Hawthorne that *The Scarlet Letter* was worthy of publication. As one trade historian has recently observed, publishers' efforts at cultivating an image of virtue were so successful that even today their largesse is fondly remembered. "Their questionable treatment of widows and old maids," however, "has been largely forgotten."[35]

Almost from the beginning of their troubles with Mrs. Hawthorne, Ticknor & Fields had suggested that the matter be turned over to some impartial arbiter (such as Oliver Wendell Holmes), who could determine whether their accounts were accurately and fairly rendered. When Mrs. Hawthorne threatened to take her case to the courts, the firm reiterated a preference for more discreet arbitration:

> To explain fully our actions . . . would necessitate going into all the details of publication. Having offered to lay these details before some competent person, and take his judgment of what[,] in equity, we should do, both as regards our past and future accounting to you for copy[righ]t on Mr. Hawthorne's works, we do not feel that it is incumbent upon us to exhibit, for general inspection, some of the private matters of our business.[36]

Mrs. Hawthorne eventually relented and authorized her sister, the venerable Boston bluestocking Elizabeth Peabody, to go over the evidence. It is hard to imagine the transcendental Miss Peabody scanning account ledgers in pursuit of knowledge, but her conclusions were sobering: for the entire period under review (1850–67), the actual sale of Hawthorne's works had been so small that neither publisher nor author had received, on average, even one thousand dollars a year.

Except during those years when a new volume was published, Peabody found that "the whole profit of all this first rate literary art [did] not assure to Hawthorne's family a *hundred dollars* a year."[37] Peabody nevertheless rebuked Ticknor & Fields for their careless treatment of Mrs. Hawthorne, even though their actions seemed to be within the boundaries of law. A new contract was eventually drawn up, paying the estate a royalty of 10 percent on the retail price of all Hawthorne's books and guaranteeing Ticknor & Fields the right to publish all of his remaining manuscripts and notebooks.[38]

Ticknor & Fields were less polite to Mary Abigail Dodge, who, after all, had no Hawthorne manuscripts in her pocket. At first the firm suggested that, if she were dissatisfied, she could simply take her books elsewhere; but when the spectre of potentially damaging publicity was raised by Mrs. Hawthorne, Ticknor & Fields also offered to submit her friend's complaints to a third party for arbitration. Negotiations became protracted, however, and Dodge's discontent soon escalated into open warfare—the chronicle of which, appropriately titled *A Battle of the Books,* she published in 1870.

Dodge's exposé is a thinly veiled *roman à clef,* crudely written, but quite revealing in its less hysterical moments. The plural in her title raises the fundamental question of accountability in the publishing world:

whose books can be trusted—a publisher's record of sales and earnings, or a writer's reckoning of his expected share of his work's profit? The author confessed that for years she had stupidly trusted her publisher; but the sorry evidence of the trade's abuses, abundantly provided by her own and Mrs. Hawthorne's difficulties, had finally opened her eyes. Her sermon was aimed less at publishers, whose ways were probably beyond redemption, than at authors whose distaste for the commercial aspects of the literary marketplace prevented them from conducting their affairs intelligently:

> the only royal road to justice is for authors, in the beginning, to be intelligent, prompt, exact and exacting on all business matters which come within their scope. This seems a little thing, but it would work a revolution in the literary world. Let writers deal with publishers, not like women and idiots, but as business men with business men. If an author chooses to relinquish all pecuniary rewards from his books and to make an outright gift of the profits to his publishers, he may leave the whole matter in their hands; but if he condescends to take any part in the spoils, he thereby becomes a business partner, and the only question is whether he shall be a good business man or a poor one.[39]

Most genteel Bostonians probably shook their heads in disbelief when they discovered Dodge's unabashed concern for money; nevertheless, one modern historian has recognized that her conclusions set the tone for the author-publisher relationship for the next hundred years.[40] The effect was by no means immediate and widespread, but, at least in Boston, reverberations echoed loudly for many years. As soon as the book appeared, James's mother dispatched a deprecating account of it to her son:

> Gail Hamilton is out in the most disgraceful way before the public in her "Battle of the Books."—Her object is to revenge herself upon Ticknor & Fields for some injustice in a pecuniary way she *says* she has received at their hands. The Fields who were her warm and personal friends! From what I hear she has ruined herself by it, and will find it hard in future to get a publisher.[41]

Even if Dodge were justified in her complaints, the idea of airing them publicly offended Mrs. James. If her son read the book from a writer's point of view, however, his verdict was probably less conventional. What Mary Abigail Dodge had done with bold publicity James would do in quiet confidence for the rest of his career.

It is probably impossible to know whether James actually read Dodge's book from cover to cover, but he was doubtless familiar with its contents.[42] *A Battle of the Books* supplied ample grist for the literary gossip mills of Boston, and the depressing history of the Hawthorne family's troubled fortunes soon became the best-kept open secret in town. In his introduction to *The Scarlet Letter,* Hawthorne had begged for deliverance from the family's legendary curse, but his unfortunate descendants apparently did not escape its effects.

Hawthorne's legacy of poverty and failure seemed particularly apparent to Henry James, who never spoke of the family in his letters without mentioning their dismal prospects. In the midst of a season during which he was dining out at an almost record-breaking pace, comfortably working his way into fashionable English society, James reported to his parents:

> I hear poor Julian Hawthorne is (somewhere near London) in great destitution & distress; & wonder greatly that he doesn't go home. Is it true that poor little [George Parsons] Lathrop has been dismissed from the *Atlantic* & is separated from his wife [Rose Hawthorne]? So I heard sometime since, I forget how.[43]

The contrast in their circumstances was not lost on Julian Hawthorne, whose path in England James never crossed until self-interest altered his course. "Had a letter this morning from Henry James Junior," Julian entered in his journal on 14 January 1879,

> who wishes to pump me on his biography of my father. . . . I don't know that I can tell him anything useful; however I shall be glad to see him; he has hitherto kept out of my way, either purposely or not; but now that he thinks I can serve him, he finds out my address. Well, that is all right and natural; we shall see what sort of an impression we make upon each other.[44]

James visited Hawthorne at Hastings in February, but their impressions were not much changed on closer acquaintance. James complained mildly to his brother that Julian gave him "little satisfaction or information about his father."[45] Julian's journal reveals, however, that another subject was much on James's mind: "pecuniary relations with publishers."[46]

At this point in his career, James certainly could profit from the professional experience of Julian Hawthorne, whose aggressive attitude toward publishers descended from Mary Abigail Dodge rather than from his preprofessional father. Julian was surprised to discover the disparity between James's fame and fortune: "he has been paid far worse than I have," Julian confided to his journal, "owing in large degree, I fancy, to his negligence in looking after his affairs."[47] Julian Hawthorne's impression may well have been colored by James's confirmed practice of exaggerating his incapacity (and unconcern) for business. Both English and American publishers would soon learn that James was hardly "negligent in looking after his affairs" when *Confidence* was ready for the press—but that revealing affair occurred after James' interview with Julian Hawthorne and possibly was determined by it. In a very real sense, the preparation of the biography completed James's professional education.

If the novelist benefited personally from Julian's advice, his study of Hawthorne was affected by it as well. Nathaniel Hawthorne was never more "provincial" than in his "pecuniary relations with publishers." His life, James remarked, was "singularly exempt from worldly preoccupations and vulgar efforts. It [was] as pure, as simple, as unsophisticated, as his work" (p. 165). On the other hand, Americans of James's generation—professional writers among them—had "eaten of the tree of knowledge": "eventualities, as the late Emperor of the French used to say, [would] not find [them] intellectually unprepared" (p. 135). James's *Hawthorne,* in fact, was flavored by the fruit of that tree. Writing the book prepared him "intellectually" for the "eventualities" of the modern literary marketplace.

V

Melodrama in the Marketplace: The Making of The Bostonians

Almost as if to demonstrate the validity of *Hawthorne*'s assertions, Henry James's capacity for dealing with the "eventualities" of the literary marketplace was rigorously tested in the years to come, particularly during the decade of the 1880s, when his income from writing fluctuated wildly (see Appendix B). Leon Edel long ago deflated the myth that James did not really have to live by his pen,[1] but few critics have attempted to demonstrate the particular ways in which the novelist's creative life was influenced by social or economic forces. Edel himself tends to slight such determinants of viewpoint in favor of narrowly personal ones. This critical oversight has distorted most noticeably our view of James's middle period, the years of bold artistic and professional experiment demarcated by the achievement of *The Portrait of a Lady* (1881) and the debacle of James's interlude in the theatre that culminated with the momentous failure of *Guy Domville* in 1895.

Important throughout this period is James's effort to create and maintain an audience for his work. Characteristically, his ambitions were divided between conflicting ideals—between the private seriousness of the artist's imagination and a concomitant desire for public understanding of his intentions. Almost all of James's fictions in the decade of the eighties—especially the three major novels, *The Bostonians, The Princess Casamassima,* and *The Tragic Muse*—are peopled by characters who struggle to find a common ground between their private and public roles. This, too, was James's dilemma as his rising fame transformed him into a kind of literary ambassador from the new world to the old. His celebrity status was rather shortlived (though James quickly recognized its potential dangers to the artist, as he would later testify in "The Death of the Lion"), but for a time he enjoyed the greatest popularity of his career both in England and in America.[2] The peculiar success of "Daisy Miller" stimulated a new appetitie for fiction based on the "international situation," and James was immediately heralded as its creator. His books were widely discussed; he associated freely with the best literary circles in London; and in America he was welcomed home as a prominent man of letters. From Washington he wrote an English friend in the early days of 1882, "I too am 'someone' here, and it will be at a terrible sacrifice of vanity that I return to England and walk in to dinner after every one, alone, instead of marching with the hostess or the prettiest woman present! But I love my London better than my vanity, and expect to turn up there about the month of May."[3]

Flushed with the apparent triumph of *The Portrait of a Lady,* James had returned to America in the fall of 1881. Sailing from Liverpool, he despatched a quick note to Frederick Macmillan, expressing hope that the publisher would sell five thousand copies of his works during his absence: "I see them in *all* the shopwindows (booksellers' of course) here; which makes me feel as if I had not only started but arrived."[4] James's confidence was bolstered further by the novel's success in America, where it was "selling—largely," he told Macmillan.[5] A sense of large accomplishment gave James the courage to request that the American contracts for his books be renegotiated. "Ten per cent. royalty on the retail price of my volumes seems to me a very beggarly profit," he told Houghton, Mifflin:

> Let me request then that it be raised then to [*fifty* crossed out] twenty. My next half-yearly account in that case will present a less meagre appearance than the last you sent me [which totaled $23]. Please let me receive your assent to this.[6]

At the same time, James responded aggressively to an invitation to write a serial novel for Thomas Bailey Aldrich, the new editor of the *Atlantic Monthly.* James's terms were steep, $300 an installment, 20 percent more than for *The Portrait,* with the condition that the work be published simultaneously in an English magazine. Despite the favorable reception of James's last *Atlantic* novel, Aldrich penciled "I decline this offer" in the margin of the author's letter and responded in kind.[7] Houghton, Mifflin (who now controlled the magazine) also balked at the novelist's request for higher royalties.

For a time, James was not especially ruffled by these setbacks. Unexpectedly free of commitments to write fiction, James had time to rework "Daisy Miller" into dramatic form, an ill-fated enterprise that gave him his first unpleasant brush with the commercial theatre. His labor was not entirely profitless—*Daisy Miller: A Comedy* eventually found its way into the pages of the *Atlantic*—but James soon became frustrated by his reduced productivity. Several months after his American sojourn (perhaps with the truncated shadow of Hawthorne behind him), James reconsecrated his artistic ambition in the notebooks he had only recently begun to fill:

> If I can only *concentrate* myself: this is the great lesson of life. I have hours of unspeakable reaction against my smallness of production; my wretched habits of work—or of un-work; my levity, my vagueness of mind, my perpetual failure to focus my attention, to absorb myself, to look things in the face, to invent, to produce, in a word. I shall be 40 years old in April next: it is a horrible fact! I believe however that I have learned how to work and that it is in moments of forced idleness, almost alone, that these melancholy reflections seize me. When I am really at work, I'm happy, I feel strong, I see many opportunities ahead. It is the only thing that makes life endurable. I must make some great efforts during the next few years, however, if I wish not to have been on the whole a failure. I shall have been a failure unless I do something *great!*[8]

The "something great" that James hungered to do could only be writing a major novel, although it would be several years before he could attempt to redeem the pledge. The rapid decline and death of Henry James, Sr. in the winter of 1882 abruptly brought the writer back to America, where he was destined to remain for several months settling the terms of his father's estate. Despite the complications that his service as executor entailed, such as reconciling his brother William to a more equitable division of the estate among the five children, James pushed ahead with a surprisingly large number of publishing projects. The year before William Dean Howells had reported James's dissatisfaction with Houghton, Mifflin & Company to James R. Osgood, who lost no time in resuming his relationship with the novelist. By offering James a sliding-scale contract for the dramatic version of *Daisy Miller* and a generous 20 percent royalty on *The Siege of London*—terms that Houghton, Mifflin refused to match—Osgood once again became James's official publisher in America.[9]

Howells's continued advocacy, however, was also the source of some embarrassment to James. In the November 1882 *Century,* which enjoyed considerable circulation in England, Howells had published an article on "Henry James, Jr.," in which he credited his American friend with advancing the art of the novel beyond the achievements of Dickens and Thackeray. Howells's flattering tribute precipitated a critical brouhaha in the fervidly nationalistic London press. James was in Paris at the time, where he missed the ruckus produced by the article, but he told Howells not to worry:

> You are accused of having sacrificed—in your patiotic passion for the works of H. J. Jr.—*Vanity Fair* and *Henry Esmond* to *Daisy Miller* and *Poor Richard!* The indictment is rubbish—all your text says is that the "confidential" manner of Thackery [*sic*] would not be tolerable today in a younger school,

> which should attempt to reproduce it. . . . But don't let the . . . matter bother you; it is infinitesimally small and the affair of three fourths of a minute.[10]

Unfortunately, the reverberations provoked by Howells's ill-starred amiabilities echoed for months rather than minutes. Subsequent judgments of James's work in the English press tended to link James with Howells more frequently and to be colored by indignation at the American upstart's remark. Even Edmund Gosse, a friend of both James and Howells, took issue with the *Century* piece and wrote to its author, "So you have demolished poor old Dickens and Thackeray, have you? Well, I am glad I was born in the good old times when they were thought good enough week-day reading." Gosse also included a scrap of doggerel "by a candid friend":

Motto for the American Critic

Ho! the old school! Thackeray, Dickens!
Throw them out to feed the chickens.—
Ho! the new school! James and ———
Lay the flattery on with trowels.[11]

Despite James's assurances, the storm of damaging publicity took Howells by surprise. He himself was not worried about the affair, but, aware of his friend's limited public, was chiefly concerned because he had disturbed James's precarious relation with his audience.

The immediate effect of Howells's overcharged appreciation was to cloud James's plans for publishing a volume of travel pieces that were buried in old numbers of various American periodicals. "A collection of these," he told Osgood, "would be feasible and I think, entertaining. The trouble is that the best of these things are the sketches of England—which motives of delicacy absolutely prohibit my reprinting, *in toto,* at present." James added that he "could reprint portions of them (the flattering ones!)" and felt that there was enough material on other subjects to flesh out the book. To Macmillan, James insisted that he would be willing to publish the book in England only if it seemed "overwhelmingly *genial.*"[12] When the time came for him to prepare the manuscript of *Portraits of Places,* he instructed the type-copyist to leave a considerable margin, owing to the substantial revisions he intended to make. James not only reworked the collection extensively but prefaced it with an additional disclaimer to remind his audience that the sketches had been written primarily for Americans. At least with respect to his English public, James was on the defensive.

Some critics have alleged that throughout the 1880s an increasingly defensive tone emerged in James's fiction as well. Donald D. Stone observes that in most of James's work in this decade, the author betrays "a constant need to explain, without drawing attention to, himself and a fruitless desire to become popular by turning to the writing of topical books in a conventional style with real endings."[13] The seriousness of this charge is somewhat muted by the fact that it does not adequately describe the range of the writer's intentions. As long as he was dependent on the literary marketplace for his living, James's motives were almost always mixed; if a "fruitless desire to become popular" crippled much of his fiction during this period, the same hope also inspired and, to some extent, shaped his creative imagination.

To begin with, James's negotiations and publishing contracts for his work became rather unconventional after the proven appeal of *The Portrait of a Lady.* For his next novel—envisioned as a twelve-month serial—he had tried the *Atlantic,* whose editor, perhaps satiated with Jamesian prose after fourteen installments of *The Portrait,* declined his offer. After a host of other projects were either published or well under way—*Daisy Miller: A Comedy* (1882), *The Siege of London* (1883), the first Macmillan Collective Edition (1883), *Portraits of Places* (1883), and *A Little Tour in France* (1884)—James again proposed a novel, this time to the *Century.* Though he left the terms to the editors, James confided to Howells, they also refused. "I should add that this refusal has since been somewhat modified. But in the meantime I have virtually (though not yet formally) engaged to give my next thing to Osgood to dispose of as he lists, & that if they take it they will have [to] do so on his terms."[14]

The arrangement with which James was experimenting was English in origin—a lease of copyright for a fixed term of years similar to the one he had negotiated with Chatto & Windus for *Confidence.* Such a contract had it advantages to James: it simplified negotiations by disposing simultaneously of serial and book rights; it guaranteed a substantial sum of money down on publication; and, as considerable experience had demonstrated, a lease for a modest number of years was virtually coterminous with the life span of profitability for James's titles. Just as he had brought American customs to the British publishing scene, James returned to his native land with a determination to profit from his experience with foreign publishers.

Although the leaders of the American book trade pointed with pride to the more progressive royalty contracts they signed with their authors, they discouraged as dangerously speculative the practice of advancing sums of money in anticipation of future sales. The royalty contract, they maintained, ensured that, in time, an author would receive his appropriate share of a book's returns. The delay, however, could be considerable. Most houses rendered statements only once or twice a year and then deferred the payment of royalties for another four to six months. From 1878 to 1892 the Harpers settled their account with Henry James only five times.[15] Under the half-profits system, remuneration from English publishers was equally slow, but their willingness also to lease copyrights for a fixed sum distinguished them from their American counterparts. For an author like Henry James, who relied on each successive book to

Agreement made this 13th day of April, A.D. 1883, between Henry James of the first part, and James R. Osgood & Co. of the second part, both of the City of Boston, Mass.

1. Said James agrees to write for said Osgood & Co. the following literary works; viz. one novel of plot and plan generally as described in his letter to them of April 8. 1883, substantially of the length of one hundred and fifty (150) "Atlantic Monthly" pages; one sketch or story (at present entitled "Lady Barberina" and generally as described in said letter) of the length of about fifty (50) "Atlantic" pages; and two shorter stories of about twentyfive (25) "Atlantic" pages each.

2. Said James hereby assigns and transfers to said Osgood & Co. absolutely and forever any and all rights of copy, publication and sale in and for said works in any and all forms in any and all countries other than the United States of America.

3. It is agreed that the United States copyrights for said works shall be entered in the

Memorandum of Agreement dated 13 April 1883 between Henry James and James R. Osgood & Co. for *The Bostonians* and *Tales of Three Cities.* James's preference to lease the domestic copyright in these works and sell the foreign rights altogether (Clauses 2–4) reveals the influence of his publishing experience in England. Such practices were alien to the American trade; hence, name of said James and shall belong to him subject only to the rights of publication and sale conferred on said Osgood & Co. under this agreement. And said James hereby assigns and transfers to said Osgood & Co. the entire and exclusive right of publication and sale of said works in serial form in the United States without any restriction whatever. He also assigns and transfers to said Osgood & Co. the entire and exclusive right of publication and sale of said works in book form in the United States for the term of five years from the date of such publication in book form.

4. At the expiration of five years from the date of publication in book form in the United States said Osgood & Co. may continue the publication of said works in the United States upon the payment to said James of such consideration for the use of his copyright as shall then be mutually agreed upon. In the case of failure to agree upon such consideration, said James shall have the right to take the stereotype plates of said works and the copies then on hand paying

a holograph contract had to be drawn up in place of the standard, pre-printed form that Osgood normally used. Unfortunately, Osgood's untimely bankruptcy in 1885 rendered the terms of this agreement "insanely unprofitable" for James.

therefor their value upon a fair appraisal and to discontinue their publication with said Osgood & Co.

5. It is agreed that the said works shall take precedence of any other works of fiction to be written by said James, and shall be furnished as rapidly as possible, the shorter stories first and the novel soon after and while no time is definitely agreed on it is generally understood that the stories will be furnished during the summer and autumn of the present year, and a substantial part of the novel during the first two months of the year 1884. And it is further agreed that for purposes of book publication in the United States said Osgood & Co. are at liberty to include without further payment in the volume containing the three short stories a story by said James heretofore published and entitled "Four Meetings."

6. In consideration of the premises and the agreements of said James said Osgood & Co. agree to pay to said James the sum of Four thousand dollars ($4000.) for the long story named above, and Two thousand dollars ($2000.) for the three

shorter stories, upon the delivery of the completed manuscripts respectively.

In witness whereof the said parties have hereunto set their hands on the day and year first above mentioned.

Henry James.

James R. Osgood & Co

1. Tales of Three Cities pub^d. Oct. 17, 1884
2. Bostonians – surrendered to author

We hereby assign to Houghton, Mifflin and Company all our right and interest under this contract.

Boston, Mass
May 1, 1889.

Ticknor & Co.

pay his way, the ready money up front made quite a difference. By combining aspects of both English and American publishing conventions, James was working toward a form of agreement recognized today as the industry standard—a royalty contract that stipulates payment of a fixed sum of money in advance of sales.

Even in physical form the contract James eventually signed with Osgood for *Tales of Three Cities* (1884) and *The Bostonians* (1886) departs from established convention. Earlier letters of agreement with Osgood, the Harpers, and Houghton, Mifflin were typical of standard trade practice—preprinted forms with appropriate spaces for the author's name and the title of his book, but with a royalty rate of 10 percent fixed in cold type.[16] The contract for *Tales of Three Cities* and *The Bostonians* is a four-page document, entirely in longhand, that bears almost no resemblance to its predecessors. As James had told Howells, his plan was to dispose of all rights in his next novel for a fixed sum. The same strategy applied to the collection of short stories that James was anxious to write first, so both were included in the arrangement with Osgood. The novel, which James had outlined to his publisher in a letter of 8 April 1883 that served as the basis for their contract, was to be "substantially of the length of one hundred and fifty (150) *'Atlantic Monthly'* pages" (or six installments); the short stories included one "at present entitled *'Lady Barbarina'* . . . of the length of about fifty (50) *'Atlantic'* pages" and two of about twenty-five pages each still to be written. James surrendered all foreign rights in these works to Osgood as well as the American serial rights; license to publish them in book form in America was granted for five years from the date of issue. At the end of that term, James had the option of renewing the contract with Osgood or taking the books elsewhere. In exchange Osgood agreed to pay James $4000 for the novel and $2000 for the three short stories upon delivery of the completed manuscripts.[17]

For 250 pages of material James had made a good bargain, although the sums he agreed to were slightly less than what he first demanded ($4500 for the novel and $2500 for the stories). This compromise and the actual wording of the contract illustrate Osgood's shrewdness, too—particularly the inclusion of all foreign rights for one comprehensive price. When James first made his proposal, he reminded Osgood, "I shall also have to hear from you how my property in the *copyright* of the productions in question is affected by the arrangement we are discussing. I don't suppose I make it over to you *forever?* That is an idea from which I shrink."[18] In turn, Osgood agreed to a lease on the American rights but reserved foreign rights to his firm. James quickly advised Macmillan that he had "parted with the English copyright (prospective) in two books which I am to write as speedily as possible for my American publisher . . . as to which . . . you will have to treat with him—not with me." For his part Osgood lost no time in selling the English copyrights. Macmillan agreed to pay the American publisher £150 ($725) for each of the volumes when they were ready—£50 more if either sold more than 3000 copies. These sums, together with what he could get from American magazines for serialization, guaranteed Osgood a decent return on his investment.[19]

To prod Osgood along with the deal, James had stressed that the sale of the serial rights (at least for his international tales) would be easy money. "The other day," James told his publisher, "[Richard Watson] Gilder (of the *Century*) said in writing to me—'Haven't you got any more short stories in you: short as *Four Meetings* & as good?' I mention this to show you that there is a demand for those productions. He had asked me this two or three times before." With a ready market for his short fiction, James was eager to complete "Lady Barberina" and the two other stories first. The first installment of *The Bostonians* could be ready "by *about* the New Year. This will give me more time for that story," James pregnantly added, "which, as I think over it, I should a good deal prefer to have."[20]

The period of gestation that James felt he needed for *The Bostonians* had, as everyone knows, a disastrous effect on his planned economy of scale. The six installments he envisioned for the novel ballooned to thirteen; the serial grew ponderous; and like the later books of the eighties it was marred by a problem of completion. As Edmund Wilson has bluntly observed, "there is a point—usually about half-way through—at which every one of these novels begins strangely to run into the sands; the excitement of the story lapses at the same time as the treatment becomes more abstract and the colour fades from the picture. The ends are never up to the beginnings."[21] Other critics have sometimes apologized for James's digressive treatment of his subjects, but few have offered convincing explanations for them.

The case of *The Bostonians* seems especially problematic in view of the author's original intention to write "a shortish novel" that was, he told Grace Norton, "to mark a new era in my career, and usher in a series of works of superior value to any I have yet produced." In fact, the amplitude of *The Bostonians* increased directly in proportion to James's delay in writing it. In his letter to Norton he deprecated his other recent short stories as "the mechanical working off of an old, unprofitable contract"—"you will . . . not care for them any more than I do."[22] What he did care for was the chance to do "something great," to complete a substantial fiction. As he told his brother William several months later,

> I am happy to say I am drawing to the close of various short things I have lately had to write—& am attacking two novels—one serial of six months in the *Century*, & one, to run a year (but not to begin till July 1885) in the *Atlantic*. The subjects of both, thank God, are big & important; & the treatment will be equally so.[23]

Both the subject of *The Bostonians* and its treatment were bigger and more important than a six-month serial could contain. An unexpected opportunity to make money from another source reconciled James to the novel's inexorable expansion.

Work on *The Bostonians* was postponed by a lucrative offer for more short stories that the novelist could not afford to pass up. Charles Dana, the enterprising editor of the New York *Sun,* invited James and other prominent writers to contribute a number of tales to his Sunday editions and for distribution to other American newspapers. Syndication of serial fiction was a new development in American journalism, and Dana was one of the first American editors to recognize the need for news and features appealing to a growing audience of feminine readers.[24] Even though James had completed the three stories he had promised to Osgood, the terms of his contract stipulated that they and *The Bostonians* take precedence over any other works of fiction he might care to write. With Dana's offer in hand, however, James wrote to Osgood for an extension. His reason was simple—"want of money":

> I have not enough ready money to carry me through the time it will take me to complete my novel—as I shall not be paid for it, of course, till it is completed. I would undertake to deliver it to you in instalments, to be paid for successively, which would serve my purpose as well; but this you very possibly would not care for, & I think it best not to waste time in waiting for an answer on that point. My necessity has accidentally arisen; I did not foresee it—on the contrary—when we made our agreement. I see the *Century* does not advertise my novel for the present year—therefore I suppose that it is not in a *particular* hurry for the MS. I do not mean by this that I propose to put off the production of it; on the contrary I shall go on with it rapidly & deliver it promptly as soon as I have had time to produce a couple of short tales (of 12,000 words each) for which I have had a handsome offer, & which will enable [me] to live while I work! These things I shall of course also look to you to republish—so my request is not injurious to you.[25]

Osgood was obliging (James's inference about the *Century*'s flexibility was correct), and the novel was set aside.

Earlier in his career James had complained of the vulgarity of American magazines. Now he was descending into the newspapers! "Lately I have been doing some short things," he told Thomas Sergeant Perry, "which you will see in due time in the Century, & eke three or four in (horresco referens!) the New York Sunday *Sun!*" To James's essentially melodramatic imagination, even his own career could bear resemblance to a rake's progress. "That journal has bribed me with gold—it is a case of gold pure & simple," he insisted—but then went on to say, "moreover the reasons against exposing myself in it do not seem to me serious."[26] James's extended (and extenuating) sentence betrays the true complexity of his motives. Money, he claimed, was decisive, but the prospect of reaching an enormously expanded audience (the *Sun* alone had 150,000 readers, the other papers in the syndication scheme had thousands more) also had an unquestionable appeal. "The die is cast," he announced portentously to his sister, "but I don't in the least repent of it—as I see no shame in offering my productions to the widest public, & in their being 'brought home,' as it were, to the great American people."[27]

James's defensive letters to his family and friends could almost have been written by Matthias Pardon, the journalistic "son of his age" in *The Bostonians,* whose "passion" for Verena Tarrant, the mysteriously gifted heroine of that novel, is "not a jealous one, and include[s] a remarkable disposition to share the object of his affection with the American people."[28] The novelist's obvious contempt for Pardon becomes much more significant when we recognize that his scorn may also have been directed at certain aspects of his own character. James's posture in the marketplace, his divided ambition for both artistic integrity and popular acceptance, was frequently an embarrassment to the more purely imaginative side of his genius. His efforts to transcend the old paternal dichotomy between being and doing were never wholly successful. Self and society were like the poles of a magnet, both powerfully attractive, that left the artist in a state of charged suspension between them. The play of these two forces informs all of James's major fiction in the decade of the eighties.

Outside of his novels, James's most sustained effort at reconciling the competing claims that tugged at the artist was his definition of that figure's role in "The Art of Fiction" (1884). This essay was written in response to an address on "Fiction as One of the Fine Arts" by Walter Besant, one of the great Victorian novel-machines, who claimed to have written eighteen books in as many years. Although James agreed with Besant on many issues (that novel writing should be classed among the fine arts, for example, and duly recognized with prizes and other public honors), he could not go along with the assertion that the novel must embody a conscious moral purpose. The novelist, James felt, could hope only to record manners, not police them. "The only reason for the existence of a novel is that it does attempt to represent life. When it relinquishes this attempt, the same attempt that we see on the canvas of the painter, it will have arrived at a very strange pass."[29]

James's famous sentences—there are many others—have typically been read as the classic defense of realism in English literary history. It seems fair to say, however, that his essay was not merely an aesthetic rejoinder to Besant's address but also a professional one, since it attempted to define the novelist's social role and to clarify the attitudes and values ideally personified by the artist figure in contemporary culture. The claims James made for the novelist were essentially those allowed to the historian, whose subject had to be taken for granted and whose value could be judged solely by his method of dealing with it. "To represent and illustrate the past, the actions of men, is the task of either writer," James wrote, "and the only difference that I can see is, in proportion as he succeeds, to the honour of novelist, consisting as it does in his having more difficulty in collecting his evidence, which is so far from being purely literary."[30] In giving the novelist a legitimate role as a social historian, dismissing as irresponsible any apology for him as a mere dabbler in make-believe, James was also attempting to educate and expand his own limited audience and so ensure his own artistic freedom. Like one of Hawthorne's prefaces, only detached from the novels it preceded, "The Art of Fiction" was intended to prepare the reading public for the new kind of fiction that James was about to attempt. By asking readers to grant the artist his *donnée* and to focus instead on his treatment of it, James was anticipating and trying to deflect the major contemporary criticisms of *The Bostonians* and *The Princess Casamassima*—that their subjects, if not actually libelous or subversive, were socially inappropriate and unacceptable.

James had admitted in his essay that the high claims he was making for the novel were possibly mocked by "the enormous number of works of fiction that appeal to the credulity of our generation, for it might easily seem that there could be no great character in a commodity so quickly and easily produced." If the field suffered "discredit from overcrowding," however, the injury to the novel was "only superficial"—another testament to its remarkably elastic strength as a form of art.

> It has been vulgarized, like all other kinds of literature, like everything else to-day, and it has proved more than some kinds accessible to vulgarization. But there is as much difference as there ever was between a good novel and a bad one: the bad is swept with all the daubed canvases and spoiled marble into some unvisited limbo, or infinite rubbish-yard beneath the back-windows of the world, and the good subsists and emits its light and stimulates our desire for perfection.[31]

The theme—and even the landscape—of vulgarization is central to the meaning of *The Bostonians,* James's next exercise in the art of fiction. The unforgettably sordid vista seen from Olive Chancellor's back windows is indeed the "infinite rubbish yard" of a materialistic American civilization. As an addendum to the outline of the novel he submitted to Osgood, James stressed that "the whole thing" was to be

> as local, as American, as possible, and as full of Boston: an attempt to show that I *can* write an American story. There must, indispensably, be a type of newspaper man—the man whose ideal is the energetic reporter. I should like to *bafouer* the vulgarity and hideousness of this—the impudent invasion of privacy—the extinction of all conception of privacy, etc.

By coupling this theme with his anxieties about the feminization of American culture—"the most salient and peculiar point in our social life"—the novelist arrived at his formula for *The Bostonians.*[32] The possibilities inherent in this combination convinced James that it was "a better subject that I have ever had before, & I think," he boasted to his brother, "will be much the best thing I have done yet. . . . I shall be much abused for the title but it exactly and literally fits the story, & is much the best, simplest and most dignified I could have chosen."[33] Earlier James had told Thomas Sergeant Perry that the book was to be "a remorseless exploitation of Boston." "Look out," he warned, "in Marlborough St.; I am especially hard on the far end."[34] Marlborough's "far end," of course, points toward Charles Street, the thoroughfare in which Olive Chancellor's citadel of reform is located.

From the moment that Basil Ransom enters his cousin's drawing room, even that venerable sanctuary becomes an arena for the conflict between the demands of private and public life. "Olive will come down in about ten minutes," Mrs. Luna announces in the book's opening line—a stage direction that immediately suggests the extent to which the action of the novel will unfold in a series of public appearances, calculated entrances, and (mis)calculated exits. Almost all the private homes in the book become public forums, frequented by an "irregular army of nostrum-mongers" (p. 72). Miss Birdseye, the superannuated epitome of the New England reformer, lives in "the common residence of several persons," among whom there prevails "much vagueness of boundary" (p. 29). Verena Tarrant's innocence is all the more remarkable because it has "survived the abolition of walls and locks" in a variety of transcendental Bohemias (p. 212). American architecture would seem to be a partner in society's general conspiracy against the manhood of every one of its members (as Emerson remarked in "Self-Reliance"). It is hardly a coincidence that Ransom and Verena first experience their attraction to one another in the narrow transept of Harvard's Memorial Hall—the "most interesting" feature of the building, James tells us, "a chamber high, dim, and severe," squeezed between "a theatre, for academic ceremonies" and "a vast refectory . . . hung about with portraits and lighted by stained windows, like the halls of the colleges of Oxford" (pp. 241–42). Only in the novel's more private spaces can genuinely spontaneous emotion surface and find expression.

Under the perpetual glare of publicity, sincere expression of any sort is a remarkable achievement for the characters in *The Bostonians.* "A voice, a human voice, is what we want," declares Olive Chancellor, whose problem of finding an appropriate vehicle and style of communication is particularly acute (p. 56). Unfortunately, Olive's personal manner tends to discourage ordinary human contact. Her hand, when grasped, is "at once cold and limp"; the "curious tint of her eyes" resembles "the glitter of green ice"; and her smile, seldom seen, is likened to "a thin ray of moonlight resting upon the wall of a prison" (pp. 8, 18). Because of her "tragic shyness," Olive's own "cultivated voice" is incapable of articulating the passion of her intensely felt convictions (pp. 10, 8). With a face that seems "to plead for a remission from responsibility," she confesses to the presiding feminist in Miss Birdseye's salon, "I can't talk to those people, I can't!":

> "I want to give myself up to others; I want to know everything that lies beneath and out of sight, don't you know? I want to enter into the lives of women who are lonely, who are piteous. I want to be near to them—to help them. I want to do something—oh, I should like so to speak!"

Responding to the invitation to give a few remarks, however, Olive protests. "O dear, no, I can't speak; I have none of that sort of talent. I have no self-possession, no eloquence; I can't put three words together"—at least not in public (p. 36).

Olive's contradictory inclinations, her private ambition and public reluctance, effectively mirror her creator's. Her frustrated desire to find an audience for her feelings is surprisingly similar to James's, just as she shares his distaste for the vulgarizing influence of incessant publicity. Ransom is surprised to find his fastidious cousin among the promiscuous company of reformers who gather in Miss Birdseye's sordid drawing room; but he will never know, James confides to us, "that she mortally disliked it, and that in a career in which she was constantly exposing herself to offence and laceration, her most poignant suffering came from the injury of her taste" (p. 29). Although Olive is "preoccupied with the romance of the people" and entertains a theory of democracy that bids her to "put off invidious differences and mingle in the common life," in her heart she loathes the public streetcars that conscience urges her to ride (pp. 34, 22). James's descriptions of the "offence and laceration" that Olive must suffer could almost have been lifted from his confessional letters about publishing stories—"horresco referens!"—in the New York Sunday *Sun.* For the sake of their careers, both James and Olive must traffic with the herd.

James's ambivalent relation to the organs of publicity is also shared by Olive's primary antagonist, Basil Ransom, whose "immense desire for success," though "not of a mercenary spirit," can only be satisfied through the agency of the literary market place (p. 17). "He had always had a desire for public life," James informs us; but Ransom's legal career, which might have launched him onto "some judicial bench or political platform" (p. 4), instead condemns him to a sadly unvisited office in New York where he passes many unoccupied hours reading Tocqueville:

> He asked himself what was the use of his having an office at all, and why he might not as well carry on his profession at the Astor Library, where in his

> spare hours and on chance holidays, he did an immense deal of suggestive reading. He took copious notes and memoranda, and these things sometimes shaped themselves in a way that might possibly commend them to the editors of periodicals. Readers perhaps would come, if clients didn't. (p. 188)

Curiously enough, James ascribes to Ransom the same pattern of movement between library and office first associated with Isabel Archer in *The Portrait of a Lady.* Once again the protagonist's problem is opening an intercourse with the world, finding a sympathetic audience for his ideas.

Ransom's way, like Isabel's, is blocked—not by a bolted door, but even more emphatically by "the powers that preside over weekly and monthly publications," who decline his articles ("with thanks") and remind him that his conservative social doctrines are "about three hundred years behind the age; doubtless some magazine of the sixteenth century would have been very happy to print them" (p. 189). Once infected with the virus of authorship, Ransom is reluctant to admit defeat; he even contemplates marriage to crude but comfortably endowed Mrs. Luna, whose money would enable him to circumvent the ordinary channels of publicity:

> Images of leisure played before him, leisure in which he saw himself covering foolscap paper with his views on several subjects, and with favourable illustrations of Southern eloquence. It became tolerably vivid to him that if editors wouldn't print one's lucubrations, it would be a comfort to feel that one was able to publish them at one's own expense. (p. 197)

Ransom soon renounces life as a gentleman-author, however, just as James had rejected his father's "amateurish" habits of dealing with publishers. Willing to do battle in the literary marketplace, he continues his assault on various editorial precincts until one of his articles is accepted and his professional career has begun.

Both Olive Chancellor and Basil Ransom are impelled on their diverse paths to publicity by the example of Verena Tarrant, whose mysterious talent for moving great audiences they covet almost as much as her affection. Given Olive's frustrated desire to "know intimately some *very* poor girl," thereby to move in closer proximity to the "mysterious democracy . . . that the fortunate classes know so little about," her discovery of Verena at Miss Birdseye's promises to satisfy an intense moral craving (pp. 34, 79). "Who is that charming creature?" she impulsively inquires, when Verena's "artless enthusiasm" for the rights of women easily upstages the false theatricality of Mrs. Farrinder, the evening's featured performer (p. 52). Olive instantly recognizes the potential value of Verena's oratorical gift; when her cousin questions the propriety of parading the young girl in public, she rejoins,

> "Come out in public! . . . in public? Why, you don't imagine that pure voice is to be hushed?"

> "Oh hushed, no! it's too sweet for that [Ransom replies]. But not raised to a scream; not forced and cracked and ruined. She oughtn't to become like the others. She ought to remain apart."
>
> "Apart—*apart?*" said Miss Chancellor; "when we shall all be looking to her, gathering about her, praying for her!" There was an exceeding scorn in her voice. "If *I* can help her, she shall be an immense power for good." (p. 95)

Olive visibly swells at the prospect of involving herself in the young woman's career: "If I could take her to New York, I would take her farther," she remarks, hoping to be enigmatic. Mrs. Luna bluntly dispenses with her sister's coyness, however, and interjects prophetically, "You talk about 'taking' her, as if you were a lecture-agent. Are you getting into that business?" (p. 96). Olive cannot admit it to herself, but she is in the business already.

Ransom caustically dismisses the feminists' agitation as an "immense power for quackery," but he, too, finds Verena's "intensely personal exhibition . . . irresistibly appeal[ing]" (p. 61). Despite his obvious attraction to her, Ransom must retire humbly to New York, because he cannot offer her a comfortable marriage. The months roll by and Verena almost passes from his memory, until her image is unwittingly revived by the jealous Mrs. Luna, who scornfully mentions the girl's later (and equally impressive) appearance on the platform of a "Female Convention" in Boston (p. 202). In Mrs. Luna's eyes, Verena is "a perfect little adventuress, and quite third-rate into the bargain"; but the example of public acclamation that attends her inspirational lecture is, in fact, the immediate spur to Ransom's renewed drive for professional literary distinction. What becomes of his chauvinistic conservatism if *she* achieves a greatness beyond his grasp? One of Ransom's articles is eventually welcomed by the *Rational Review*—a journal that proves hospitable, one might suppose, to his powers of rationalization. In the face of Verena's continued success, which puts to shame his "sordid conditions," he splutters inwardly,

> Who wouldn't pay half a dollar for such an hour as he had passed at Mrs. Burrage's [the New York hostess who sponsors one of Verena's triumphant appearances]? The sort of thing she was able to do, to say, was an article for which there was more and more demand—fluent, pretty, third-rate palaver, conscious or unconscious perfected humbug; the stupid, gregarious, gullible public, the enlightened democracy of his native land, could swallow unlimited draughts of it. He was sure she could go, like that, for several years, with her portrait in the druggists' windows and her posters on the fences, and during that time would make a fortune sufficient to keep her in affluence for evermore. (pp. 319–20)[35]

Envy so completely overwhelms him that Ransom is capable of musing arrogantly, "if he should become [Verena's] husband he should know a way to strike her dumb" (p. 329). The implicit violence of Ransom's attitude ominously anticipates the menacing overtones of the novel's famous concluding line, which suggests that the tears streaming down Verena's face as she runs off with her lover are "not the last she [is] destined to shed" (p. 449).

The question of Verena's fate involves all the other characters in the novel—so much so that James first considered using her name as its title. Less imposing than *The Portrait of a Lady, Verena* would still have offered James an unusual opportunity to develop a theme of deep personal interest. "The private history of the public woman" struck the novelist as a challenging subject, one that would allow him to explore "the drama of her feelings, heart, soul, personal relations, and the shock, conflict, complication between those things and her publicity, her career, ambition, artistic life." Several months prior to starting *The Bostonians,* James wrote these words to Mrs. Humphrey Ward, whose novel about a heroine of the stage, *Miss Bretherton,* provoked his comment. As so often happened in his letters to Mrs. Ward, James immediately attempted to rewrite the novel she had just published: Mrs. Ward had failed, in James's view, to take the measure of the antagonism between Miss Bretherton's private and public aspects; the novel treated this conflict "too simply, refused perhaps even to face it."[36] Unfortunately, James himself was insufficiently tempted to face the challenging subject in *The Bostonians,* for Verena's private history remains something of a closed (and perhaps not even a particularly interesting) book.[37] The critical weakness of James's novel stems from this disproportion. Verena stands at the center of the action but does not reflect sufficiently upon it; all the other characters are defined by their relations to her, but by refusing to "go behind" and enter into Verena's consciousness, James sacrifices the remarkable psychological realism he had achieved in *The Portrait of a Lady.*

Almost by default, James diverts our attention to Olive Chancellor and Basil Ransom, who at least exhibit a certain aggressive interest. Paul John Eakin has recently observed that in their struggle for Verena, both Olive and Ransom conceive of courtship as "a drama of conversion," an avenue of salvation from unspeakable alternatives.[38] Olive has had premonitions of Ransom's latent "brutality" from which she tries earnestly to protect Verena, but the girl's youthful curiosity repeatedly defeats her companion's watchfulness. "'I don't think he's brutal; I should like to see,'' Verena remarks gaily (p. 296). Her tears come only at the end. Ransom's object, conversely, is to rescue Verena from the sterile clutches of his reform-minded cousin:

> The deepest feeling in Ransom's bosom in relation to [Verena] was the conviction that she was made for love. . . . She was profoundly unconscious of it, and another ideal, crude and thin and artificial, had interposed itself; but

> in the presence of a man she should really care for, this false, flimsy structure would rattle to her feet, and the emancipation of Olive Chancellor's sex (what sex was it, great heaven? he used profanely to ask himself) would be relegated to the land of vapours, of dead phrases. (p. 330)

His argument has a decided effect upon Verena, who is forced at last to confront her private self and see beyond the public role she has been playing; but Ransom's phrases, carefully calculated for effect and spoken in a "cool, mild, deliberate tone, as if he were demonstrating a mathematical solution," betray a certain deadness, too:

> "You stand apart [he tells her], you are unique, extraordinary; you constitute a category by yourself. In you the elements have been mixed in a manner so felicitous that I regard you as quite incorruptible. . . . [Y]ou ought to know that your connexion with all these rantings and ravings is the most unreal, accidental, illusory thing in the world. You think you care about them, but you don't at all. They were imposed upon you by circumstances, by unfortunate associations, and you accepted them as you would have accepted any other burden, on account of the sweetness of your nature. You always want to please some one, and now you go lecturing about the country, and trying to provoke demonstrations, in order to please Miss Chancellor, just as you did it before to please your father and mother. It isn't *you,* the least in the world, but an inflated little figure (very remarkable in its way too) whom you have invented and set on its feet, pulling strings, behind it, to make it move and speak, while you try to conceal and efface yourself there. Ah, Miss Tarrant, if it's a question of pleasing, how much you might please some one else by tipping your preposterous puppet over and standing forth in your freedom as well as in your loveliness!" (p. 336)

The "freedom" Ransom purportedly offers, however, would grind Verena in the very mill of the conventional. Women have "[n]o place in public," he snaps. "My plan is to keep you at home and have a better time with you than ever." "The civilization of the Turks, then, strikes you as the highest?" Verena wittily retorts; but mere repartee cannot shield her from the beguiling influence of Ransom's clever advances (pp. 334–35).

Despite James's dramatic juxtaposition of Olive and Ransom, which the novelist sustains and elaborates by shuttling Verena between them, it is important to recognize that they share certain qualities with each other and with their creator as well. David Howard reminds us that both characters are adamantly opposed to the advancing vulgarity of American life; both look back nostalgically to an age when the national culture was enriched by their respective ideals—New England's Transcendental dictum for plain living and high thinking and the chivalric code of honor enshrined by the antebellum South.[39] Few readers are likely to forget Ransom's famous declamation against the "nervous, hysterical, chattering, canting age" (p. 333), but they might overlook the fact that Miss Chancellor privately anticipates his harangue much earlier in the book:

> Olive had a standing quarrel with the levity, the good-nature, of the judgments of the day; many of them seemed to her weak to imbecility, losing sight of all measures and standards, lavishing superlatives, delighted to be fooled. The age seemed to her relaxed and demoralized, and . . . she looked to the influx of the great feminine element to make it feel and speak more sharply. (p. 125)

Olive's reflections are sparked by the presence of Matthias Pardon, the journalistic incarnation of everything that she and Ransom (and James) detest in the contemporary American scene.[40] "The whole generation is womanized; the masculine tone is passing out of the world," Ransom declares, unmistakably thinking of Pardon, whose "small, fair features . . . and pretty eyes" are obviously feminine and whose speech abounds in exclamations—" 'Goodness gracious!' and 'Mercy on us!'—not much in use among the sex whose profanity is apt to be coarse" (pp. 333, 122). Despite his effeminate manner, Pardon is Selah Tarrant's choice for Verena's hand in marriage. To Mr. Tarrant, whose nature (like Pardon's) is "pitched . . . altogether in the key of public life," the alliance seems perfectly natural. With his assured access to the widest channels of publicity, Pardon strikes Verena's father as the ideal mate for a young woman whose talent needs simply to be "worked." Indeed, the journalist is only the first of several suitors from whom Olive must deflect the girl's—or, in this case, her father's—attention. Every aspect of Verena's upbringing has prepared her for such a match. From her earliest breath she has taken in the bracing air of publicity. As Ransom immediately perceives, Verena's curious innocence carries with it "an air of being on exhibition, of [her] belonging to a troupe, of living in the gaslight" (p. 58). Olive Chancellor also recognizes the necessity of detaching Verena from an atmosphere of vulgarity she has been excessively bred to; a handsome cheque delivered into Selah Tarrant's long, slender fingers neatly does the trick. But while the two major contenders for the girl's affection seek to rescue Verena from the world of publicity, the crowning (and, ultimately, the most revealing) irony about this book is that both Ransom and Olive seek a place in that world and in the end both make compromises with it.

Witnessing the first meeting of her sister and Miss Tarrant, Mrs. Luna mockingly wonders if Olive Chancellor plans to become Verena's "lecture-agent." This unintentional prophecy is swiftly fulfilled as Olive moves to protect her interest in the girl. Discreetly generous sums of money easily reconcile Verena's parents to her transfer to Olive's household. After she is removed from her father's tutelage, Verena's path to publicity is less direct, but no less sure:

> They had no desire to be notorious [Olive muses in the plural]; they only wanted to be useful. They had no wish to make money; there would always

> be plenty of money for Miss Tarrant. Certainly, she should come before the public, and the world would acclaim her and hang upon her words; but crude, precipitate action was what both of them least desired. . . . "What we mean to do, we mean to do well," Miss Chancellor said. (p. 143)

Olive's lofty scruples prove no more successful in shielding Verena from vulgarity, however, than her watchfulness can protect the girl from Ransom's advances. As Mrs. Luna caustically remarks at one of Verena's engagements in New York, Olive "is dressed like a book-agent . . . [and] Verena, beside her, looks like a walking advertisement" (p. 259). Olive's transformation is effectively completed when she pockets the cheque for Verena's performance, "the largest . . . this young woman had ever received for an address." "To the taking of money," James notes, Olive is "now completely inured" (pp. 303–4). Her powers of rationalization, like Ransom's, are considerable.

Once again, Mrs. Luna's observations merit study, for if Olive Chancellor resembles a "book-agent," her attachment to Verena is also analogous to the contemporary relationship between publishers and authors. Just as nineteenth-century publishers asserted the claims of trade courtesy to keep productive writers under their respective imprints, Olive intends to monopolize Verena's talent by restricting competition for her affection. Indeed, one primary contender for the girl's hand addresses Olive with the same euphemistic gentility that publishers regularly invoked when speaking of their relations with authors:

> "I daresay you don't like the idea of [Verena's] marrying at all; it would break up a friendship which is so full of interest" (Olive wondered for a moment whether she had been going to say "so full of profit") "for you." (p. 304)

Olive eventually disposes of this threat from "the house of Burrage" (another publishing catch-phrase), but competition for Verena merely intensifies after the girl is brought before the public (p. 305). Ironically, Basil Ransom's suit becomes serious only after *he* breaks into print. Publication offers him more than a new career; it also gives him a new and highly effective vocabulary with which to court Verena's affection. "[T]o be published," he confesses, "makes an era in my life":

> "This will seem pitiful to you, no doubt, who publish yourself, have been before the world these several years, and, are flushed with every kind of triumph; but to me it's simply a tremendous affair. It makes me believe I may do something; it has changed the whole way I look at my future. I have been building castles in the air, and I have put you in the biggest and fairest of them." (p. 368)

Ransom's discovery of a new vocation forces Verena to reconsider hers, and privately she renounces "the old exaggerated glamour of the lecture-lamps" (p. 348). Sensing an ominous change in her companion, Olive pitches Verena immediately into rehearsal for an engagement at the Boston Music Hall. James remarks that there is nothing amateur or "superficial" about Miss Chancellor's "standard of preparation." She desperately recognizes (as does Ransom) that her only way to keep Verena is to give the girl a "fresh start which [will] commit her irretrievably . . . to the acclamations of the newspapers" (pp. 392–93).

How far Olive has strayed from the purity of her original intentions can be measured by the fact that to promote Verena's lecture she employs the techniques of modern publicity with a facility that Matthias Pardon might envy. "Photographs of Miss Tarrant—sketch of her life!" "Portraits of the Speaker—story of her career!" itinerant newsboys cry out (p. 429). The papers clamour for the most vulgar details about Verena's life. "What is she going to have for dinner?" Pardon inquires on the evening of her performance (p. 423). Ransom quickly sees that Verena herself has nothing to do with "this exhibition of enterprise and puffery"; it is all Miss Chancellor's doing. Significantly, however, he recognizes (if only for a moment) a kind of perverse heroism in his cousin's compromises with the marketplace: "what he saw was Olive, struggling and yielding, making every sacrifice of taste for the sake of the largest hearing, and conforming herself to a great popular system" (p. 430). Ransom can appreciate Olive's "struggle" because he, too, has sacrificed some portion of his artistocratic taste for the sake of obtaining an audience for his views.

Both Olive and Ransom are creatures—as well as critics—of the society that has produced them; and in the novel's shrewdly suspended climax at the Music Hall, James violently exposes their tacit accommodation to the cheapened values of the age. All the characters gather here for the momentous launching of Verena's professional career; her earlier appearances, by comparison, are merely a form of preparation for this public affirmation of her calling. The deliberate parallel to the oldest of New England's civic rituals—the public conversion of a visible saint—merely underscores the Bostonians' declension from the ideals of a bygone era. The spartan meetinghouse has given way to a garishly ornamented auditorium, which reminds Ransom of "the *vomitoria* . . . of the Colosseum" (p. 429). Not coincidentally, Miss Birdseye, the lone descendant from New England's golden day, quietly passes away during the pastoral interlude at Cape Cod that acts as a tranquil counterpoint to the cacaphonous uproar of the novel's conclusion. The death of "this frumpy little missionary," James openly tells us, effectively closes "the heroic age of New England life—the age of plain living and high thinking, of pure ideals and earnest effort, of moral passion and noble experiment" (p. 179). In another reference to that Transcendental era, James once said of Emerson that "life had never bribed him to look at anything but the soul; and indeed in the world in which he grew up and lived the bribes and lures, the beguilements and prizes, were few."[41] In the fallen world of *The*

Bostonians, however, the "bribes and lures" are many and their beguiling influence is irresistible.

In arranging his characters for the novel's final scene, James reverts to a familiar blueprint. In *The Portrait of a Lady* an unused "office" shelters Isabel Archer from the vulgar street beyond; a similar room adjoining the stage of the Music Hall performs the same function for Verena as she waits for Basil Ransom to rescue her from the "roaring crowd" that has gathered under its roof (p. 441). When the featured performer fails to appear on the platform, symptoms of suspicious irritation—"cries and groans and hisses"—proceed from the hall (p. 443). Although Olive has taken every precaution to prevent Ransom from interfering—shielding Verena behind padlocks and policemen—the terrified girl throws open the chamber's bolted door to admit her lover and effect a clandestine retreat.

Before the pair can escape, however, Ransom and Olive are again face to face. "Let her appear this once," Olive pleads, "just this once: not to ruin, not to shame! Haven't you any pity; do you want me to be hooted!" Olive's abrupt shift of emphasis to herself betrays the awful depth of her despair. "I'll do anything," she cries, "I'll be abject—I'll be vile—I'll go down in the dust!" Given her present circumstances, Olive's use of the future tense is absurd. She is abject; she has been vile (vile enough, at any rate, to keep Verena under lock and key); humiliation is moments away. Ransom's behavior, on the other hand, is hardly more commendable. To Olive's helpless request that Verena speak for just an hour, he selfishly replies, "Why for an hour, when it's all false and damnable? An hour is as bad as ten years! She's mine or she isn't, and if she's mine, she's all mine!" Condemned to face the angry mob alone, Olive tragically declares, "I'm going to be hissed and hooted and insulted!" When Verena instinctively responds to Miss Chancellor's ultimate appeal, Ransom's verbal arrogance translates into "muscular force." "[P]alpitating with his victory," he pushes Verena out the door and, to conceal her identity, buries her face in a long cloak, a gesture that suggests how forcefully he will suppress her individuality after they are married. "Ah, now I am glad!" Verena absently utters when they reach the street; but, privately, "beneath her hood," she sheds her famously pessimistic tears (pp. 442–43, 448–49).

The lurid prospect of Olive's exposure before "the thousands she had disappointed and deceived" may at least afford her the consolation of a martyr's finish. It is not apparent, however, that they are likely "to hurl the benches at her"; "even when exasperated," James cleverly remarks, "a Boston audience is not ungenerous" (pp. 448–49). Coming on the last page of the book, this observation probably expressed the novelist's private hope for a kindly reception of his own performance. Certainly, James knew that he had exasperated his American audience as the serial appeared. "Our teapot was stirred to its depths by the Birdseye sacrilege," William Dean Howells told Edmund Gosse, referring to the widely discussed charge that James had modeled his frumpy Boston reformer after Elizabeth Palmer Peabody, the venerable bluestocking whose spectacles *were* always in the wrong place.[42] Probably because of its prominence in letters between Henry and his brother William, the rumpus about Miss Peabody has long been credited for the failure of the book with the public at large.[43] This simple explanation cannot possibly be sustained, however, by any complete reading of the novel, which finally treats Miss Birdseye with remarkable tenderness. As James told his brother, "though subordinate, she is, I think, the best figure in the book, she is treated with respect throughout, and every virtue of heroism and disinterestedness is attributed to her. She is represented as the embodiment of pure, the purest philanthropy."[44] Another cause for the book's unprosperous career seems more likely.

Inflated disproportionately by the Boston press, the "idiotic & baseless" uproar about "this serial's containing 'personalities'" only confirmed James's disparaging opinion of literary gossip-mongers (like Matthias Pardon) who paraded their vulgar "material" as serious criticism.[45] As we have seen, James reserved his harshest language in the book for Pardon and the whole apparatus of publicity that he represents. Unfortunately for James, a veritable horde of Matthias Pardons would have an opportunity to avenge themselves when *The Bostonians* appeared in volume form. By every measure, they did. As George E. Brett, the Macmillan Company's New York agent, reported,

> Mr. James' story has met with the poorest measure of success. I must say that I never knew of a book being more thoroughly condemned. This abuse would not matter so much if people only read the book for themselves but the damning notices seem to have removed all the desire.

Even though the novel "started off fairly well"—with "some persistent pushing," 2000 copies of *The Bostonians* had been ordered in advance of publication—sales rapidly tapered off after the book (and its reviews) appeared. "The trouble we have had to contend with in the case of 'The Bostonians,'" Brett later confided to Macmillan,

> has been the hostility engendered towards it in the minds of certain Bostonians who are supposed to be—I know not how truly—satirised in its pages. They are a noisy and to a degree a powerful bastion and they raised an outcry against the story in its progress through the 'Century' and the curious part of it is that they induced the newspaper reviewers against Mr. James and the consequence is that no unprejudiced review of the book is now possible.[46]

Brett's repeated emphasis on the hostile attitude of the reviewers was not simply the stock response of a disappointed publisher. Such universal enmity would not have been so widely incurred had *The Bostonians'* satire been directed merely at an aging liberal dowager or a group of long-winded feminists. The sharpest arrows in the novelist's quiver were aimed elsewhere.

By writing *The Bostonians* James had hoped to redeem his pledge to do "something great."[47] The short novel he first envisioned more than doubled in size before it was ended; the book's frequently undisciplined expression eluded the artist's control. What James recorded in this magnificent but troubled narrative was the inadvertent epic of his own disaffection from the literary marketplace. To satisfy his critics he returned to an American subject involving a host of conventional character types[48] and reverted to the intrusive mannerisms of Victorian prose. But signs of stress are everywhere apparent. As Donald D. Stone had observed, by fixing his characters in place in advance, James not only sets up an uncomfortably "ironic distance" from them, but "he also barely conceals his dislike of a reading public which has forced him into this stylistic straitjacket."[49] The novelist's performance here oddly anticipates his career as a playwright, when every compromise he made with the vulgarity of his audience inexorably betrayed itself upon the stage. Almost all the characters in this novel make similar concessions, and James cannot bring himself to care for any of them deeply. In casting the fate of Olive Chancellor, he wrote the strangest prophecy of all—a curse upon himself ("to be hissed and hooted and insulted!") for succumbing to the very "bribes and lures" that prove so fatally attractive to his fictional Bostonians.

VI

Between the Worlds of Beauty and Necessity: Hyacinth Robinson's Problem of Vocation

Perhaps because Henry James conceived and began to write his next novel in tandem with the over-long *Bostonians*, it is not surprising that *The Princess Casamassima* shares many of its predecessor's concerns. The two fictions have often been linked in critical accounts of James's career, in part because they were published back to back in 1886, but also because of their explicitly sociological interest. Then, too, both books were conspicuous failures in the marketplace; they brought James, apparently, to a turning point in his career. A famous letter of 1888 (in which James remarked that *The Bostonians* and *The Princess* had "reduced the desire, and the demand, for [his] productions to zero")[1] is often cited as proof of this; but, in fact, James's keen sense of the market had warned him of danger as soon as the serial run of *The Princess* was completed. "I have lately published 2 long-winded serials," he told Howells in October 1886,

> lasting between them far more than 2 years—of which, in all that time no audible echo or reverberation of any kind, either in America or here, has come back to me. If I had not my bread and butter to earn I should lay down my pen tomorrow—hard as it is, at my age, to confess one's self a rather offensive fiasco.[2]

Because James had entertained such high hopes for his work, his confession was even more galling. With the prospect of expanding the market for his short stories to include the enormous readership of the New York Sunday *Sun,* James proudly informed the editor of the *Atlantic* "that by July 18[8]5 I expect to be in the enjoyment of a popularity that will require me to ask $500 a number for the successive instalments of *The Princess Casamassima.*"[3] James later retracted this demand "as an off-hand and indigested proposal," but he insisted that the magazine should pay at least the same rate ($15 per page) as for his other recent things. "This, kept up for a year, may not suit you," James admitted to the editor, but he refused to compromise further: "I ought to say that it is, this time, my deliberate and digested estimate of the *The Princess.* If it does not meet the idea of the publishers, we will hang her up on her peg again." The *Princess* came off her peg and James received $350 a number.[4]

James had promised to begin his serial in the July 1885 *Atlantic,* but the inexorable growth of *The Bostonians* forced him to postpone his new work. "Two months more will give me plenty of margin," he told Aldrich, "& when the 'Princess Casamassima' *does* begin it will be so magnificent that you will be delighted (so to speak) to have waited for it."[5] Once again, an accidental delay was pivotal in the imaginative shaping of James's work. Even though the early chapters of *The Princess* were drafted far in advance of his deadline (the novelist visited Millbank Prison in December 1884 to collect notes that would become the serial's first installment), his progress on the book was decisively interrupted in the spring of the following year by the collapse of James R. Osgood & Company, his American publisher.

James could hardly have suspected that Osgood was sliding toward insolvency when the publisher failed to remit a semiannual royalty cheque in January 1885. Osgood's accounting was often slipshod or delinquent; even the gentle poet Whittier occasionally dunned him.[6] This time, however, James's letters failed to elicit even an apologetic response. "I have as yet received no tidings whatever of the semi-annual account & cheque which I asked for several weeks ago," he wrote at the end of February, "but hope they are now on their way."[7] By April his patience was exhausted:

> I wrote some three months ago (my letter was to Mr. [Benjamin] Ticknor) to ask him that some half-yearly statement of account and cheque be sent me. But save a casual mention in a subsequent letter of his that he had spoken of the matter to you, I have not, though in a second letter I re-iterated my request, had to this moment any satisfaction on this point. The delay (though I don't know why it shouldn't have been explained meanwhile) has seemed to me to be perhaps owing to the fact that you were getting the *yearly* account ready, and that as so much of the year had elapsed (it has now elapsed completely), you did not think it worth while to anticipate it with a partial statement, by only a few weeks. It was on the 15th of this month, a year ago, that I last received a remittance, under this head, from you. In heaven's name, then, please send me the yearly statement, without further postponement. I have been much inconvenienced by this delay, and should have been glad if some notice—even merely explanatory—had been taken of my two requests.

Significantly, James also informed Osgood that all but the last two installments of *The Bostonians* had been sent to the *Century*. With the entire manuscript virtually delivered, he hoped now to be paid for his novel as well:

> I shall not ask you for the complete sum we agreed upon as the price of the work till the last sheet is in [editor Richard Watson] Gilder's hands; and I shall be greatly obliged to you if you send me at present the first *half* of it—i.e. $2000. I shall notify you a very short time hence of the despatch of the concluding pages (as I shall ask Gilder to do of its arrival); but meanwhile I am in pressing need of money. Please, therefore, at the earliest possible moment after the receipt of this, send me the sum above-mentioned. You will not, I trust, think this an unreasonable request. You will probably have already perceived that the *Bostonians,* like most of my things, transcends considerably the length to which I had originally intended to confine it. I consider that a wondrous bargain![8]

The "wondrous bargain" became even more wonderful two weeks later, when James discovered (in the columns of the *Times*) that Osgood had filed for bankruptcy. When the publisher failed to answer his letters, James had begun "to entertain suspicions that his solvency was not perfect"; now he knew that Osgood would never settle his obligations. Almost as Olive Chancellor and Basil Ransom do battle in the final pages of *The Bostonians,* James and his publisher soon wrangled about the novelist's rights in his book. James's dilemma was acute: how could he protect his interests without behaving like a "grasping businessman?" He immediately wrote to Frederick Macmillan for advice. Characteristically, James began his letter by confessing that the news of Osgood's bankruptcy left him "at sea in regard to one or two important facts," and it occurred to him that Macmillan, "having many lights on such matters (I have none)" might be able to answer a few of his questions. The remainder of James's query, however, effectively controverts his helpless attitude. All of the novelist's instincts about the affair, expressed in tentative questions ("Wouldn't the book become mine, as a book, to do what I please with, on the failure of J. R. O. & Co. to pay me $4000 on receipt of the whole [manuscript]?"), were later confirmed by Macmillan's solicitor. What James needed was assurance, not a "light," to guide him in the marketplace.[9]

Macmillan offered him both light and assurance as he outlined various scenarios of possible action. If James sent Osgood the last installment of *The Bostonians* without payment, he would instantly become a creditor in the bankruptcy proceedings and thus would probably receive only ten to fifteen cents on the dollar of the amount he was owed. If the novelist withheld the installment on condition of payment (Osgood, of course, being unable to deliver the full purchase price), his contract with the publisher would be void and rights to the book would revert to James. Disposing of the volume rights would not be a problem; indeed, Macmillan offered to publish *The Bostonians* in America and to pay James whatever royalty he usually received from Osgood. Finally, with regard to the older books on Osgood's list, James became a creditor for whatever amount was due him in royalties; the stereotype plates of the volumes would probably be transferred to some other publisher to whom Osgood owed money. Even though James had anticipated much that Macmillan told him, hearing his counsel echoed by one of the trade's leading representatives must have shored up his confidence.[10]

The novelist was emboldened, at any rate, immediately to offer Macmillan the entire copyright to *The Bostonians.* James knew that such a move was drastic, but his acute want of money seemed to justify it. Macmillan recognized the seriousness of James's situation and offered him a royalty of 15 percent of the retail price on both English and American sales, together with an advance of £500 (slightly less than $2500). Still, the novelist wanted more. The original sale to Osgood would have brought him more than £800, the sum for which James doggedly held out, even if he had to part with the copyright to get it. Macmillan's proposal, however, was firm: the company could not offer James a large enough sum to make it worth his while to part with the copyright entirely, nor did Macmillan advise the novelist in his own interest to sell it. "It may be," the publisher noted, "that the 'Century' people will be induced to pay enough for the serial use of the MS. not yet delivered to go some way towards making up the loss you suffer through Osgood's defection." In any event, if James were truly short of funds, the firm would gladly advance him money, particularly if his other Osgood titles (*Daisy Miller: A Comedy, The Siege of London, Portraits of Places, A Little Tour in France, Tales of Three Cities,* and *The Author of Beltraffio*) were given to Macmillan for American distribution.[11]

Before James decided which course to follow, he cautiously waited to hear more news from America. He had asked his brother William to consult with the family's attorney, Joseph Bangs Warner, and to report back on the options available to him. "It's a godsend," William relayed,

> you've still got your own end of the story to hang on to—as that practically puts the game into your own hands. Your alternative seems to be, (1) to get Osgood to cancel the agreement, in which case you lose apparently all proceeds from him & gain only such as you may extort from the Century for the end of the novel, leaving them to sue him for damages, and owning your own copyright; or (2) to extort, etc, from them *without* cancelling, and still get your fifty cents on the dollar or whatever Osgood pays if he is put through bankruptcy. In either case you ought not to lose. I should think the latter course would be the more dignified on the whole. I doubt whether Osgood will be willing to cancel. He said he hoped the creditors would allow them to continue business, but I imagine they will not. . . . Osgood said yours was the

> hardest case of all, and seemed to feel pretty badly about it. Your various copyright contracts revert to you if arrears are not paid in full, and Osgood cannot sell his rights in them to anyone who does not pay you all arrears. . . . Altogether you will probably lose little, if anything, and will be only inconvenienced by delay. How great the inconvenience may be I don't know. Osgood said that if they were allowed to go on, payments would begin in a couple of months.[12]

Warner's opinion merely repeated what the novelist already knew. His brother's optimistic advice James instantly repudiated. "I shall never have a penny of the money from [Osgood]," he told Howells. "Fortunately I shall recover the book—but the *Century,* I fear, will have enjoyed my calumnious prose for nothing (as far as I am concerned)."[13]

James privately resolved that no one else should enjoy his calumnious prose for so little. Even though Macmillan was pressing him for a response to his proposal, James kept the publisher at bay until more news arrived from America. Benjamin Ticknor, one of Osgood's associates, apparently intended to reorganize the firm, and he was eager to keep James on his list of authors. "I have heard from my lawyer in Boston & from the *Century* about the Bostonians," James told Macmillan in early June, "but inconclusively. That is, Osgood's assignees [Ticknor & Co.] appear inclined to maintain his offer & take the book, giving the money down, *if I insist.* But I don't insist & have telegraphed on the subject. I expect an answer tonight, & if the agreement *is* cancelled shall probably accept your offer."[14] Ticknor's continued reluctance to surrender the book—the expected cancellation was not forthcoming—prodded James to rethink his strategy. Very much like its heroine, Verena Tarrant, *The Bostonians* was becoming the focus of peculiar competition.

In the wake of Osgood's collapse, Frederick Macmillan had directed his New York agent, George E. Brett, to keep an eye on the papers and an ear to the ground for news concerning James's Osgood titles. On 2 June, Brett reported that no decision had been reached about Osgood's affairs, although it was rumored that Benjamin Ticknor would take over the business with outside help. "As regards Mr. James's books," Brett continued,

> an expert here tells me that the most popular novelists here now—quoting them in the order of their popularity—are
>
> [E. P.] Roe
> [F. Marion] Crawford
> Howells
> James
>
> Mr. James coming fourth on a list of seven or eight names which I gave. James would be a first class name to add to our list—much superior in my estimation to Mr. Crawford's, and I should strongly advocate the purchase [of Osgood's stereotype plates] if it can be made at not too high a figure. But

> we should have to move in the matter with a great deal of circumspection for if our hand was seen in the matter every effort would be made to keep the books out of our hands or else to pay dearly for them. Perhaps Mr. James himself could be made the medium of purchase.[15]

Brett's shrewd (and unusually candid) advice openly acknowledged the hostility that the Macmillan Company felt from established publishing houses in the United States. Competition, especially from foreigners (whose labor costs were much lower), was anathema to the American trade. If Macmillan wanted James's books, he would have to move surreptitiously to get them.[16]

On the other hand, Benjamin Ticknor wanted to keep James, especially since a portion of the old contract (covering *Tales of Three Cities*) had been satisfactorily fulfilled. On 6 June, William James cabled his brother that Osgood's successors were unwilling to break the original contract.[17] Sensing his new advantage, the novelist pressed Ticknor for better terms. If he paid the $4000 down, Ticknor could still have *The Bostonians,* but James insisted on one important alteration in the old arrangement. For the English market James wanted freedom to negotiate a separate contract (presumably with Macmillan). His reasons were simple:

> My original contract with your former firm was so insanely unprofitable for me that I must claim this relief now that that firm is broken up. If it had lasted I should have swallowed my mistake in silence, though greatly repenting of it: but I must rectify it in some small degree, in these altered conditions. The changes I ask for still leave you the book on tremendously low terms. The *Atlantic* gives me $4200 for the *simple serial* use of the novel I begin there in September; & for the $4000 now in suspension between us you will have had the serial use of the *Bostonians* & the American sales, which I am sure will be larger than those of any other book of mine, for the long period I mention (5 years) into the bargain. I trust you will see the justice of the alterations I desire; in which case I shall, as I say, be very glad to leave you the book.[18]

James's confidence in the American demand for his novel was somewhat misplaced, but his new stipulation regarding the English copyright gave Ticknor pause. After all, James had signed a contract ceding all foreign rights; if Ticknor could come up with $4000 the English market was legally his. To verify his claim, Ticknor directed a query to the Macmillan Company, with whom Osgood had conducted preliminary negotiations about the English rights to *The Bostonians* in 1883. The English publisher affirmed that serial publication of the novel in Great Britain prior to its appearance in volume form would be enough to secure the English copyright for *The Bostonians.* Since *The Century* did come out simultaneously in England, the English rights to James's work remained with his publisher.[19] Perhaps James was pushing his advantage too far?

The novelist, at any rate, didn't think so. Earlier in the year, when finances were tight, Henry had borrowed $1000 from his brother, which he intended to repay when the deal with Ticknor was completed. "My transaction with Osgood's successor has dragged out long," he told William on 24 July, "partly through a delay, at the last, of my own; but before you get this he will to all appearance have paid over $4000 to Warner for me." A week later his confidence was still unshaken: "I have already written to [Warner] to pay you back the $1000 you advanced me, out [of] the $4000 he will (I trust by this time) be receiving for me."[20] Within a few days, however, Warner cabled that the deal was off; Ticknor refused to renegotiate the contract and was cancelling the agreement to publish *The Bostonians.*

After months of haggling, the novel was at last in James's hands. But not for long: on 5 August, Frederick Macmillan deposited £500 in the novelist's bank account as an advance on future royalties from the book. The sum indeed was handy, but James understandably was disappointed. "This year has been disastrous," he honestly lamented:

> Ticknor's cancellation has come, unfortunately too late to be of the same service to me that it would 3 months ago—though I am still glad of it, as it restores me the copyright of the book. The merit of his cancelling 3 months ago was that it would have enabled me instantly to get a sum of money from Macmillan, of which I was much in need, instead of waiting—an indefinite time—for his, Ticknor's, $4000. Not to get the $4000 after I *have* waited so many weeks is a little provoking, for of course the money Macmillan has given me for the book alone is *not* $4000—the sum Osgood was to give me for serial *and* the book. It is however considerable enough to be very welcome, & I shall have 15 percent on future sales in the 2 countries, instead of having nothing at all in either, from that source, as from Ticknor.[21]

Unfortunately, the novelist's professional consolation remained largely theoretical. The book's contract was more rewarding to him than its sales; returns on *The Bostonians* never exceeded Macmillan's advance.[22] Admittedly discouraged by its poor showing, James depended upon his next novel to restore his standing in the marketplace. "The *Princess* will, I trust, appear more 'popular,'" he told William:

> I fear the *Bostonians* will be, as a finished work, a fiasco, as not a word, echo or comment on the serial (save your remarks) have come to me (since the row about [Miss Birdseye in] the first two numbers) from any quarter whatever. This deathly silence seems to indicate that it has fallen flat. I hoped much of it, and shall be disappointed—having got no money for it I hoped for a little glory.[23]

Critics of *The Princess Casamassima* frequently have attempted to confirm the political intelligence of the novel by examining the historical and sociological validity of James's excursion "beneath the vast smug surface" of London society.[24] Well versed in the history of European radicalism, Lionel Trilling once claimed that "there is not a political event of *The Princess Casamassima,* not a detail of oath or mystery or danger, which is not confirmed by multitudinous records." W. H. Tilley has diligently combed the files of the London *Times* to show why James's audience would have found his subject credible. More recently, Marcia Jacobson has asserted that the appearance of *The Princess* in the James canon is to be explained by James's desire to write a topical novel, the study of working-class life having become a popular genre in the eighties in England.[25]

Whatever their merits, none of these approaches to the novel adequately measures the impact that Osgood's collapse had on the evolution of *The Princess.* James himself could not divorce the two; as he worked on the novel, the demands of the market threatened to overwhelm the imperatives of art. Weeks of financial uncertainty turned into months. The novelist's self-confidence was mocked by developments (such as Ticknor's last minute cancellation of the agreement to publish *The Bostonians*) that eluded his control. On 10 August 1885 James confided to his journal:

> It is absolutely necessary that at this point I should make the future evolution of the *Princess Casamassima* more clear to myself. I have never yet become engaged in a novel in which, after I had begun to write and send off my MS., the details had remained so vague. This is partly—or indeed wholly—owing to the fact that I have been so terribly preoccupied—up to so lately—with the unhappy *Bostonians,* born under an evil star.

The novelist admitted that he had "plunged in rather blindly, and got a good many characters on [his] hands"; but these would "fall into their places" if he could "keep cool and think it out. Oh art, art, what difficulties are like thine," James wondered; "but, at the same time, what consolations and encouragements, also, are like thine?"[26]

Perhaps at no other time in his career were the sacred and profane aspects of the artist's life so vividly juxtaposed. He had begun a novel about the London poor; suddenly, his own financial security was seriously threatened.[27] He had planned to spend the summer on the continent; now he had to content himself with the fictional travels of Hyacinth Robinson.[28] Indeed, in the history of his little London bookbinder, James embodied many of the paradoxical elements of his own professional life. As Leon Edel has suggested, the novelist's identification with his protagonist seems to have been considerable. James came from a privileged if not an aristocratic family, but, like Hyacinth, he had also to labor for his bread. He could count members of the nobility among his friends, and his social connections among the English upper middle class were legendary. Yet unlike most of his acquaintances, whose social status derived from inherited wealth, James derived an income through steady employment of his pen. For six hours every day he was pledged to the task of writing, and this professional discipline was never more critical than during the months when serial installments of *The Bostonians* and *The Princess* were running back to back.[29]

In keeping with James's express desire to infuse the English novel with the clinical methods of continental literary naturalism, Hyacinth's divided nature is apparently determined by his mixed birth. The bastard son of an English lord and a French shop-girl, Hyacinth is torn by conflicting social loyalties. As James suggestively remarks, when Hyacinth is not "letting his imagination wander among the haunts of the aristocracy, and fancying himself stretched in the shadow of an ancestral beech, reading the last number of the *Revue des Deux Mondes,*" he is "occupied with contemplations of very different order":

> he was absorbed in the struggles and sufferings of the millions whose life flowed in the same current as his, and who, though they constantly excited his disgust, and made him shrink and turn away, had the power to chain his sympathy, to make it glow to a kind of ecstasy, to convince him, for the time at least, that real success in the world would be to do something with them and for them.[30]

Despite the novel's naturalistic overtones, Hyacinth's divided consciousness derives less from an accident of biology than from the conflicting ambitions of his maker. "There were times when he said to himself that it might very well be his fate to be divided, to the point of torture, to be split open by sympathies that pulled him in different ways": James easily might have been describing his own ambiguous status in the marketplace instead of his protagonist's unfortunate destiny (p. 126). Indeed, many careful readers have come to view the book (in Clinton Oliver's words) as "an elaborate experiment in autobiography," in which James projects himself into the personality of his protagonist.[31]

Hyacinth is a binder of books who privately yearns to write them; like James, he dreams of achieving "literary distinction" (p. 67). At the same time, Hyacinth senses that "real success in the world" involves "do[ing] something with [the people] and for them." James himself recognized the horns of this dilemma in his argumentative exposition of "The Art of Fiction" in 1884. Describing the differences between James's and Walter Besant's views on the subject, John Goode has correctly pointed out that Besant placed the audience at the center of his aesthetic by emphasizing what the novel could do for the reader, what it could give him, teach him, preach to him. The novel, wrote Besant,

> converts abstract ideas into living models; it gives ideas, it strengthens faith, it preaches a higher morality than is seen in the actual world; . . . it is the universal teacher; it is the only book which the great mass of mankind ever

> do read; it is the only way in which people can learn what other men and women are like; it redeems their lives from dulness, puts thoughts, desires, knowledge and even ambitions into their hearts: it teaches them to talk and enriches their speech with epigrams, anecdotes, and illustrations. It is an unfailing delight to millions, happily not too critical.

On Besant's terms the novel can hardly be differentiated from the sermon in its purpose. What distinguishes it is a style of presentation calculated to amuse rather than to forewarn. At least by implication, then, James's famous rejoinder to Besant rejected the centrality of the reader in defining the novelist's aims. Like Besant, James was concerned with the relation between fiction and its readers, but (as Goode properly observes) he was "less concerned with the effect of the novel on the public than with the effect of the public on the novel."[32]

As long as James was dependent on the market for his livelihood, however, he could not entirely repudiate the demands of popular taste. "[T]he most improved criticism," he wisely noted, would never abolish the "primitive"—yet "ultimate"—test of "'liking' a work of art or not liking it."[33] James longed to find a public that could accept his art on its own demanding terms—thereby to win "the praises of the London press," "the caresses of the British aristocracy," and "the literary suffrages of the American people"[34]—but he early learned that "literary distinction" and popular acclaim did not always go hand in hand. James was not alone in recognizing the division between the serious novel and the best-seller, which became so acute in the decade of the eighties. Like George Moore, Thomas Hardy, and George Gissing, whose careers were also seriously affected by the same bifurcation of sensibility, James felt that the position of the artist in the modern marketplace was radically different from that of his Victorian predecessors.

Another measure of James's radical difference is indicated simply by his choice of subject in *The Princess Casamassima.* Besant had warned writers from the lower middle class against introducing their characters into "society"; but by making Hyacinth Robinson a youth from the slums "on whom nothing [is] lost" (p. 124), James refutes his theoretical antagonist with the very language of "The Art of Fiction." In fact, important sections of James's novel read almost like paraphrases of the earlier essay. Far more important to the artist "than any accident of residence or place in the social scale," James wrote in 1884, was the

> power to guess the unseen from the seen, to trace the implication of things, to judge the whole piece by the pattern, the condition of feeling life in general so completely that you are well on your way to knowing any particular corner of it—this cluster of gifts may almost be said to constitute experience, and they occur in country and in town, and in the most differing stages of education.

His word is made flesh in Hyacinth Robinson:

> For this unfortunate but remarkably organized youth, every displeasure or gratification of the visual sense coloured his whole mind, and though he lived in Pentonville and worked in Soho, though he was poor and obscure and cramped and full of unattainable desires, it may be said of him that what was most important in life for him was simply his impressions. They came from everything he touched, they kept him thrilling and throbbing during a considerable part of his waking consciousness, and they constituted, as yet, the principal events and stages of his career. (p. 117)

"If experience consists of impressions," James concluded in "The Art of Fiction," "it may be said that impressions *are* experience, just as (have we not seen it?) they are the very air we breathe."[35] The rich verbal texture of *The Princess Casamassima* derives from this remark.

As we have seen, the ramifications of James's quarrel with Besant extended beyond matters of technique to the writer's conception of his vocation. Was the novel to be considered a form of art, or merely an article of commerce? Was authorship a profession or a trade? "The Art of Fiction" dealt with these issues largely by implication, but *The Princess Casamassima* has at its center a kind of vocational debate. Hyacinth's surrogate parents, Amanda Pynsent and Anastasius Vetch, apprentice him to a bookbinder as a means of reconciling the claims of his two social affinities and of rescuing him from the vulgarity of "retail business" (p. 73).[36] But Millicent Henning, Hyacinth's childhood friend, simply sneers at this choice:

> "A bookbinder? Laws! . . . Do you mean they get them up for the shops? Well, I always thought he would have something to do with books. . . . But I didn't think he would ever follow a trade."
>
> "A trade?" cried Miss Pynsent. "You should hear Mr. Robinson speak of it. He considers it one of the fine arts." (p. 50)

Indeed he does. As a "disciple" of Eustace Poupin, a Parisian master exiled in London because of his radical politics, Hyacinth has been converted to "the religion of conscientious craftsmanship" (pp. 76, 81). The stubbornly Philistine Miss Henning may condescend to him as a journeyman who earns his bread with his hands, but Hyacinth is abundantly aware of the limits of her taste. When she asks to see some examples of his work, he bluntly rejoinds, "You wouldn't know how good they are" (p. 66).[37]

In an age of encroaching vulgarity and machine technology, Hyacinth rightfully anticipates that, in the not too distant future, his bindings "would be passed from hand to hand as specimens of rare work, while connoisseurs bent their heads over them, smiling and murmuring, handling them delicately" (p. 465). The novelist might have been predicting the posthumous recovery of his own reputation as a craftsman of words;

but this indulgent attitude toward Hyacinth also reveals James's abiding concern about the technical standards of the book trade, a side to his professional character that has seldom been appreciated. Because of higher labor costs in the United States, American publishers pioneered most of the technical innovations in the book trade after the Civil War. The transformation of the industry was so rapid and far-reaching that by the late 1880s there was not a single process in the traditional sequence of operations in hand binding that could not be done by machine. Once it was perfected in the 1890s, the new technology was soon exported to England and other countries. Hyacinth's concern for the future of his craft could not have been better timed.[38]

When he first arrived in London in the 1870s, James carried letters of introduction to William Morris and other leaders of the arts and crafts movement, who inspired the late-Victorian revival of interest in printing and book design. Morris had also embraced socialist philosophy and committed himself to the reformation of an industrial system that had obliterated the distinctive value of the individual laborer's handiwork or skill. In "The Art of Fiction" James had suggested that the novelist might serve unofficially as the social historian of his place and time. Throughout *The Princess Casamassima* he fulfilled that role with remarkable accuracy. In London of the 1880s, revolution may not have been in the air, but it was probably on the lips of more than one bookbinder's apprentice. Historians have long recognized that the movement for trade unionism originated with printers and pressmen, workers for whom literacy was a necessity. With virtually guaranteed access to enlightened opinions, these groups were effectively organized even before the Industrial Revolution transformed the nature of the modern workplace.

Perhaps the best testament to the novel's verisimilitude can be read in the journals of Thomas James Cobden-Sanderson (1840–1922), a London bookbinder of exquisite taste and tremendous pride in his craft. A friend of William Morris, Cobden-Sanderson also dedicated his life and work to the principles of socialism and dreamed of an apocalyptic transformation of English society. A survey of his reading is instructive. Among the authors he studied reverently were Henry George, Robert Owen, Friedrich Engels, and Edward Bellamy—and, with them, Walter Pater! Hyacinth Robinson could not have improved upon his choices.[39] At first glance, *Marius the Epicurean* may seem a curious complement to *The Condition of the Working Class in England,* but to Cobden-Sanderson the combination was natural. Art, at least, might achieve what Marx and Engels prophesied for the social order—an ideal arrangement of competitive forces working in harmony for the benefit of all. Within the limits of his trade, Cobden-Sanderson strove to realize this synthesis in "the book beautiful," an artistic ideal in which every decorative aspect of a volume's design would be subordinated to the author's text and the spirit behind it. Here was a man after the novelist's own heart. James's correspondence with his publishers consistently reveals his abiding concern for the book as an object of art. His fastidiousness as an artist did not stop at the fashioning of his prose style, but extended to the creation of the finished volume as a cultural artifact.[40]

Such data from the history of the book trade do more than corroborate certain claims that occasionally are made (usually without hard evidence) for James's reliability as an annalist of social facts. They also suggest that he was saturated with every detail of the profession of authorship. Indeed, if James had needed a prototype for a hero whose vocation left him suspended between art and trade, the novelist wouldn't have had far to look. His own experience as a writer, by no means unique, revealed again and again the dual allegiance of his calling. The literary artist, as Howells perceptively wrote, was in a "transition state":

> He is really of the masses, but they do not know it, and what is worse, they do not know him; as yet the common people do not hear him gladly or hear him at all. He is apparently of the classes; they know him, and they listen to him; he often amuses them very much; but he is not quite at ease among them; whether they know it or not, he knows that he is not of their kind. Perhaps he will never be at home anywhere in the world as long as there are masses whom he ought to consort with, and classes whom he cannot consort with.[41]

Even to its implicitly despairing conclusion, Howells's analysis of "The Man of Letters as a Man of Business" reads like a gloss of *The Princess Casamassima.*

Throughout the 1880s men of letters in both England and America debated the nature of their calling, particularly as the expanding literary marketplace created new opportunities for wealth that openly challenged older (and occasionally more genteel) assumptions about the writer's status in society. Signs of a new professional self-consciousness were everywhere. Critical organs catering to the literati—such as the *Dial* (1880) and the *Critic* (1881)—appeared; and they were quickly followed by publications like the *Writer* (1887) and the *Author* (1889), whose unabashed function was to keep magazinists posted on the markets for their wares. As publishers launched an unprecendented number of new periodicals—priced at all levels and targeted at varying levels of taste—the competitive rush to capture segments of the expanding reading public demonstrated to authors that rights to literary property were a valuable commodity. Particularly in England, where publishing practices (such as the outright sale of copyright) tended to alienate writers from the new sources of wealth, authors moved aggressively to protect their interests. With surprising facility, literary men cast off the historical legacy of dilettantism that previously had weakened their resistance to abuses in the publishing trade. They soon began to voice their discontents publicly and to press for reform. No doubt these men of letters gathered in more fashionable places than the back room at the Sun and Moon Café, but the collective airing of perceived injustice had the same effect on authorship as class-conscious labor agitation had on the proletariat. Isolated and helpless resentments were centralized and made effective. "With supply and demand, those dear old friends, we have no intention of quarrelling," Edmund Gosse announced in 1887, "but we think, without any absurd sentimentality, that there may be some portions of the professional careers of a man of letters which organization may take under its protection and may improve."[42] Clarification of publishers' agreements, the defense of authors' literary property, and the promotion of international copyright were key items on his agenda.

The concerns Gosse articulated had been in the air for several years. and the group he addressed, the Incorporated Society of Authors, was formed in 1883 to offer counsel and support to victims of publishing malpractice. Henry James was an honorary American fellow of the Society from its inception (and a resident member after 1888),[43] even though he occasionally took issue with its vociferous president, Walter Besant, and generally assumed a minor role in the organization's public activities. Privately, however, in the discreet confidence of London's literary haunts and clubrooms, James played the part of a professional ambassador, informing his English friends (especially Gosse and Robert Louis Stevenson) about publishing opportunities in the United States and keeping them abreast of literary news as it was conveyed to him by his family, his friend Howells, and other American literati. Acutely conscious of journalism's encroachment upon the literary life, James deliberately avoided the glare of publicity that was so actively courted by the Society's leaders; nevertheless, behind the scenes he worked diligently for many goals similar to theirs.[44]

James's active affiliation with the organization broke down, however, when he realized that the Society's leaders (especially Besant) were too narrowly restricting its focus of concern. Like any other writer worth his salt, James wanted the public to reward him with "laurels and shekels";[45] but he also felt that other standards besides income should determine a writer's status and shape his attitude toward his craft. By concerning itself almost exclusively with the protection and better marketing of literary property, the Society of Authors limited itself to the view that literature was a trade. Besant regarded fiction, in particular, as a consumer commodity and therefore did nothing to discourage the Society's members (and younger writers generally) from catering to the desires of an uncultivated mass audience. Besant's attitude, which became even more abject as the Society prospered, was one that Henry James could not abide.[46]

In *The Princess Casamassima,* James projected his alienation from the demands of an unenlightened democracy of readers in Hyacinth Robinson's gradual disaffection from the egalitarian impulse that presumably inspires the anarchist movement. From the moment he arrives at Medley, the country house that the Princess rents to escape the London "season" (society obeying its own unnatural calendar), Hyacinth partakes of a new communion with the existing social order: "The cup of an exquisite experience . . . was at his lips; it was purple with the wine of novelty, of civilization, and he couldn't push it aside without drinking. He might go home ashamed, but he would have for evermore in his mouth the taste of nectar" (p.303).

The echo from Keats is appropriate, because Hyacinth's initiation to the amenities of culture occurs in Medley's library:

> It was an old brown room, of great extent—even the ceiling was brown, though there were figures in it dimly gilt—where row upon row of finely-lettered backs returned his discriminating professional gaze. A fire of logs crackled in a great chimney, and there were alcoves with deep window-seats, and arm-chairs such as he had never seen, luxurious, leather-covered, with an adjustment for holding one's volume; and a vast writing-table, before one of the windows, furnished with a perfect magazine of paper and pens, ink-stands and blotters, seals, stamps, candlesticks, reels of twine, paper-weights, book-knives. Hyacinth had never imagined so many aids to correspondence, and before he turned away he had written a note to Millicent, in a hand even more beautiful than usual—his penmanship was very minute, but at the same time wonderfully free and fair—largely for the pleasure of seeing "Medley Hall" stamped in crimson, heraldic-looking characters at the top of his paper. In the course of an hour he had ravaged the collection, taken down almost every book, wishing he could keep it a week, and put it back quickly, as his eye caught the next, which appeared even more desirable. He discovered many rare bindings, and gathered several ideas from an inspection of them—ideas which he felt himself perfectly capable of reproducing. Altogether, his vision of true happiness, at that moment, was that, for a month or two, he should be locked into the library at Medley. He forgot the outer world, and the morning waned—the beautiful vernal Sunday—while he lingered there. (p. 279)

Through a masterly use of detail, James once again evokes a sense of antagonism between the library as a citadel of art and the demands of the "outer world." Whereas in *The Portrait of a Lady* James's herione carries her books from the library into the "office"—and even, on occasion, feels drawn to the "vulgar street" beyond it—the library to Hyacinth is distinctly a refuge from those quarters. Even though they are often frustrated or defeated by it, James's earlier protagonists confidently assert themselves in the "outer world." In *The Princess* that confidence is missing.[47]

Even Hyacinth's brash commitment to the anarchist movement is a kind of involuntary reflex that betrays his desperate need to establish a fixed social identity. There can be "no peace for him," James observes, "between the two currents that [flow] in his nature, the blood of his passionate, plebeian mother and that of his long-descended, supercivilized sire." They continue to "toss him from one side to the other" and array him "in intolerable defiances and revenges against himself" (p. 471). After he experiences the artistic glories of Paris and Venice (enjoying the itinerary that Osgood's failure denied James), Hyacinth's internal conflict becomes unresolvable. The face of Europe may be scarred by "want and toil and suffering" ("the constant lot of the immense majority of the human race"), but Hyacinth is even more impressed by "the great achievements of which man has been capable in spite of them"—"the treasures, the felicities, the splendours, the successes, of the world" (pp. 380, 434). Feeling a need to balance his accounts, Hyacinth eventually recognizes that, at its root, egalitarianism springs from a seed of "invidious jealousy" (p. 380). When the protagonist returns to London and rejoins his fellow conspirators, he sees "everywhere . . . the ulcer of envy" (p. 390). Despite his pledge of allegiance to the underground movement, Hyacinth is no longer absorbed with "the idea of how the society that surrounded him should be destroyed"; instead, he is struck by "the sense of the wonderful, precious things it had produced, of the brilliant, impressive fabric it had raised" (p. 365).

Significantly, as the pitch of Hyacinth's conflict intensifies, almost the sole consolation of which he can avail himself is the pleasure of his craft. When Hyacinth returns to the bindery from his continental sojourn, his feelings, unavoidably, are "mingled." After saturating his senses with the pleasures of Paris and Venice, Hyacinth cannot help finding Crookenden's workshop "loathesome," but there is still "something delightful in handling his tools." Indeed, his imagination is quickly overrun by a "pleasant swarm" of new ideas:

> They came in still brighter, more suggestive form, and he had the satisfaction of feeling that his taste had improved, that it had been purified by experience, and that the covers of a book might be made to express an astonishing number of high conceptions. Strange enough it was, and a proof, surely, of our little hero's being a genuine artist, that the impressions he had accumulated during the last few months appeared to mingle and confound themselves with the very sources of his craft and to be susceptible of technical representation. (pp. 387–88)

For the moment Hyacinth feels that "his trade [is] a resource, an undiminished resource" (pp. 388). He will soon come to recognize, however, that its exercise is lonely and its reward largely spiritual.

"Oh art, art, what difficulties are like thine," James had pondered in his journal; "but, at the same time, what consolation and encouragements, also are like thine? Without thee, for me, the world would be, to the avowedly disharmonic intentions of the anarchists. As the novel progresses, the disjunction between Hyacinth's growing appreciation of the cumulative achievements of civilization and his commitment to the democratic leveling of society eventually overwhelms him. When he receives his calling from Hoffendahl (to repay the hospitality of a certain Duke with a pistol shot), he cannot face the discordant music and turns his weapon against himself.

Irving Howe has seen that, through the mysterious alchemy of the artist's imagination, James has come upon a problem that lies at the very center of political life. "Hyacinth is trapped in the heart-struggle between beauty and necessity: he wants only to live, only to respond, but it is his very awareness of the unmediated clash between beauty and necessity that destroys him." Howe is honestly baffled, though, by the process of discovery that led James to this recognition. ("I shall not even try to guess how [James came upon it], except to note that he knew only too well what it meant to live between two worlds.)[49] The "worlds" to which Howe was referring, of course, were England and America; in 1957 the issue of James's expatriation was still alive and kicking. Perhaps unconsciously, however, the critic hit upon a more revealing truth: James also knew—only too well—what it meant to live between the worlds of beauty and necessity, between art and the marketplace. The disjunction of *those* realms offered the novelist his imaginative footing to plumb the depths of Hyacinth Robinson's vocational dilemma.

indeed, a howling desert."[48] Hyacinth Robinson's world rapidly be a howling desert, when, at the moment of his crisis, one by one his ships wither. The Princess diverts her attention (as Madame Bra her venerable companion, has warned) to a new house, new clothe new acquaintances—all deliberately less fashionable than the last Muniment, whose friendship Hyacinth has pathetically coveted, ac without a flicker of emotion the bookbinder's potentially fatal sacrif his liberty. "How could he—how *could* he——?" Hyacinth asks hir with tears in his eyes. "It may be explained," James parenthetically n "that 'he' was a reference to Paul Muniment; for Hyacinth had drea of the religion of friendship" (p. 377). Hyacinth's dream is fu betrayed when he inadvertently discovers that Muniment has become Princess Casamassima's latest (and possibly most intimate) prot Weighed down by a "sense of supersession," the bookbinder tries stick to [his] tools," but his art (unlike James's) cannot see him thro (pp. 571–72). "Oh yes, I recognise your work when I see it," Mr. Ve cheerfully tells him:

> there are always certain little finer touches. You have a manner, like a master With such a talent, such a taste, your future leaves nothing to be desired. You will make a fortune and become a great celebrity. (p. 563)

As the novel slides towards its fatal conclusion, however, Vetch's nervou assurances merely foreshadow their inevitable reversal.

Only a few years before, Henry James had offered similarly optimisti prophecies about his own career to an eager audience in Quincy Street He too would "make a fortune and become a great celebrity." Now his future—like Hyacinth's—seemed unsure. For James's bookbinder the problem of vocation transcends the practical question of earning a living (though this, too, is obviously important). Because of his conflicting social sympathies, Hyacinth is also forced to ponder the meaning of a specifically political *vocation*—in fact, the entire action of the book hinges upon the root sense of the word (from the Latin *vocare,* "to call"). From the moment that he mortgages his freedom to the shadowy Diedrich Hoffendahl, Hyacinth is pledged to await the call of the anarchist leader, the "great musician" who

> treated all things, persons, institutions, ideas, as so many notes in his great symphonic revolt. The day would come when Hyacinth, far down in the treble, would feel himself touched by the little finger of the composer, would become audible (with a small, sharp crack) for a second. (p. 313)

At this early stage of his radical engagement, Hyacinth's language of consciousness reveals that he cannot easily distinguish between the pleasures of culture and the grim demands of his political commitment. His symphonic metaphor is passionately suggestive, but curiously inappropriate

VII

Accommodating Art and the World: The Primary Motive of The Tragic Muse

When Henry James sat down to write the prefaces for the New York Edition of his novels and tales, he confessed to a curious blankness about *The Tragic Muse.* Failing to recall the "productive germ" that spawned this sprawling fiction, James could only look upon it "as a poor fatherless and motherless, a sort of unregistered and unacknowledged birth." Critics have since recognized that, far from being a literary orphan, *The Tragic Muse* is, in fact, a lineal descendant of James's other large novels of the eighties—*The Bostonians* and *The Princess Casamassima.* Despite their dissimilar settings and subjects, all three books portray the conflict (as James said in *The Bostonians*) between the individual's "genuine vocation" and society's "hollow and factitious ideal." *The Tragic Muse* makes explicit a theme that James had suggested symbolically in his earlier novels—that art is "a human complication and a social stumbling-block," and that the life of the imagination, "having to be not altogether easily paid for," can only be secured on "difficult terms." The conflict between art and the world, as James phrased it, was "one of the half-dozen great primary motives" available to the novelist.[1] Small wonder it should take so many different forms in his prodigious output: James had more than a half-dozen novels in him to write.

This modest tally of the artist's "primary motives" does not explain, however, why the conflict between art and the world surfaces repeatedly in James's fiction during the latter half of the 1880s. The balance sheets from his publishers provide more salient clues. As we have seen, James voiced his skepticism about the public reception of *The Princess Casamassima* as soon as its serial run was completed. His optimistic prophecy about sales of *The Bostonians* had been thoroughly discredited; he nursed fewer illusions about his next book. "I hope the Princess will have a career," he halfheartedly told Macmillan, "& almost think it probable—though I am cured of presumption."[2] In his zeal to capture the American market for James's books after the failure of J. R. Osgood & Company, Macmillan had offered the novelist a generous advance (£500) on royalties of *The Bostonians,* a sum that was never earned back. Now the publisher, too, was "cured of presumption" about the market for James's books. For *The Princess* he accepted the writer's preference for the same arrangement as was made for *The Bostonians,* a royalty of 15 percent on English and American sales, but he reduced the advance from £500 to £400.[3] Through the end of the decade, Macmillan's advances continued to shrink, despite the publisher's efforts to expand James's English audience by issuing his books in cheaper formats.

After a triple-decker had run its course with the circulating libraries (usually within a year), English publishers typically issued the novel in a single volume, priced at six shillings, that was intended to be bought rather than borrowed. Six shillings was certainly a far cry from the deliberately prohibitive price of a novel in three volumes (a guinea and a half), but it still kept most new books beyond the reach of an ever-expanding market. In the 1880s Macmillan experimented with a new format for reprints, bound in paper boards and priced at two shillings, that more readers could afford. The two-shilling books were "as showy as the ordinary 'yellow back,'" he boasted to James, "but not as vulgar." Appropriately, *The Princess Casamassima* was the first book of James's to appear in this more easily obtainable form. To convince the novelist of the wisdom of this move, Macmillan told James that a two-shilling issue probably would not interfere with the sales of his more expensive editions (these sales unfortunately were small any way), but might even help them "by making your work more widely known & so educating readers for your future books." The two-shilling *Princess* sold well (Smith and Sons, who had a monopoly on railway bookstalls, alone ordered 700 copies), and Macmillian followed it up with some of James's earlier titles—*Daisy Miller* (predictably), *The Madonna of the Future,* and *Washington Square.*[4] Sales of these editions were cheering to the novelist, but it is difficult to gauge their efficacy in "educating" the public for James's future work. By perpetuating the author's reputation as the chronicler of "the American girl," these editions actually may have contributed to the public's frustration with James's later attempts to move away from that subject, which he had come to see as necessarily restrictive.

In a famous letter written to Howells at the beginning of 1888, James complained that he remained "irremediably unpublished." Essays and stories had poured from his pen but they were nowhere to be seen. After the successive failures of *The Bostonians* and *The Princess Casamassima,* the novelist feared that magazine editors were ashamed of his work and were holding it back. Perhaps Howells, who was more familiar with editorial practice, could offer some advice? Then, too, it was likely that some day all of his "buried prose" would "kick off its various tombstones at once."[5] This letter has frequently been quoted out of context in order to illustrate a precipitous decline in James's market, but Leon Edel assuredly is right in suggesting that "James's mournful complaint to Howells was that of an impatient rather than of an unpublished and unpopular author."[6] The tombstones fell like dominoes later in the year as piece after piece appeared and book after book rolled from Macmillan's presses. *Partial Portraits, The Reverberator,* and *The Aspern Papers*—all were published in a five-month interval from May to September; *A London Life* came the following spring. "With what a torrent it has come at last!" Robert Louis Stevenson exclaimed. Wherever he looked, the magazines were filled with James's work. The published volumes came in quick and majestic succession.[7]

Although the "torrent" of James's prose came in a great flood of print, the author's royalties, by comparison, were reduced to a trickle. For each of James's new titles Macmillan maintained his customary offer of a 15 percent royalty on English and American sales, but the advances he put forward progressively diminished. James knew that *The Princess,* while faring better than *The Bostonians* ("born under an evil star"), had not fully justified Macmillan's payment of £400. His new books, moreover, were of lesser magnitude and would not appear in the ever-so-profitable three-volume form; even as first editions, each was priced at six shillings per volume. Nevertheless, James informed Macmillan that his "aspirations" in regard to the spate of recent books would "not have been fulfilled" unless he received "something 'down'—a certain sum in advance, of course I mean, on that 15 per cent royalty which I should otherwise have a long time to wait for."[8] For *Partial Portraits* and *The Reverberator,* Macmillan sent James £125. The publisher also wanted to issue *The Aspern Papers* together with a number of other short stories, but he advised a slight delay; otherwise, sales of *The Reverberator* might be hurt. "The 'circulating library' life of a book is not very long," he shrewdly observed, "but while it lasts it should be treated tenderly."[9]

Without a running serial to yield him a monthly income, however, James soon felt pressed for money. Once again he assumed the pose of supplicant. Even though many of his recent stories and articles had not yet appeared serially, James proceeded to organize his considerable output into three prospective tables of contents. These he sent to Macmillan with the express desire of obtaining an advance against future sales. One of James's stories was called "The Modern Warning," and he received a very modern warning from his publisher. "I am sorry," Macmillan promptly responded,

> that the sale of your books does not enable me to be as liberal in our advances as we should like to be but of course in matters of this kind we have to look facts in the face. If it will be of any assistance to you I shall be glad to send you a cheque for £200 on account of royalties to come from the three books you mention viz (1) The Aspern Papers, (2) A London Life, (3) The Lesson of the Master.

The publisher's retreating confidence was reflected in his modest offer. Nevertheless, James quickly accepted these terms, although it would be years before he fulfilled his end of the bargain (*The Lesson of the Master* not appearing until 1892).[10]

Macmillan's embarrassing reference to the meager demand for James's work did not take the novelist by surprise: the fate of *The Bostonians* and *The Princess* had given him the true measure of *that.* If the public treated him indifferently, however, James would gladly return the favor. When Charles Eliot Norton published an edition of Carlyle's letters in 1886, James commended the editor on a job well done; but he doubted whether the "general public" would "bite at it very eagerly. I don't know why I allude to this," James continued, "for the general public has small sense and less taste, and its likes and dislikes, I think, must mostly make the judicious grieve."[11] Two months later he thanked Howells for the "real delight" of *The Minister's Charge:*

> If anything I happen to say consoles you in any degree for the stupidity of the age, you are a thousand times welcome to it. The vulgar-mindedness of the public to which one offers the fruits of one's brain would chill the artist's breast if those fruits were not so sweet to his own palate! One mustn't think of the public *at all,* I find—or one would be nowhere & do nothing.[12]

The novelist offered similar advice—and, occasionally, consolation—to many other correspondents. Quite unwittingly, however, James's incessant reference to the public belies his professed indifference to it. "I don't know why I allude to this," he ingenuously told Norton. James alluded to the public—again and again—because he couldn't honestly avoid it. "[T]o write for the public is to follow the scent of a red herring," he imperiously told Howells. But to Macmillan James referred more humbly to another of his senses: "The book is charmingly pretty," he said of *The Aspern Papers,* "& if the public would only show some practical agreement in this estimate there would be no wormwood mingled with my honey."[13]

The public's appetite for James's work was promptly satisfied, however; for each of the new volumes sales were steady but modest.[14] This unspectacular record simply confirmed the novelist's dependence on the serial market for reliable income. Sales of his books quickly tapered off and rarely yielded substantial returns beyond their advances. Roger Gard has observed that, during his lifetime, James had neither the benefits of the transitory best-seller nor those of the steadily emerging classic; but these same benefits were frequently denied to other writers, and it would certainly be a mistake to exaggerate the distinctiveness of James's unsalability. His dependence on the magazines makes his career representive rather than exceptional.[15]

At any rate, renewed evidence of that dependence forced James to change his plans for *The Tragic Muse.* Exhausted by his two "long-winded" serials, James originally intended his next novel to be "about half as long (thank God!) as the *Princess.*" In the summer of 1887 he confided to Grace Norton that the book would "probably appear, at no very distant day, as a volume, without preliminary publication in a magazine. It will be called (probably) *The Tragic Muse;* but don't tell of it."[16] Norton kept the secret, and so did James, because friction with the market soon forced the writer to respond instead to the comic muse who beckoned him to write another short novel *(The Reverberator)* for serialization in *Macmillan's Magazine.* How readily James turned that friction to account is evidenced by the fact that he sketched an outline for the book into his journal on 17 November 1887 and two weeks later had sold it to Macmillan.[17] The story was small (James conceived it as a three-part tale), and the magazine made it smaller (by publishing it, he complained, "in terribly short snippets"); but Macmillan accepted it *"immediately,"* James informed another editor who wanted the serial, "which was my bribe."[18]

Macmillan also "bribed" him by agreeing to James's stipulations on "the great money-question." James had first discussed the serialization of *The Reverberator* with Mowbray Morris, who edited *Macmillan's Magazine,* but the novelist preferred to talk business with Macmillan himself. Morris had told him that Macmillan had recently agreed to pay the popular novelist Annie Thackeray Ritchie £2.10.0 ($12) per page for one of her contributions, and James held out for comparable terms. This was still considerably less than James could get from a periodical in the United States, but Macmillan could have the story if he would also agree to send advance sheets to *Harper's Weekly* (which did not circulate in England). The publisher accepted these terms, but the Harpers, apparently, didn't; *The Reverberator* never appeared serially in America. Timing was probably a factor, because illustrations could not have been prepared for the *Weekly*'s pages by the date at which Macmillan wanted to begin publication. The same problem had delayed the American serialization of some of James's earlier material. With income from his published volumes steadily declining, James could not afford to pass up an offer of ready cash for magazine work.[19]

The same incentive prompted James to abandon his early conception of an abbreviated *Tragic Muse;* the book eventually became his longest serial, running through seventeen monthly installments. James had offered a briefer version of *The Tragic Muse* to the *Atlantic,* but Thomas Bailey Aldrich, the editor, induced him to accept a larger assignment. "I succumb to your arguments," James responded, "and will undertake to manage a serial for the full twelvemonth of 1889 . . . [to] be paid for at the same rate as the *Princess*—i.e. $15 per page." To achieve the desired length James revealed that he would "run two stories (i.e. two subjects I have had in my head) together, interweaving their threads."[20] The structure of the novel and the conditions that gave rise to it were similarly interwoven. By asking James to rethink his plan for the book, Aldrich indirectly forced the novelist to deviate from his usual narrative technique. To fuse his two stories into one, James realized that the book had "to get itself done in dramatic, or at least in scenic conditions," to "move in the light of *alternation.*" Scenic consistency, James later wrote, could only be achieved through "the multiplication of *aspects,*" the careful restriction (and alternation) of narrative points of view—the same technical innovation that inspired the works of the so-called major phase.[21]

The Tragic Muse was to begin it's run in January 1889, and James had promised to deliver his first installment by October of the preceding year. As the deadline approached, Aldrich also sounded James on the question of book rights to his serial. The clever Yankees of Houghton, Mifflin & Company, who published the *Atlantic,* were not eager to sacrifice the publicity value of serialization to another house (especially a foreign competitor like Macmillan), and they expected a contributor to give the firm at least first refusal of volume rights to serial work. With advances from Macmillan on the decline, the author gave the matter more serious consideration than he had a few years earlier, when the house of Scribner renewed its invitation to publish his work after Osgood's collapse. Though flattered by Scribner's offer (a "friendly disposition [was] always gratifying"), James had informed the American publisher that "Messrs. Macmillan, who have a house in New York, are now doing for me there as well as here, & are likely to continue to do so. I find a great convenience in being able to deal with my publishers face to face (instead of merely by letter,) & I think it insured me by this arrangement."[22] Whatever its merits, the "arrangement" with Macmillan no longer "insured" James quick profits, and he was willing to give another firm at least the American rights to his new book. Provided certain conditions were met, that is. James rarely hesitated to press an advantage when he was conscious of one, and he told Houghton, Mifflin that they could have *The Tragic Muse* if the serial were paid for on receipt of the manuscript, rather than on publication. James wanted—and needed—his money promptly.

Such unusual departures from standard business practice were rarely smiled upon in Park Street (the Boston address of Houghton, Mifflin), and James knew he was taking a chance. "I hope you have found Messrs.

H. & M. responsive to my little condition," he inquired encouragingly of Aldrich, in a note despatched with his first installment. Three weeks later another and more anxious letter arrived on the editor's desk, but Aldrich now could reassure the novelist by sending James a handsome cheque for the first chapters of his serial. James was delighted, of course, to have his money, but he was even more encouraged by the publisher's additional suggestion that his novel be extended to run an additional two or three months, thus timing more advantageously its publication in volume form. "I shall be glad—very glad to avail myself of your license to take 14 to 15 months," the author eagerly replied, "& I appreciate the better position made for my novel as a volume by its coming out in the spring of '90 rather than just after Xmas."[23] James was rightly pleased with his new margin of freedom. Every trip to the Post Office (to mail another installment) guaranteed him another trip to the bank: the novel itself exudes a kind of breezy confidence. Whatever his quarrels with the public, James was still on firm ground with editors and publishers.

The novelist's arrangement with Houghton, Mifflin was convenient and remunerative: serialization of *The Tragic Muse* netted him almost $5000 over a span of sixteen months. In exchange for such favorable treatment from the *Atlantic,* however, James had to make certain concessions when it was time to publish the novel in volume form. For several years Macmillan had paid him a royalty of 15 percent together with an advance on future sales of his books. Houghton, Mifflin refused to budge from their more conservative standard—a 10 percent royalty with no advance. The trade-off, in fact, cost James little. Macmillan's advances, which covered both English and American markets, kept getting smaller; and so, James had to admit, were his sales. Even with a 15 percent royalty, his income from published volumes was not considerable. A reduced rate of return on American sales of *The Tragic Muse* would have almost no effect on James's overall income, and the arrangement with Houghton, Mifflin would still leave him the English volume rights to dispose of. His compromise was larger on paper than in life.

James probably was inclined to give the English market of his book to Macmillan, whose friendship had always been an asset. The novelist refrained, however, from making the first move toward an agreement. When the serial run was almost over, Houghton, Mifflin notified Macmillan of their intended publication date, so that the book could be issued simultaneously in both countries (to secure the English copyright). Such information usually would have come from James himself, and Macmillan was put on guard. "You have not yet said anything to us about this book," he politely inquired of James, "but I presume (& hope) that you intend to have it published in England."[24] Of course this was James's plan, but the question of who should publish the novel was apparently not yet settled in his own mind.

In February 1890 James asked Houghton, Mifflin to let him know "as soon as possible *when* the book is to appear in the U.S., as I must make that perfectly definite to any publisher here. In that case I will attend to the question of simultaneity."[25] The novelist carefully avoided mentioning an English publisher by name, but Houghton, Mifflin must have assumed that he intended to keep the book with Macmillan; therefore, they directed their response to the publisher. But James had other plans in mind. Macmillan's query came to him on 22 March. On 24 March James notified the publisher that he would send revised serial proofs of the novel to Bedford Street the following morning, so Macmillan could estimate how long the book was likely to be.[26] No words had yet been spoken about terms; but, as if to remind Macmillan of his lofty professional status, the novelist confirmed a rumor that the publisher had heard. "Oh yes," James wrote,

> I translated three months ago an unpublished Tartarin novel of Daudet's [*Port Tarascon*], the last, killing the hero off, for the Harpers, who are to produce it as a six-months serial (and then as a book) in their magazine in advance of its issue in France. It begins in the U.S. I think in June—and appears in France only for Christmas. I was bribed with gold—more gold than the translator (as I suppose) is accustomed to receive.[27]

"The book," he added, "is charming," and so was James's strategy. The ball was in Macmillan's court. James deliberately waited for him to make an offer, to indicate the tangible measure of his desire for *The Tragic Muse*.

Macmillan's situation was uncomfortable. His previous advances to James had proven overly generous; and for *The Tragic Muse* the firm would be getting only the English market. Despite his large personal affection for James, Macmillan had always emphasized the necessity of looking certain facts in the face: "there is nothing we like so much as paying large sums to authors," he declared in 1885, "but our ability to do so must depend on the liberality of the British book buyer." The British book buyer, however, had not been very liberal toward James, nor was he likely to become so. Macmillan would gladly publish *The Tragic Muse* if James agreed "to be paid by results, and . . . accept *two thirds* of whatever profits there may be."[28] No royalty contract. No advance. Macmillan's proposal reverted to the kind of agreement he had first used with James in the 1870s.

The day that Macmillan's offer arrived, James again asked Houghton, Mifflin to inform him of their publication schedule.[29] Only if he knew exactly when the book would be ready could James bargain effectively with other English publishers. The novelist found Macmillan's offer of "two thirds profits in the future" unacceptable. "That future is practically remote," James told him, "and I am much concerned with the present":

> What I desire is to obtain a sum of money "down"—and I am loth to perish without a struggle—that is without trying to obtain one. I gather that the terms you mention are an ultimatum excluding, for yourselves, the idea of anything down—which is why I make this declaration of my alternative. But I should be sorry to pursue that alternative without hearing from you again—though I don't flatter myself that I hold the knife at your throat.[30]

Even if at arm's length, James still held the door ajar. Macmillan quickly calculated that two-thirds of the profit on a first edition of 500 copies (in three volumes at 31 shillings and 6 pence) would be £70 and he now offered this sum as an advance. His reason, he explained, for reverting to a rather archaic form of agreement

> was not any objection on our part to pay promptly, but a desire to guard against loss. I am sorry to say that this caution arises from the fact that the commercial result of the last few books we have published for you has been anything but satisfactory. At the same time we like to be your publishers and are anxious to fall in with your wishes about terms so far as we can prudently do so.[31]

James's response, justly famous, deserves to be quoted in its entirety:

> I thank you for your note and the offer of £70.0.0. Don't, however, think my pretensions monstrous if I say that, in spite of what you tell me of the poor success of my recent books, I still do desire to get a larger sum, and have determined to take what steps I can in this direction. These steps I know will carry me away from you, but it comes over me that that is after all better, even with a due and grateful recognition of the readiness you express to go on with me, unprofitable as I am. I say it is "better" because I had far rather that in those circumstances you should *not* go on with me. I would rather not be published at all than be published and not pay—other people at least. The latter alternative makes me uncomfortable and the former makes me, of the two, feel least like a failure; the failure that, at this time of day, it is too humiliating to consent to be without trying, at least, as they say in America, to "know more about it." Unless I can put the matter on a more renumerative footing all round I shall give up my English "market"—heaven save the market! and confine myself to my American. But I must experiment a bit first—and to experiment is of course to say farewell to you. Farewell then, my dear Macmillan, with great respect—but with the sustaining cheer of all the links in the chain that remain still unbroken.[32]

The experiment James had in mind was not, as Leon Edel has suggested, his anticipated entrance into the theatre as a playwright;[33] it was, instead, his use of a literary agent to dispose of the English rights to *The Tragic Muse.*

James had first entertained the idea of employing an agent during the dark months of 1887–88, the season in which his spirits were brought low by the unremitting failure of his last two novels. His letters from this time (such as the famous one to Howells: "I have fallen upon evil days . . . ")

are unusually somber, though his gloomy professional outlook is occasionally relieved by touches of self-deprecating humor ("Very likely . . . all my buried prose will kick off its various tombstones at once"). On the evening of 23 December 1887, James visited with his friend Edmund Gosse, who sounded out the depths of the novelist's despair. The public had repudiated *The Bostonians* and *The Princess,* but at least magazine editors had accepted them. Now James feared that he had lost *their* confidence as well. What could he do? The talk was long and lugubrious. Perhaps, Gosse suggested, the Society of Authors could be of assistance. James recoiled instantly from the idea: he had no desire to publicize his vocational problems—and what else was the Society but a vast machine for publicity, run by a clique of self-appointed "professionals" who cared more for money than for literature? Gosse shared James's distaste for the occasionally vulgar excesses of the Society's proceedings, but he himself had addressed the group earlier that year in an effort to define its appropriate mission. "The person whom we wish, if possible, to do something to help," Gosse maintained, "is the half-successful writer, the person who has a right to exist, and who yet cannot force himself, or herself, strongly upon the public."[34] He might easily have been thinking of his friend Henry James. Couldn't the Society help James now, when even "half-success" seemed remote?

The following morning James relented:

> An impulse not morbid, I trust, leads me to send you three words on this (supposedly) genial Xmas card, in correction of my plaintive accents of last night. . . . I feel as if I had whined, & am ashamed of it—having, as I am resolved, a considerable future in my . . . guts! So have you—don't doubt of that! It is a good thing from time to time, in the floundering gallop of existence, to have to take a fence: let us therefore, at these moments, exchange jovial & stimulating cries. There is in all difficulties an excitement which it would be poor to be without. So, in short, I still propose to succeed, & let me have the pleasure of observing that you do the same. Even this dim morning is garish enough to float, as I recall them, my lamplit remarks on the celebrated "clique." What I meant was so little that it was scarcely worth meaning at all; & the tongue magnifies things as it wags, & it is all accidental. Heaven bless them all; I wish them, vague as I am about their identity, every compliment of the Season.

James was "vague" about the identity of the Society's members, but he knew one of them (the president, Walter Besant), if only too well. In James's view, Besant may have known nothing about the art of fiction, but he certainly had mastered the art of selling it, which he did largely through an agent. James added in a postscript to Gosse, "If you *should* speak to Besant I don't mind, after all, your telling him that it is for me you do it. If I profit, in fact, by any suggestion of his, it is better that he should know I owe it to him."[35] Besant simply pointed to the moral of his own prolific career. He suggested, through Gosse, that James hire an agent to market his wares and referred him to A. P. Watt, a genuine pioneer in the field.

One publisher has called Watt an authorial David, "armed with a sling called a contract and a smooth pebble called advance royalty."[36] James himself was familiar with these weapons and had already employed them with considerable effectiveness, but the rise of the literary agent (Watt was the first to have a lasting impact on the marketplace) signaled a fundamental shift in the relations between authors and publishers. Historians have recognized that the rapid diversification of the literary marketplace made the rise of agenting inevitable (particularly after the adoption of an Anglo-American copyright convention in 1891).[37] When they first appeared, however, agents were vilified as leeches on the body of literature, "sucking blood entirely out of proportion" to the value of their services.[38]

Not surprisingly, the appearance of literary agents disturbed publishers more than it did authors, who were their clients. For Henry James, however, the move toward hiring an agent was reluctantly arrived at. "I tremble on the verge of Mr. Watt," the novelist told Gosse, "but shan't write to him till I can ask you, *viva voce,* two or three questions about him—as for instance whether I might interview him in a purely experimental or tentative manner without putting myself in his hands. I am beset with certain doubts and fears." Using an agent presumably would force an author to sacrifice some measure of freedom. If money were the sole arbiter of the fate of his manuscripts (and by what other light could a literary broker operate?), what would this imply about the writer's art—or the writer himself? Still, James was glad that Gosse had acted promptly. "It was immensely obliging of you," James acknowledged,

> to take the field with so little delay and I appreciate your benevolence. You are right in supposing that my talk with you the other night made me feel better. It quite set me up, as if I had received a cheque for £1000.[39]

A. P. Watt never presented James with such a princely sum; indeed, the extent to which the writer availed himself of Watt's help remains somewhat obscure. In February 1888 the novelist told his brother William that Watt would handle only the serial rights to his new work—arranging terms particularly with the English magazines. (James himself knew better how to handle the American market.) Although basically straightforward, his explanation was also tinged with a degree of defensive apology, as if his reliance on another man to handle some of his business affairs connoted weakness or incapacity:

> I have lately put my literary affairs (so far as they are connected with magazines) largely into the hands of an *agent,* one Mr. A. P. Watt, who places & arranges for all the productions of Walter Besant, Rider Haggard, Wm. Black,

> Bret Harte, James Payn, & Wilkie Collins. He appeared eager to undertake *me,* & I am promised remarkably good results from it. He is to make one's bargains & take charge of one's productions generally—but especially over here. He takes 10 per cent. of what he gets for me, but I am advised that his favourable action on one's market & business generally more than makes up for this—& that even if it didn't the relief & comfort of having him take all the mercenary & selling side off one's mind is well worth the cost. I debated a long time, but the other day he came to see me, & after a talk seemed so much impressed with the fact that I have done much less well for myself than I ought to be done for that I entered into relations with him. There is nothing hard & fast in them & they can be terminated at any moment if they don't do.[40]

Whether there was *anything* "hard & fast" in James's dealings with Watt is difficult to say.[41] Most of James's serials that appeared in 1888 had been contracted for earlier; and the English share of his income from periodicals over the next three years was small indeed (about $1200, which can be compared directly with the $6000 James received from American magazines during the same period). Watt's disposal of the English book rights to *The Tragic Muse* may well have been his major service to Henry James.

The novelist thought that his "experiment" with an agent would carry him away from his old publisher; in fact, it netted him an attractive new offer from Macmillan. James said "Farewell" and turned the book over to Watt, but the agent shrewdly picked up where the professional writer left off. James was accustomed to receiving a royalty contract and an advance. Macmillan had offered instead a generous share of the profits (assuming there were any). Watt suggested an alternative agreement: a five-year lease on the copyright. Eager to keep James on his list, Macmillan accepted Watt's new proposal and agreed to pay £250 for exclusive rights to *The Tragic Muse* in England and the British Dominions. The whole affair was settled within a matter of days. "I hear with pleasure from you that you have so promptly arranged the matter of the Tragic Muse," James told Watt on 2 April. "I am quite content with this result." James's brief experiment was an obvious success.[42]

The Tragic Muse is a novel about success, about the problems of defining and achieving it. Like any abstract ideal, the image of success is formed in the eye of the beholder. The discrepancies among its many versions in the novel are the source of the book's abundant humor and narrative interest. James engages all his important characters in spirited debate about the subject: but, by refusing to enter into the contest, he both complicates and extends the significance of his theme. In the end, the reader is no better off than any of the characters in the sense of having privileged answers to the vital questions that the novel raises.

What constitutes success is the riddle that each of James's men and women must solve. Though they differ widely on particulars, all of the characters would seem to agree that a certain ambition is fundamental to achieving it. "I will, I will, I will . . . I will succeed," the actress Miriam Rooth declares: "I will be great."[43] Her friend Peter Sherringham is slightly amused by her outburst ("You'll do what you want, evidently"), if only because he conceals his own vocational drive beneath a more politic façade. With the discretion befitting an aspiring diplomat, Sherringham will never allow such passionate words to escape from his lips. Appropriately, we must enter his consciousness to discover the touchstone of his behavior:

> There was only one thing in life that his mind had been very much made up to, but on this question he had never wavered: he would get on, to the utmost, in his profession. (p. 341)

Nick Dormer, on the other hand, wavers between two professions, which makes his problem of "getting on" even more acute. Nick shows every sign of prospering as a liberal politician and understands perfectly the inner workings of public life. But this role has been imposed upon him by others—by his mother (Lady Agnes), his eventual fiancée (Julia Dallow), and his wealthy party patron (Mr. Carteret). "The difficulty," as Nick explains to Lady Agnes, "is that I'm two men; it's the strangest thing that ever was. . . . One man wins the seat [in Parliament], but it's the other fellow who sits in it" (p. 267). If Nick were perfectly honest, he would have said "sits *restlessly,*" because the "other fellow"—the artistic side of his nature—will soon lead him to give up his political post and devote himself to painting.

The price of renunciation comes high for Nick, because in abandoning politics he must also relinquish the prospect of a magnificent settlement from Mr. Carteret. "The pencil—the brush?" this befuddled political veteran moans when Nick discloses his new vocation, "They're not the weapons of a gentleman" (p. 591). Weapons they still are, however, and Mr. Carteret promptly makes use of the former to write Nick Dormer out of his will. As James would say in his preface, the artist's freedom can only be had on difficult terms. Those terms become even more demanding for the struggling painter after Julia Dallow (herself "the incarnation of politics") severs their engagement (p. 487). Julia's pockets are stuffed with money from her first marriage to a wealthy connoisseur, but "her late husband's flat, inglorious taste for pretty things, his indifference to every chance to play a public part," has also filled her heart with bitterness. "I hate art," she tersely declares to Nick, and "passionately" accuses him of practicing it as if painting were a kind of infidelity. "You're an artist," she exclaims, "you are, you are!" (p. 483).

Nick must shoulder the burden of implicit betrayal from the very beginning, when we first discover the Dormers in Paris at the annual exhibition of the Salon. With masterful economy, James places these sturdy representatives of the "tweed-and-waterproof class" in a setting that best discloses their idiosyncrasies and betrays their private antagonisms (p. 2). For Lady Agnes and her daughter Grace, the pursuit of culture is a kind of unpleasant duty, and they clearly disapprove of Nick's more sensuous appreciation of the art work that, uncomfortably, surrounds them. Nick wants to show his younger sister Biddy around the sculpture garden; but, in the presence of the frankly nude, Mrs. Dormer intervenes. Everything to her "seems very dreadful. I should think Biddy had better sit still. Hasn't she seen enough horrors up above?" The "horrible" pictures in the upper galleries have only excited the girl's imagination (she, too, has a modest talent for art), and she begs her mother's permission. "Do you really think it's necessary to the child's development?" Lady Agnes demands, when Nick attempts to override his mother's objections. "She ought to see good work," Nick answers. "I leave it to your sense of responsibility," Lady Agnes rather majestically returns. With typical irrelevance, Grace begins to chatter about luncheon, but, sensing Nick's embarrassment, Mrs. Dormer returns to the charge: "You used to have so much," she went on; "but sometimes I don't know what has become of it—it seems all, *all* gone!" Her speeches are separated by a page of print, but the ponderous weight of Mrs. Dormer's antecedent—*responsibility*—carries its meaning forward.

From Lady Agnes's point of view, Nick is something of a fugitive for refusing to commit himself enthusiastically to a political vocation. Eventually, she is joined in this opinion by Julia Dallow and Mr. Carteret—the three of them, taken together, representing the Philistine stolidity of English civilization. "Ah, dear mother," Nick says reprovingly at the Palais de l'Industrie, "don't do the British matron!" (p. 12). A joke at the nation's expense, however, does not strike her as funny. Nick's humor is also lost on Julia and Mr. Carteret, who take political affairs with far greater seriousness than their elected representative. Nick tells Julia that she is "a very accomplished woman and a very zealous one; but you haven't an idea, you know—to call an idea." "I have an idea that's as good as any of yours," she rather vacuously responds, "the simple idea that one ought to do something or other for one's country." Nick can easily dispose of Julia's patriotism:

> "'Something or other' certainly covers all the ground. There is one thing one can always do for one's country, which is not to be afraid."
>
> "Afraid of what?"
>
> Nick Dormer hesitated a moment, laughing; then he said, "I'll tell you another time." (p. 117)

Mr. Carteret's patriotism, however, manifests itself on a larger scale. Indeed, everything at Beauclere, Carteret's country estate, appears to Nick

> to be on a larger scale than anywhere else—the tea-cups, the knives and forks, the door-handles, the chair-backs, the legs of mutton, the candles and the lumps of coal. . . . Nowhere were the boiled eggs, at breakfast, so big or in such big receptacles; his own shoes, arranged in his room, looked to him vaster there than at home. (pp. 315–16)

Figuratively speaking, the shoes Nick cannot fill belong to his deceased father, Sir Nicholas, a politician who, like Mr. Carteret, "had been of the same general type—a type so pure, so disinterested, so anxious about the public good" (p. 322). Nick privately admits that he feels like "a great hypocrite" whenever he visits Beauclere; but, lacking the courage he boasts of to Julia, he cannot bring himself to disappoint his elderly patron by telling Mr. Carteret the truth about his desire to become a painter (p. 321). When Nick finally decides to give up his seat in Parliament, that disappointment becomes inevitable. "Do you turn against your father?" the bewildered old man inquires:

> "Do you give up your name, do you give up your country?"
> "If I do something good my country may like it," Nick contended.
> "Do you regard them as equal, the two glories? . . . Do you pretend there is a nobler life than a high political career?"
> "I think the noble life [Nick simply declares] is doing one's work well." (p. 592)

To Mr. Carteret the "two glories" of art and politics are alien and incompatible. And in a sense they are: "It *is* fascinating," Nick admits to Julia, "to be a great man before the people—to be loved by them, to be followed by them. An artist isn't—never, never" (pp. 487–88). But in painting as well as in politics, there are degrees of success; whatever his distinctiveness, the artist is never wholly immune from the judgment of others. Success depends on the artist's relationship with an audience; it is decidedly a social construct, not necessarily contingent upon or proportional to solitary effort. No politician, actress, portrait painter (or novelist) can afford to ignore this. Each is a type of performer who cannot function without registering some kind of public approval.

Measuring the validity of these social claims against the self becomes one of the novel's major preoccupations. Certainly no one ridicules them more consistently than Nick Dormer's friend Gabriel Nash. More than any other character in the book, Nash refuses to be constrained by the envelope of social circumstance. Early in the novel Biddy Dormer wonders who he is and what he does, but Nash gleefully responds, "I've *no* profession, my dear young lady. I've no *état civil*. . . . Merely to be is such a *métier;* to live is such an art; to feel is such a career!" (p. 35). "I really think I'm perfectly independent," Nash later confides to Nick. One of the "regenerate," as he calls them, who jump overboard ("in search of better fun") from life's ship of conventional fools, Nash relishes the expansiveness of open water: "I've grown a tail, if you will; I'm the merman wandering free. It's a delightful trade!" (pp. 184–85).

Nash crows deliberately to wake his Philistine neighbors up, for, like Thoreau, he takes an irreverent view of conventional vocations. James carefully reveals, however, that Nash has no true neighbors and can be found at no address. When visiting London he stays at the Anonymous Club. At the conclusion of the novel, Nash vanishes without a trace. Even his likeness fades from the canvas that Nick has attempted. "Nash has melted back into the elements," the painter observes to Biddy, whose curiosity about her brother's aesthetic friend has never been satisfied; "he is part of the ambient air" (p. 858).

The ethereal nature of Gabriel Nash contrasts vividly with the gross catalogue of things that delimits a man like Mr. Carteret. Indeed, these two figures would seem to represent the antinomies of Jamesian existence—the fixed fool of conventional society and the free fate of unencumbered selfhood. The book's other figures (like most of us) work out their destinies somewhere between these extremes. In this respect, *The Tragic Muse* is one of James's most humane novels, because its broad canvas includes such a wide variety of characters, all of whom are pursuing basically sympathetic goals: a decent standard of living, a comfortable marriage, and, not lastly, the satisfaction of "doing one's work well."

Despite the carefree cynicism of Gabriel Nash, *The Tragic Muse* insists that we recognize the importance of vocation in the quest for human fulfillment. Miriam Rooth and Peter Sherringham illustrate this fact most aggressively in their climactic midnight encounter, when Peter asks Miriam to chuck her career as an actress and become a diplomat's wife. "Give it up—give it up!" he implores, just when Miriam has triumphed in a new play; "I'll marry you tomorrow if you'll renounce." "Renounce," Miriam questions, "after tonight?" (p. 770). Sherringham proceeds to make a mockery of her extraordinary premiere. Of course she succeeds—in a second-rate workhorse revival—and the same facile success will follow her for the rest of her days. Managers and box-office men will exploit her magnificent talent and confine her to the most vulgar repertoire imaginable. Sherringham offers to rescue Miriam from the debasing conditions of the stage, on which she will be forced to perform (Peter has the pleasure of quoting her) "like a contortionist at a country fair." Miriam spurns him, however, with superior intelligence and equal force:

> "I don't know what I may have said [in the past]," replied Miriam, whose steady flight was not arrested by this ineffectual bolt; "I was, no doubt, already wonderful for talking of things I know nothing about. I was only on

the brink of the stream and I perhaps thought the water colder than it is. One warms it a bit one's self, when once one is in. Of course I'm a contortionist and of course there's a hateful side: but don't you see how that very fact puts a price on every compensation, on the help of those who are ready to insist on the *other* side, the grand one, and especially on the sympathy of the person who is ready to insist most and to keep before us the great thing, the element that makes up for everything?"

"The element?" Peter questioned with a vagueness which was pardonably exaggerated. "Do you mean your success?"

"I mean what you've so often been eloquent about," the girl returned, with an indulgent shrug—"the way we simply stir people's souls." (pp. 788–89)

Miriam summons up the kind of professional eloquence that failed Verena Tarrant at *her* hour of need, and she makes Sherringham's ears burn with words that probably should have been directed at Basil Ransom: "how much," she incredulously declares, "you seem to take for granted one must like you!" (p. 795).

Sherringham's misplaced confidence stems from a kind of vocational hubris. What is art, after all, but a fiction? "I'll give you a larger life than the largest you can get in any other way," he says enticingly.

> "The stage is great, no doubt, but the world is greater. It's a bigger theatre than any of those places in the Strand. We'll go in for realities instead of fables, and you'll do them far better than you do the fables." (pp. 773–74)

Asserting that her stage is preferable to Sherringham's, Miriam turns the tables and asks the diplomat to "come off [his] own." The diplomat clings to his double standard. "The cases are not equal," he blandly responds. "You would make me the husband of an actress. I should make of you the wife of an ambassador" (p. 776). Because of the compromises that Miriam must make with the theatre, Sherringham cannot conceive of her vocation as anything but lowering. (Conveniently, he can regard his own degrading stint at a nameless banana republic as a service to crown and country.)

What Sherringham cannot fathom is Miriam's genuinely enlightened acceptance of the theatre's shortcomings. Aware of its limitations, how can she go on? What drives her to perform? One possible clue, Sherringham smugly observes, is probably racial, for the tragic muse is also a Jewish one—at once mercenary and aesthetic. Indeed, as Nick Dormer observes, Miriam intends to make the public pay—and pay dearly—but not just for the price of admission. "Precisely," she affirms: "make it pay, without mercy—squeeze it dry. That's what it's meant for—to pay for art. Ah, if it wasn't for that!" (p. 454).

Through unremitting labor, both Miriam and Nick eventually gain a kind of professional wisdom that is forever denied to Peter Sherringham. By his own admission, Sherringham relishes "the results, the finished thing, the dish perfectly seasoned and served: not the mess of preparation"—a fastidious ideal that only a dilettante can indulge (p. 245). During his assignment in Paris, the diplomat devotes himself to Madame Carré, the great dowager of the Théâtre Français; but he never fully appreciates the lessons of this master, for whom an artist's most interesting qualities are "not the gifts, but the conquests—the effects the actor had worked hard for, had wrested by unwearing study." "Work—work—work!" she insists to Miriam, who rises to the challenge with a zeal (and literally parallel determination: "I will, I will, I will") that surprises everyone but herself (pp. 142, 145).

Miriam's relentless ambition (and her obvious physical charm) temporarily stifles Sherringham's skepticism about the nature of her talent. Gabriel Nash, however, remains a patronizing antagonist. Nash's opinion of the English stage is so low that he cannot bring himself to take Miriam seriously. How could he after this lurid indictment?

> "The *omnium gatherum* of the population of a big commercial city, at the hour of the day when their taste is at its lowest, flocking out of hideous hotels and restaurants, gorged with food, stultified with buying and selling and with all the other sordid preoccupations of the day, squeezed together in a sweltering mass, disappointed in their seats, timing the author, timing the actor, wishing to get their money back on the spot, before eleven o'clock. Fancy putting the exquisite before such a tribunal as that! There's not even a question of it." (p.72)

Nash promulgates the charge and promptly drops it. Miriam stoops to pick it up and heroically defies it. The actress is hardly blind to the theatre's deficiencies, but she responds to them in a creatively adversarial way. She accepts the limited intelligence of her audience as a given, but prefers to consider the restrictions of the stage as a practical challenge to her powers. The artist must struggle against confinement, and James endorses this antagonism as a stimulus to his instinctive desire for freedom.

Miriam certainly confirms this observation when she finally takes to the stage. She frankly recognizes that "such a life as hers could only be a fighting life" and actually looks forward to the "fine uses" to which she will put her "faculty for making a row":

> She rejoiced that she had this faculty, for she knew what to do with it; and though there might be a certain swagger in taking such a stand in advance, when one had done the infinitely little that she had done, yet she trusted to the future to show how right she should have been in believing that a pack of idiots would never hold out against her, would know that they couldn't afford to. . . . [S]he would drive her coadjutors in front of her like sheep. (pp. 670–71)

Significantly, the pressure of Miriam's professional achievement also drives Gabriel Nash from sight. Sherringham has every reason to blush when Miriam tells him why Nash is absent from her premiere: "Oh, he says he doesn't like the kitchen fire—he only wants the pudding!" (p. 673). Sherringham, too, has primly excused himself from the "mess of preparation." The red in his cheek, James cleverly notes, must come from handling the saucepans.

Almost as if he were an allegorical caricature of the elder Henry James's philosophy, Nash contents himself with being and feeling. The idea of doing leaves him helpless and discomfited. He has written a very clever novel, we are told, but vows never to repeat the mistake. "Literature," he explains, "is for the convenience of others. It requires the most abject concessions. It plays such mischief with one's style that really I have had to give it up" (p. 36). Many critics have heard the voice of Henry James in this speech and in Nash's other diatribes against the restrictions imposed on the artist by "the essentially brutal nature of the modern audience" (p. 72). Undoubtedly, James chafed against those limits; partly because of them, he told his friends, *The Tragic Muse* would be the last long novel he would ever write. But James also knew that an artist's relation to his audience kept him in touch with reality and even acted as a vital antidote to the potentially fatal egoism of the creative imagination.[44] "[W]e are often reminded," he would later say in "The Lesson of Balzac," that "there is no art at all . . . that is not on too many sides an abject compromise. The element of compromise is always there; it is of the essence; we live with it, and it may serve to keep us humble."[45]

By rejecting the element of compromise, Gabriel Nash remains almost arrogantly free. Such liberty is "always provoking," Nick laughs (p. 183), as he and his friend stroll through the streets of Paris on a summer night. It is also rather provoking to Nick, who occasionally wonders to what positive uses Nash's freedom is put. Nash, of course, rejects the criterion of achievement as a Philistine encroachment; the beautiful, to him, remains a kind of rare abstraction. In the looming presence of Notre Dame, however, Nash's polished phrases ring hollow in Nick's ears:

> "Ah, the beautiful—there it stands, over there!" said Nick Dormer. "I am not so sure about yours—I don't know what I've got hold of. But Notre Dame *is* solid; Notre Dame *is* wise; on Notre Dame the distracted mind can rest! Come over and look at her!"
>
> They had come abreast of the low island from which the great cathedral, disengaged today from her old contacts and adhesions, rises high and fair, with her front of beauty and her majestic mass, darkened at that hour, or at least simplified, under the stars, but only more serene and sublime for her happy union, far aloft, with the cool distance and the night. Our young men, gossiping as profitably as I leave the reader to estimate, crossed the wide, short bridge which made them face toward the monuments of old Paris—the

> Palais de Justice, the Conciergerie, the holy chapel of Saint Louis. They came out before the church, which looks down on a square where the past, once so thick in the very heart of Paris, has been made rather a blank, pervaded, however, by the everlasting freshness of the great cathedral-face. It greeted Nick Dormer and Gabriel Nash with a kindness which the centuries had done nothing to dim. The lamplight of the great city washed its foundations, but the towers and buttresses, the arches, the galleries, the statues, the vast rose-window, the large, full composition, seemed to grow clearer as they climbed higher, as if they had a conscious benevolent answer for the upward gaze of men.
>
> "How it straightens things out and blows away one's vapors—anything that's *done!*" said Nick while his companion exclaimed, blandly and affectionately:
>
> "The dear old thing!"
>
> "The great point is to do something, instead of muddling and questioning; and, by Jove, it makes me want to!" (pp. 190–91)

The great point is to do something—and the point, James might have added, is to do something great. As Nick eventually learns, the only way the professional artist can achieve this end is to "sit quietly down and bend over his task. . . . [H]is actual job [is] not a crusade, with bugles and banners, but a gray, sedentary grind, whose charm [is] all at the core" (pp. 608–9). Nick's private maxim is to peg away and not mind.

Almost everyone who has pegged away at *The Tragic Muse* minds the novel's conclusion, because the element of compromise is everywhere apparent. As Gabriel Nash predicts, Miriam marries the man in the box office, Basil Dashwood. Sherringham, in turn, settles for Biddy Dormer; and Nick apparently intends to resume his engagement to Julia Dallow. Like the other novels we have examined, *The Tragic Muse* suffers from a problem of completion.[46] Many readers have accepted rather uncritically, however, the simple dichotomy between art and the world that James addressed in his 1908 preface. Seen through that distorting lens, the novel necessarily ends on an unequivocally pessimistic note. The dualistic logic behind such interpretations—that one must choose between art and the world, opt either for artistic integrity or popular success—falsely converts a richly ironic novel into simple melodrama.

The confident voice of James's later preface is extremely deceptive; the novel itself betrays the absence of controlling authority. All the characters stumble along the classically comic obstacle course to the altar, but the marriages all round seem motivated less by love than by convenience. Likewise, while the resolution of the novel ensures that art will prosper, no one can safely predict whether it will also be any good. In the end we must take James—and his art—on faith. Nevertheless, our sense of reconciliation is very profound, as profound as at the end of all great comedies; as Kenneth Graham intelligently observes, "the profundity is that of James's eventual submission to life and its limiting conditions."[47]

Even as he struggled to master them, Henry James accepted the "limiting conditions" of the writer's trade. Its joys and disappointments, seldom far apart, imbue *The Tragic Muse* with a consistently realized vitality. As the serial made its way through the *Atlantic,* James was haunted by familiar fears. "Not a single echo of it has come back to me from the public," he confided.[48] But any sign of genuine appreciation found him eager to respond. "I am touched & gratified more than I can say by your friendly & charming letter," he told an old Cambridge acquaintance; "for of course, after all, one writes for success, & your genial words [about *The Tragic Muse*], your writing to me at all, give me a high sense of that."[49]

VIII
The Eclectic Architecture of Henry James's New York Edition

When Henry James turned to the theatre after completing *The Tragic Muse,* he was unusually frank about his motives. "It isn't the love of art and the pursuit of truth that have goaded me into such miry ways," he told Howells; "it is the definite necessity of making, for my palsied old age, more money than literature has ever consented or evidently *will* ever consent, to yield me. My books simply don't sell—ecco."[1] As everyone knows, the pathetic history of James's dramatic years did nothing to reverse the decline in his sales or literary income. Frustrated by diminishing royalties from his books and spurned by the theatre public, James still felt the necessity of saving and maintaining at least a modest capital reserve for the day when his pen would no longer support him—an anxiety periodically stimulated by brusque reminders of an impending retirement from his brother William.[2] It may come as a surprise, however, to discover that Henry James looked to the sales of his magnum opus, the New York Edition of his novels and tales, to provide for "the bread of [his] vieux jours."[3]

The decade between James's withdrawal from the theatre and the culmination of his American lecture tour (1895–1905) has typically been viewed as the novelist's "major phase." And with good reason. The writer's painful experience as a playwright only made more rigorous his exacting professional discipline; indeed, it seems that James recovered from his humiliation on the stage through the self-prescribed anodyne of labor. "Oh, soul of my soul—oh, sacred beneficence of *doing!*" The invocation in James's *Notebooks* got results. He would publish seventeen books in the next ten years.[4]

As always, though, statistics can be misleading. One would hardly guess from this remarkable tally that during these same years James found it increasingly difficult to serialize his work and to find publishers who would take the risk of issuing his books. Signs of the scramble are evident in the pages of the *Bibliography.* For the first time in his career, James was forced to publish stories and major novels without the benefit of serialization ("In the Cage" and "The Beast in the Jungle," for example, together with *The Sacred Fount, The Wings of the Dove,* and *The Golden Bowl*). Among them, the published volumes bear no less than ten different English and American imprints. In England James's work was divided largely between Heinemann and Methuen, but Blackwood, Constable, and Duckworth each picked up a title. In America the distribution was even broader: Scribner's, Macmillan, and Houghton, Mifflin each brought out four books; the Harpers published three; and the avant-garde press of Herbert Stone issued two.

This pattern of diversification is symptomatic of a fundamental change, not only in James's professional career, but also in the nature of the literary marketplace. When the United States and Great Britain signed the first Anglo-American copyright agreement in 1891, the transatlantic market for literary works instantly expanded. Fully to take advantage of the new opportunities that resulted, authors turned to literary agents, paid professionals who kept abreast of rapidly changing market conditions and maintained a vast network of contacts in editorial and publishing offices. Characteristically, Henry James was among the first writers to make use of an agent's valuable services. A. P. Watt had disposed of *The Tragic Muse;* and Wolcott Balestier, a young American publicist, had helped the struggling playwright in his dealings with theatrical producers and managers; but in James Brand Pinker, whom the novelist engaged in 1898, James found his staunchest ally in an increasingly complex business arena.

Not surprisingly, many publishers resented the agent's appearance on the literary scene, since they now were forced to compete more vigorously for manuscripts. William Heinemann refused even to acknowledge Pinker's existence, a rude fact that cost him James's friendship and the chance to publish his books. Whereas Heinemann spurned the literary agent as a parasite who could only disrupt the traditional (and presumably cordial) relations between authors and publishers, many newer firms saw that men like Pinker served a positive function in the marketplace. The agent's rise was not necessarily a lamentable sign of commercialization, as so many older publishers complained, but rather a symptom of modernization. Of course, writers could handle all business arrangements for themselves—and wisely, too—if they were willing to devote ample time to a study of the marketplace. But their time was better spent writing rather than hawking their wares. A few prescient observers realized that, by directing manuscripts to the houses most likely to want them, agents could help bring order to an industry that could barely keep pace with the quantity of work submitted for editorial consideration.[5]

Whatever its impact on Heinemann, Pinker's presence certainly had a salutary effect on James, who announced to his friends that, with an agent to handle his business affairs, he had embarked on a wholly new career. This was something of an exaggeration, since Pinker's practice of soliciting more than one publisher was not alien to James's experience. The author had long recognized that if editors and publishers competed for his work, rewards would multiply. We have seen how, at the height of his popularity, he ably turned such wisdom to account. After his trial in the theatre, however, James shrewdly sensed that being *un*popular, unsalable at any price, had a cachet of its own—one that publishers, curiously, might bid for. In his famous tales of the literary life, James played with several variations on this theme. "The Next Time" (1895), for example, is the story of an artist who tries heroically to do something vulgar, "to take the measure of the huge, flat foot of the public," but, for all his effort, can't make a sow's ear out of a silk purse.[6] The temptation to read these tales autobiographically is almost overwhelming—many critics have fallen into the trap—but, unlike his doomed protagonists, James had no intention of being martyred by the marketplace. If the pressure to achieve best-seller status was made more acute by the evolution of a truly mass audience, the same conditions eventually fostered the recognition that smaller, more discriminating publics existed in tandem with it and might be capable of supporting writers of distinction. Even if James's books didn't sell, his name added an indisputable aura of quality to a publisher's list. (Not coincidentally, one of his volumes of short stories from this period was called *The Better Sort.*) With Pinker's assistance, James came to see that quite a few firms were willing to pay for the privilege of publishing one of the better sort.

Even as he helped to create an audience of uncommon readers, James was unwilling to limit himself strictly to them.[7] To earn the freedom he needed to write his masterpieces, James submitted to the necessity of producing potboilers of all kinds. The major phase, we should remember, consists not only of *The Ambassadors, The Wings of the Dove,* and *The Golden Bowl,* but also of *The Other House,* "The Turn of the Screw" ("the most abject, down-on-all-fours pot-boiler, pure & simple, that a proud man brought low ever perpetrated"),[8] and *English Hours.*

In light of the disastrous sales history of the New York Edition, most critics have considered that series as a kind of monument to James's artistic integrity. Indeed, virtually all James scholars have accepted Leon Edel's argument that the novelist's plan for the Edition, "fixed upon from the outset," was modeled after the twenty-three volumes of Balzac's *Comédie Humaine.*[9] In fact, the Edition's initial architecture was decidedly more modest. Like so many other works by James, its publication history exemplifies, as the author himself once had occasion to remark, "that benefit of *friction with the market* which is so true a one for solitary artists too much steeped in their mere personal dreams."[10]

Henry James gave voice to one of his most deeply felt and personal dreams in "The Middle Years" (1893), a touching story about a dying writer who, just coming to the fullness of his powers, longs for another go, a better chance. James's own career can be read as the best revision of this tale, for in preparing his texts for the New York Edition, he got what Dencombe is denied. The second chance was now the public's—"the chance to find the point of view, to pick up the pearl!"[11] To assist the public in its search and to satisfy its craving for novelty, James was eager to embellish his Edition with prefaces and frontispieces and to rework his earlier fictions. To captivate a publisher and the public, James was prepared to frame his artistic goals in distinctly marketable form.

Was the public curious about this reclusive author? Unashamed, he would write for each volume "a freely colloquial and even, perhaps . . . confidential preface or introduction," having no doubt that such a novelty would add greatly to the interest of the series.[12] Did his audience prefer the earlier manner of such stories as "Daisy Miller"? Then, he would include them, according to his amanuensis, "more from a necessary, though deprecated, respect for the declared taste of the reading public than because he loved them for their own sake."[13] Was a truly comprehensive Edition out of the question because no publisher would assume the risk of issuing the thirty-five volumes necessary for such an undertaking? Then gladly would James be "selective as well as collective; [wanting] to quietly disown a few things by not thus supremely adopting them."[14]

From the start James knew that "friction with the market" was inevitable. As early as the summer of 1904 he had been approached, or so his agent claimed, with various proposals regarding a collected edition; but the novelist preferred to postpone any definite arrangements until Pinker had the opportunity to discuss the matter with Edward L. Burlingame and Charles Scribner in New York.[15] Burlingame, a senior editor at Scribner's, had long admired James's work and had already spoken informally with Pinker about the prospects for a collected edition. After Pinker's first move toward more serious negotiations, however, Burlingame retreated rather cautiously:

> While we still look with much personal interest upon any project for a collected edition of Mr. James's books and from every point of view of literature should hope that it might be made, it is undeniable that the commercial situation is much less favorable than at the time I first made my inquiry of you. This is true both as regards his own works and in the light of the general experience of the last few years. . . . Your letter is of course so entirely preliminary that I hope you will look on this also as of the same kind; as I under-

> stand the subject is only to be brought up definitely after Mr. James has himself looked into the conditions. There may then be elements in what he proposes to change our present feeling.[16]

When James did look into the conditions the following year, he quickly realized that the Edition would be a gamble for any publisher, and he planned from the start to confine himself within fairly modest limits. As his agent wrote to the Macmillan Company on 17 July 1905: "I may say that Mr. Henry James does not contemplate the inclusion of all his writings, as he intends to make the edition selective as well as collective, and so far as we can see at present it will not run to more than 16 volumes."[17] Sixteen volumes—not twenty-three—at least initially; the larger number was arrived at later, as we shall see.

James had very good reasons to be conservative. He wanted, of course, "to quietly disown" a great many of his earlier productions. When an ardent young book-lover asked James for assistance in compiling a bibliography of his work in 1904, the novelist declared that authors "in general do not find themselves interested in a mercilessly complete resuscitation of their writings."[18] No such resuscitation was planned for the Edition; if anything, James intended to be mercilessly exclusive in preparing its table of contents. As he wrote to Robert Herrick when the Edition began to appear, "by the mere fact of leaving out certain things (I have tried to read over *Washington Square* and I *can't,* and I fear it must go!) I exercise a control, a discrimination, I treat certain portions of my work as unhappy accidents. (Many portions of many—of all—men's work are)."[19]

James's artistic scruples were, nonetheless, squarely reinforced by market considerations. Besides being financially and editorially cumbersome, a truly comprehensive Edition would have involved extremely difficult negotiations with other publishers who had competing interests in James's work. Even for the drastically diminished series he envisioned, James was forced to settle many old and troublesome accounts. In spite of slackening popular interest in his fiction after his interlude in the theatre, James was still capable of demanding and receiving comparatively high royalty advances on the future sales of his work. But by the time the Edition was in preparation, not a few of his titles had failed to recoup their publishers' speculative generosity. For these books to appear in a new and uniquely attractive format would only diminish their already slim chance for profitability. James and Pinker had to confront this obstacle even before the novelist returned to England after his successful American tour of 1904–5, during which his agent had begun serious planning for the Edition with Scribner's.

Skeptical from the start about the financial prospects for the Edition, Scribner and Burlingame reminded Pinker of the difficulties engendered by the competing interests of James's scattered publishers. Pinker tried to convince Scribner and Burlingame that for a writer of James's stature, the cooperation of his other publishers would be assured. Nevertheless, James felt compelled to apologize for his agent's embarrassment:

> Let me only say meanwhile how sorry I am for the up-hill moments, in New York, that you found yourself again comdemned to. You will tell me more about them, and I shall feel but the more obliged to you for having successfully dealt with them. I shall write to [Colonel George B. M.] Harvey [president of Harper and Brothers] as you suggest, making our situation in respect to the Scribners a perfectly definite obligation (in the premises).[20]

James could exert some pressure on Harvey, with whom he had negotiated good terms for a "Book of Impressions" and a projected novel about American life, by making his firm's cooperation with Scribner's a prerequisite ("a perfectly definite obligation") for prompt delivery of the serial installments that would make up *The American Scene.*[21] To maintain friendly relations with James, Harvey was decidedly accommodating. Even though advances on *The Private Life* (1893) and *The Wheel of Time* (1893) had not yet been recovered, the firm granted James complete freedom to incorporate in the Edition any of his titles on its list.[22]

Macmillan of New York, however, put a price on such freedom. Despite the popularity of such stories as "The Figure in the Carpet" and "The Real Right Thing," the volumes in which they were republished—*Embarrassments* (1896) and *The Soft Side* (1900)—had not returned the sums that George P. Brett, Macmillan's president, had advanced to James. Sales of James's earlier books—as far back as *The Bostonians* (1886)—had also been disappointing. The civility of Brett's response to Pinker's query did not conceal the red ink on the bottom line:

> In reply to your esteemed inquiry we may say that we shall be glad to allow Mr. Henry James to use any part, or the whole, of any material of his that we publish in a uniform collected edition of his works to be published by the Messrs. Charles Scribner's Sons, and to be sold in this country in sets by subscription only, provided that he will pay us the sum of one hundred pounds (£100) at this time. We are glad to meet your wishes in this matter in this way and have put our price at the sum named because it represents the loss to us on our ledgers up to this time on our publication of these works by Mr. James.[23]

Pinker went so far as to suggest that Scribner's assume this cost, and a bill was promptly tendered; but the firm balked at the outright payment of such a large sum (almost $500) before James had even submitted an exact list of the titles he wished to include. Even more troubling, however, was the fact that such payment was contrary to the terms already discussed with Pinker: for those volumes of the Edition containing works whose copyrights were held by Macmillan, James was to receive a modestly increased royalty to help compensate him for the steep permissions fee. This royalty compromise was eventually written into the formal agreement with Scribner's, but the arrangements for the Edition would entail many more "up-hill moments" for James and his agent before it emerged from the press.[24]

Within three months Houghton, Mifflin & Company, James's only other important American publisher, threw a wrench in the gears. For the volumes to which they held legal claim—virtually all the early novels up to *The Portrait of a Lady,* as well as several collections of short stories, *The Tragic Muse,* and *The Spoils of Poynton*—Houghton, Mifflin insisted that all presswork and binding be subcontracted to the Riverside Press in Cambridge and that the stereotype plates remain Houghton, Mifflin's property. Their decision was based on a good Yankee principle—"that the plates of any book on which we hold the publishing rights for the term of copyright shall be made by us, and shall remain in our possession, and that all copies printed and bound therefrom shall be manufactured by us"—but even sober principle could be augmented by wounded pride.[25] Houghton, Mifflin had been hurt by James's defection to other American houses, who had shamelessly ignored the unwritten policy of trade courtesy that was intended to govern the relations between authors and publishers. Harper's and Macmillan's concessions notwithstanding, the Boston firm intended to punish James for the sake of example: "We believe," they told Scribner's,

> that you feel no less strongly than we the desirability, both from the author's and the publisher's standpoint, that the books of a productive author should be kept under one imprint, and that the method inaugurated by literary brokers of pitting one house against another and selling their client to the highest bidder is not one to be encouraged. But we have noticed that authors who thus seek to collect their works after they have been issued by four or five different houses are surprised that there can be any difficulties or obstacles in the way, and have given no thought to the plates and stock in which the publisher has invested. The principle for which we have contended in such cases is that the publisher who has contracted for the sale of an author's works for the full term of copyright should have also the sole right of manufacturing the books whether for himself or for issue under another imprint, and if he is prepared to make the book in the style and on the lines proposed by the publisher of the uniform edition, it seems to us that he has done all that can reasonably be expected.[26]

In the face of such stern opposition, which necessarily would drive the cost of production beyond what the firm could bear, Scribner's decided to scrap the Edition. As Charles Scribner explained to Pinker, his company had just invested a vast amount of capital in a large manufacturing plant, and to send the presswork elsewhere would be ruinous: "These conditions are for us so unfavorable to the enterprise that we hardly see how we can undertake it. We fear that this will cause disappointment to Mr. James and yourself and the result is unexpected to us, but as you know we have never looked upon the proposed publication as one likely to prove very profitable and were prepared to take it up upon the most favorable conditions only."[27]

James and Pinker, immediately taking action to salvage the affair, sped proposals and appeals to George H. Mifflin, the senior executive of the Boston firm. Within a month Pinker had negotiated a compromise that granted Houghton, Mifflin the right to manufacture for three years the volumes of the Edition to which they held copyright. In addition, Scribner's agreed to pay Houghton, Mifflin a royalty of 5 percent on the retail price of each volume sold by them. To compensate Scribner's for the additional expense of these volumes, James accepted a reduced royalty of 7½ percent on most of the titles controlled by Houghton, Mifflin.[28]

Descent into the marketplace indeed! Even before the formal plan of the Edition was conceived, the fruit of James's best intentions had almost withered on the vine. His final harvest, still to be gathered, was certainly affected by the market forces at work around him.

That the plan of the Edition was still tentative in April 1906 is suggested by the phrasing of the written accord between Houghton, Mifflin and Scribner's. According to that agreement, no royalty was payable "on such few short stories as may be included in the same volume with stories issued by other publishers." But royalties to Houghton, Mifflin would accrue on:

> *The American*
> *The Europeans*
> *The Portrait of a Lady*
> *The Siege of London*
> ["The Siege of London," "The Pension Beaurepas," and "The Point of View"]
> *Tales of Three Cities*
> ["The Impressions of a Cousin," "Lady Barbarina," and "A New England Winter"]
> *Confidence*[29]

From this document we can see that James had not yet decided which titles he intended quietly to disown. Of his youthful novels, only *Watch and Ward* was clearly ruled out from the start.[30] At the time the agreement was negotiated, *The Europeans* and *Confidence* were conspicuously included as possibilities; therefore, whatever doubts James intrinsically had about them may have been reinforced by the fact that he would receive only modest returns from their inclusion. Because space in the Edition was decidedly limited, the weakest and least profitable titles would have to go.

Among Houghton, Mifflin's property, James revised and included only those works that promised to give the Edition particular appeal. The hours spent rewriting *The Europeans* and *Confidence* would not be remunerative. For *The American* and *The Portrait of a Lady,* however, what James sacrificed in his rate of return he hoped to recoup in sales, especially since he considered his extensive revisions of these novels a distinct marketing advantage. Of the revised *Portrait* he wrote, "I shall have hugely *improved* the book—& I mean not only for myself, but for the public: this is beyond question."[31] When the finished volumes were in his hands, he found them "so charming & enticing that I don't see how tens of thousands of people can help buying [them]. May they *not* help!"[32] Although critics have often regretted the extent to which James meddled with the texts of his early novels—an attitude shared even by Charles Scribner himself—the author clearly thought that the public would prefer a thoroughly revised canon.[33]

Even though the formal memorandum of Houghton, Mifflin's agreement with Scribner's was not dated until 5 April 1906, James was probably familiar with its general provisions from the moment he and his agent intervened to save the Edition during the preceding winter. Pinker's diplomacy was crucial at this stage, and he certainly kept James informed of all legal and technical developments that might affect his client's planning. In drafting their agreement, Houghton, Mifflin blatantly ignored *The Tragic Muse* (1890) and *The Spoils of Poynton* (1897) because they believed James's earlier productions to be "among his more successful and most appreciated works."[34] Surely these would be included in any collected edition. But by pushing so aggressively to protect their interest in the earlier titles, Houghton, Mifflin unwittingly gave James good reason to exclude them. Having once come to the brink of losing his chance for the Edition altogether, he needed no reminder of the friction the market could offer. Even with Houghton, Mifflin's concessions, Scribner's potential margin of profit had narrowed considerably. James was anxious to oblige his publishers in keeping costs down: better an abbreviated Edition than no Edition at all.

When Leon Edel analyzed the meaning of the New York Edition's "architecture," he underestimated the constraints James felt from his descent into the marketplace. Discovery of Scribner's prospectus—which announced the set's completion in twenty-three volumes—led Edel to ponder the significance of the Edition's curious size. Despite James's confessed regret over certain omissions "that [were] crowded out by want of space and by the rigour of the 23 vols., and 23 only, which were the condition of my being able to arrange the matter with the Scribners at all," Edel concluded from his search of the Scribner archive that "it was James who determined the scope and the extent of his New York Edition. . . . The 'rigour of the 23 volumes' was his own."[35] Twenty years later in the concluding volume of his biography, Edel asserted that "Scribner's were ready to print all of James's fiction," and that only at the novelist's insistence was the number of volumes confined to twenty-three:

> "I quite adhere," [James] wrote to Scribner's, "to my original idea as to the total number of volumes and as to the number of those for my shorter productions. I regard 23 volumes as sufficient for the series and have no wish to transcend it. I shall make what I wish to 'preserve' fit into the number and only desire to sift and resift, in selection—so as to leave nothing but fine gold!"[36]

James's letter must be read, however, in its proper context. When he wrote to his publishers on 9 May 1906, it was to reassure them that the Edition would not exceed the limit that they had imposed. Robert Herrick surmised this sixty years ago after conversing with James about the Edition's unfortunate omissions. When pressed on the issue, James "emphasized the quality of selectiveness which the new edition was to exemplify: it was to be 'severely-sifted,' and also embellished. 'Indeed,' he said, 'it was only on that condition that I consented to its being undertaken at all.'" But Herrick could see that the violence of James's reaction betrayed an irritation of his professional pride: "Knowing even in my inexperience of those days something of the ways of publishers with authors whose success is more of esteem than of dollars, I added the necessary grain of salt to this presentation of the situation, in which view I am fortified by discovering among the *Letters* a frank complaint to Howells of the restrictions to which the American publishers were forcing him by confining the New York Edition to twenty-three (ultimately twenty-four) volumes."[37]

James's frank complaint must be taken seriously. As negotiations for the Edition proceeded, the novelist became more hopeful that his initial proposal for sixteen volumes could be expanded. Shrewdly, he had begun with a conservative estimate of his needs. When Scribner's affirmed their serious interest, his demands began to multiply. First, he wanted time and freedom to revise his texts. To this Scribner's eventually consented. Second, he wanted an attractive page, with ample margins and readable type. With copies of Scribner's Outward Bound Edition of Kipling before him, James hoped to improve upon its format. He confided to Pinker, "The margin for revision meanwhile accruing is very welcome to me; and welcome also, I think, the prospect of a size greater than the Kipling. Let us be as great as possible!"[38] A larger page would accommodate a greater number of words, and thereby enhance James's freedom to include more titles within the compass of his limited number of volumes. But when James began to tally his table of contents, his ambitions exceeded Scribner's expectations.

James's agent had written to Macmillan in the summer of 1905 that the proposed Edition would not run to more than sixteen volumes. In all likelihood this was the number first discussed with Scribner's, but it seems that the firm was willing to increase the total to eighteen. From the beginning James seems to have envisioned that he would need eight volumes for his shorter novels and tales. Another eight would yield the carefully balanced sixteen suggested to Macmillan; but this plan also would have necessitated the omission of many important works. The arrangement with Scribner's presumably would have accommodated the ten major novels—

Roderick Hudson
The American
The Portrait of a Lady
The Bostonians
The Princess Casamassima
The Tragic Muse
The Awkward Age
The Ambassadors
The Wings of the Dove
The Golden Bowl

—and left four volumes each, as James requested, for the shorter novels and tales.

When James's preferences with respect to page styling and design were taken into account, however, the size of the Edition ballooned. With comfortable margins and attractive type, all those hefty Victorian triple-deckers burst the seams of a one-volume format. Scribner's response to James deserves to be quoted at length.

> We have gone very carefully into the various conditions affecting the selection of a type-page for the subscription edition of your works. It has been difficult to secure a page which would meet the varied requirements, but after a number of trials we have decided upon one of the same type as the enclosed sample, but the page itself [is] slightly larger, being one line longer and one *m* wider. We have had before us your original memorandum sent through Mr. Pinker and, having in mind the fact that you have expressed a preference for a page somewhat similar to that used in our edition of Mr. Kipling's works, have selected a type which, though not quite as large as that used in the Kipling set, is very similar.
>
> We also enclose a memorandum showing the approximate number of words in each novel. You will see from this that it would be impossible to put the longer novels in a single volume and we have accordingly divided six of these, as indicated on the memorandum, into two volumes each. Under this arrangement the largest volume will be RODERICK HUDSON (about 150,000 words) and the shortest will be Volumes I & II of THE AMBASSADORS (about 83,000 words). With the use of the proposed page we estimate that the former

will make approximately 550 pages and the latter 300 pages. Though this difference in size is very considerable, these are the extremes and we can make the thickness of the volumes very nearly the same. Under this arrangement, and with the four volumes proposed by you to include the shorter novels and the four volumes to include the short stories, the total number of volumes will be 23. *This is in excess of what was proposed* and we think it will be better not to consider at present the including of THE BOSTONIANS. This can be taken up at any time later if it seems desirable.

We should like to have your assurance that, as the set has developed, you have adhered to your original proposal as to the number of volumes of shorter novels and short stories, and we would also ask you to let us know the approximate number of words in these volumes in order that we may be sure that they do not introduce any new feature which will disturb the arrangement. We should add that our expectation is that these volumes will not be longer than the average of the volumes already before us.

[To which the following memorandum was attached:]

THE GOLDEN BOWL	212,000 [words]	
THE WINGS OF THE DOVE	186,000	
THE AMBASSADORS	166,000	
THE TRAGIC MUSE	212,000	
PORTRAIT OF A LADY	229,000	
PRINCESS CASAMASSIMA	224,000	
2 volumes each		12 volumes
RODERICK HUDSON	150,000	
THE AWKWARD AGE	130,500	
THE AMERICAN	145,000	
1 volume each		3 volumes
Four Volumes Shorter Novels	?	
1 volume each		4 volumes
Four Volumes Short Stories	?	
1 volume each		4 volumes
		Total 23 volumes[39]

Now the meaning of James's critical letter becomes clear. The resulting twenty-three volumes were "in excess of what was proposed," and Scribner's wanted James's strict assurance that the eight volumes reserved for his shorter novels and tales would not be transcended. James felt the implicit anxiety in Scribner's letter, and his response was calculated to mollify it: "I regard 23 volumes as sufficient for the series & have no wish to transcend it. I shall *make* what I wish to 'preserve' fit into the number . . . [and] am quite content, in fact much relieved, to postpone the question of the *Bostonians* for the present."[40]

Read in its proper context, James's letter is almost an apology for the prodigality of his genius. When he says, for example, "I quite adhere to my original idea as to the total number of volumes and as to the number of those for my shorter productions," he simply reiterates his desire to keep the size of the Edition within manageable bounds. His "original idea as to the total number of volumes" was for considerably fewer than twenty-three; but now that the limit was obligingly extended, he would respect it unfailingly. As James shortly wrote to Pinker, "I have engaged to keep down the 8 vols. of the shorter fictions to 120,000 words. This will necessitate marked and invidious omissions, but it is inevitable."[41] The rigor of the twenty-three volumes was not his alone.

Not surprisingly, James was privately pleased about the Edition's expanded size. Twenty-three volumes did seem "a fairly blatant array," he boasted to Howells; and the liberal dimensions of page and type made for a handsome and charming series, abating nothing of "the *dignity* of aspect which was, for this presentment of my books, my dream & desire."[42] If a twist of fate had pushed the scope of the Edition to Balzacian magnitude, James could accept fate cheerfully. Whether he actually noticed the coincidental parallel with the *Comédie Humaine* is more difficult to say.

Even with the enlarged size of the Edition, James still had to be selective in his editorial judgments. But when the novelist had to make specific decisions about the order and arrangement of the twenty-three volumes, he remained open to outside suggestions. Most striking is his surrender of *The Bostonians.* Already somewhat exhausted from the extensive working of his other early novels, James could set that book aside without much regret when Scribner's requested its deletion. He told Edmund Gosse many years later that revising it "loomed peculiarly formidable and time-consuming (for intrinsic reasons), and as other things were more pressing and more promptly feasible I allowed it to stand over—with the best intentions, and also in company with a small number more of provisional omissions."[43]

At other times James was so eager to accommodate his publisher's wishes that the Edition began to resemble a kind of Push-Me-Pull-U. For example, when Scribner's announced in their prospectus that all the long novels were to be issued without interruption, thus comprising volumes I to XV of the Edition, James happily accepted a marked deviation from his original intentions: "I see your Prospectus . . . announces the later Long Novels as publishable directly after The Awkward Age—making this succession, in other words, uninterrupted by any volume of Shorter Things. This I hadn't quite understood to be your view; but, on consideration, I am entirely ready to make it my own—I in fact seem to see it as so much better an arrangement (to make a sequence of all the regular Novels together) that I wonder I had taken anything else for granted."[44] The situation became almost comic, however, when Scribner's discovered James's willingness to shift ground. The prospectus had been drafted in error, W. C. Brownell quickly wrote back, "our own notion from the first having been that the chronological order of your writings was more important to preserve them than any artificial arrangement based upon their comparative length. We very much hope that your ready adoption of what was really our error is not so complete as to make you unwilling to return to our original and unchanged opinion."[45] So James returned to the original outline upon which both parties had agreed. But the entire episode demonstrates how responsive James could be to his publisher's suggestions as the Edition took shape.

Even more revealing, however, was the novelist's initial reaction to Scribner's insistence on having suitable subjects for the Edition's frontispieces. James trembled as he wrote to Pinker:

> I recoil with terror from the enterprise of first finding and then causing to be consummately captured the twenty subjects (and all having to be photographic!) for the rest of the series. [Two had already been arranged, in addition to the photograph of James that would grace the first volume of the series.] When it comes to the volumes of short tales, and to the various little fictions the scene of which is laid abroad, this preliminary *find* of the right, the representative or symbolic, scene or object, really looms so monstrous, that I am hoping our friends won't insist on it, or else take it into their own hands. If they could get one really artistic and charming figure-piece for each book, I would resign myself; but it's not for me to say whom they can get it *from*—in any form above the mere usual magazine average, or even maximum: which wouldn't be good enough. I'm accordingly praying they may become discouraged. Have you any encouragement to counteract my alarm?[46]

Pinker's response reanimated and inspired James, and the zeal with which he later accompanied Alvin Langdon Coburn on his quest for each "marvel of an accidental rightness" is well known.[47] Friction with the market, at first a discomfort, ultimately kindled the fire of James's artistic imagination.

With major revision of the early novels behind him, his prefaces gradually taking shape, and the ingenious young Coburn handling the frontispieces, James was left with the Herculean task of sifting and resifting his shorter novels and tales and arranging them in the eight remaining volumes. The first four (volumes X to XIII of the Edition) fell together without much effort; the others proved more taxing. The critical factor was space, since each volume could accommodate only a set number of words, but estimating a revised story's length from typescript was difficult. Publisher's arithmetic and artistic intention would not always square. In giving a tentative table of contents to Scribner's, James reminded them that:

> the composition of each of these Volumes of different pieces has been very difficult to arrive at neatly and rightly; since I have had as much as possible

> to take account of precedence by *length,* of congruity of subject and tone, that is of classification, and also in a general way of chronology, (*rigid* time-order absolutely defeated by other necessary adjustments), and yet make the individual volume attractive, and make, above all, these combinations of things square and fit with the appointed number of words (for each volume.) This to explain some collocations, some oddities of order, that you may not immediately understand. I have had to do, with much trying and transposing, what is *on the whole* best—to make the "choice of evils" presenting fewest objections.[48]

When problems arose as the stories were set up in type, James reiterated his plea for patience and understanding; to choose, regrettably among "evils," was painfully difficult. "My inevitable exclusions and omissions, from the whole array," he told Scribner's, "are already costing me some few pangs."[49] But the cutting of stories and reconstitution of volumes continued.

How complex this process became for James can be seen from the following lists that trace the evolution of his design for each volume from its inception through publication.[50] Despite an abiding concern for the Edition's "architecture," James clearly had no preconceived notions about its ultimate arrangement. Stories were shuffled and reshuffled according to his often conflicting criteria of length, thematic classification, chronology, and "the illustration-question."[51] The original tables of contents show what James would have included had space been available. Titles in brackets are stories that did not figure in any of the published volumes; those followed by asterisks eventually migrated to different books in the series.

VOLUME XIII

26 February 1908

The Reverberator
Madame de Mauves
A Passionate Pilgrim
The Madonna of the Future
The Author of 'Beltraffio'*
Louisa Pallant

20 June 1908 and Publication

The Reverberator
Madame de Mauves
A Passionate Pilgrim
The Madonna of the Future
Louisa Pallant

VOLUME XIV

26 February 1908

Lady Barbarina
The Siege of London
Miss Gunton of Poughkeepsie*
Fordham Castle*
An International Episode
Pandora*
The Point of View
A Bundle of Letters
The Pension Beaurepas
[A New England Winter]
'Europe'*

20 July 1908

Lady Barbarina
The Siege of London
An International Episode
The Pension Beaurepas
A Bundle of Letters
The Point of View
Miss Gunton of Poughkeepsie*
'Europe'*

23 October 1908 and Publication

Lady Barbarina
The Siege of London
An International Episode
The Pension Beaurepas
A Bundle of Letters
The Point of View

VOLUME XV

26 February 1908

The Lesson of the Master
The Next Time
The Figure in the Carpet
The Coxon Fund
The Death of the Lion
The Middle Years*
Greville Fane*
The Story in It*
The Tree of Knowledge*
Broken Wings*
The Abasement of the Northmores*
The Great Good Place*

14 July 1908

The Lesson of the Master
The Death of the Lion
The Figure in the Carpet
The Next Time
The Coxon Fund
The Middle Years*
Greville Fane*
The Author of 'Beltraffio'*
Broken Wings*
The Abasement of the Northmores*
The Great Good Place*

Publication

The Lesson of the Master
The Death of the Lion
The Next Time
The Figure in the Carpet
The Coxon Fund

VOLUME XVI

26 February 1908

The Altar of the Dead*
The Beast in the Jungle*
The Birthplace*
The Jolly Corner*
The Way It Came [retitled The Friends of the Friends]*
The Real Right Thing*
The Private Life*
Owen Wingrave*
The Beldonald Holbein*
Flickerbridge*
Four Meetings

Publication

The Author of Beltraffio
The Middle Years
Greville Fane
Broken Wings
The Tree of Knowledge
The Abasement of the Northmores
The Great Good Place
Four Meetings
Paste
Europe
Miss Gunton of Poughkeepsie
Fordham Castle

VOLUME XVII

26 February 1908

Daisy Miller*
Julia Bride
[The Papers]
The Real Thing*
Brooksmith*
Paste*
[The Solution]
[The Path of Duty]
[Glasses]
[The Diary of a Man of Fifty]
The Patagonia*

23 October 1908

Daisy Miller*
Pandora*
The Patagonia*
The Marriages*
The Real Thing*
Brooksmith*
Flickerbridge*
The Beldonald Holbein*
The Story in It*
Paste*
'Europe'*
Miss Gunton of Poughkeepsie*
Forham Castle*
Julia Bride

Publication

The Altar of the Dead
The Beast in the Jungle
The Birthplace
The Private Life
Owen Wingrave
The Friends of the Friends
Sir Edmund Orme
The Real Right Thing
The Jolly Corner
Julia Bride

VOLUME XVIII

Publication

Daisy Miller
Pandora
The Patagonia
The Marriages
The Real Thing
Brooksmith
The Beldonald Holbein
The Story in It
Flickerbridge
Mrs. Medwin

In shaping the collective volumes, James's primary artistic goal was to defeat his publisher's natural preference for strict chronology of presentation—an organizing principle that might have been appropriate to a complete reissue of his work but that had little relevance to a selective *édition définitive.* In his preface to *The Spoils of Poynton,* which began the series of grouped stories, James announced that his purpose was "to class [his] reprintable productions as far as possible according to their kinds."[52] The cautious wording here betrays James's loose conception of the shape of future volumes. At the time he wrote this preface, he was still unsure which titles would be "reprintable." Like one of his early serials, which had started on its course while much was still unwritten, or the gridiron plan of the city that lent the series its name, the New York Edition grew and developed in ways that James could neither wholly foresee nor control. If the architecture of the Edition was "well-dissimulated," as Edel claimed, it was partly because James continually revised the blueprint as he went along.[53]

The disparities between James's last announced intentions and the published form of each volume resulted from his ultimate surrender to the frictions of the market. Contrary to Edel's assertion that James was responsible for the final dismemberment and regrouping of the stories, unpublished correspondence reveals that the weary novelist simply collapsed into the arms of his editor, W. C. Brownell. When Brownell wrote to inform James that the Edition's contents were going to spill into a twenty-fourth volume, thus prolonging his labors, the novelist threw in the towel:

> [I] am now resigned to anything (if you will only just let your own responsibility intervene—as to which I give you, as I say, *carte blanche;*) for the sim-

> ple reason that I feel at last, over the whole business of the preparation and putting-through of the Edition, rather completely *spent!* It has cost me a more intense expenditure of diligence and ingenuity than I can well express to you, or than any one but myself can know,—and I fully believe it will quite (eventually!) justify everyone concerned. For the present, however, I am almost as much economically as artistically "spent"—through my way having inevitably been quite continually blocked for producing anything else of any consequence. Thus the sense of being pretty well finished and voided, in connection with it, is strong upon me; and thus—I repeat—I ask you not to fear to make the new subdivision and extension in what may seem to your advised judgment the simplest and most obvious way. My own—with only myself to advise it!—refuses, verily, to give another kick![54]

If another volume and further rearrangement were necessary, Brownell would have to handle these matters by himself.

The published form of the Edition reveals that Brownell's final judgments greatly altered the design of its primary architect. A particularly overcrowded fifteenth volume burst the editorial dikes, and its contents spilled into the sixteenth. Since Coburn's charming frontispiece of the tree-and-fence-lined New England street had already been prepared, "Four Meetings" was still placed in the sixteenth volume, despite the story's incongruous relation to the surplus tales of the literary life. In fact, "Four Meetings" was sandwiched between the overflow from both its neighboring volumes, since the remainder of the reconstituted sixteenth came from James's revised contents for volume XVII. The rest of the series was then pushed ahead into renumbered volumes. Sixteen ("Tales of the Supernatural") became seventeen, with some chronological reshuffling and the rather awkward addition of "Julia Bride." And seventeen, which had always been something of a catchall, became eighteen, although Brownell attempted to correct its formal chronology. When the volume was composed, however, and available space discovered, James resuscitated "Mrs. Medwin," which had not figured in previous calculations, to fill it out. "Rigid time-order" again was defeated, but James at least had the satisfaction of including an otherwise overlooked little masterpiece. By the time the last volume came from the press, the architecture of the New York Edition was as eclectic as that of the city in which it was published.

As James's letter to Brownell pregnantly suggests, his despair about the Edition's organization was aggravated by its apparent failure in the marketplace. In the two years that James devoted to revising his books, writing the prefaces, and tinkering with editorial arrangements, he had produced very little other salable material. Substantial royalty advances on *The American Scene* buoyed his income in 1907, but the following year was lean; what hopes James had were pinned on sales of the Edition, the first two volumes of which had appeared in December 1907 and which were published two at a time between then and July 1909. Knowing that his client was "sensitive on these matters," Pinker secretly wrote to Charles Scribner for help.[55] Anticipating the firm's usual time for settling accounts, Pinker hoped that Scribner's could send him an early remittance from the Edition's royalties. But the initial sale was disappointing. "We never expected a rapid sale," Scribner confessed, "indeed, as you know, we were never too sanguine of a paying sale, but I believe the sale will continue."[56]

When the bad news arrived, a vulnerable Henry James reeled from the blow. "I return you the Scribner's documents," he wrote Pinker, "which have knocked me rather flat—a greater disappointment than I have been prepared for; & after my long & devoted labour a great, I confess, & a bitter grief. I hadn't built *high* hopes—had done everything to keep them down; but feel as if comparatively I have been living in a fool's paradise."[57] Leon Edel published a more confident letter to Pinker, posted three days later, but even here what could be called James's hopeful resignation about the Edition was shadowed by resentment of its apparently endless prerogative on his time: "I am now, as it were, prepared for the worst, and as soon as I can get my [decks] *absolutely* clear (for, like the convolutions of a vast smothering boa-constrictor, such voluminosities of Proof—of the Edition—to be carefully read—still keep rolling in,) that mere fact will by itself considerably relieve me."[58] When the "smothering boa-constrictor" again threatened to tighten its grasp, as twenty-three volumes grew into twenty-four, James broke away completely.

Leaving all future decisions about the Edition's published form to Scribner's, James anxiously turned to new work; he took up his "*own* old pen again—the pen of all [his] old unforgettable efforts and sacred struggles."[59] Those words were written in the darkness that had engulfed him after the fiasco of *Guy Domville,* and the lessons of that failure were not forgotten. When the Edition seemed fated for a similarly poor reception by the public, James renewed his artistic faith by plunging immediately into the novel of American life for which he had contracted with Harvey when the agreement for *The American Scene* was signed. As he confessed wryly to Howells, "I've just had the pleasure of hearing from the Scribners that though the Edition began to appear some 13 or 14 months ago, there is, on the volumes already out, no penny of profit owing me—of that profit to which I had partly been looking to pay my New Year's bills! It will have landed me in Bankruptcy—unless it picks up; for it has prevented my doing any other work whatever; which indeed must now begin."[60] Still confident of his powers, James began to compose his preliminary notes for *The Ivory Tower.* For Henry James, the creative life of the mind could always ease the frictions of the market, if only by absorbing them.

Appendix A
Henry James and the Movement for International Copyright

Although Henry James was deeply committed to improving the material conditions of authorship, he left the "speechifying and palaver" to others. Probably the best example of James's quiet diplomacy was his consistent effort on behalf of an Anglo-American copyright agreement. When a group of American authors led by Brander Matthews and E. C. Stedman gathered in New York in the spring of 1883 to organize the American Copyright League, Henry James was present, though largely inconspicuous. As one observer (Laurence Hutton) later testified,

> Various suggestions were being made when a guest, sitting in a corner of the room by the window, suddenly arose and addressed the assembled authors. He had attracted very little attention, and it was only noticed that he had been absorbed apparently in a book on his lap. The Chairman, not recognising him, turned to me in an inquiring way, and I whispered:
>
> "Mr. Henry James."
>
> Every head was turned in his direction, surprise was on every face, and the scene was as effective as is that in Bulwer's play *Money,* when the entire *dramatis personae* push back their chairs to gaze upon Alfred Evelyn as the unexpected heir of the will.
>
> For ten or fifteen minutes the speaker, known to every man present by his work, unknown in a personal way to most of his hearers, talked of things *à propos* of the matter in hand, in a manner absolutely to the point and carrying great weight. He made as great an impression as a speaker as he had ever made as a writer; and for the first time, after a long residence abroad, he was brought into intimate contact with the men of his own guild in his own country.[1]

As an American residing in London, James could safeguard his work in both England and America, thanks to the more tolerant standards of

British copyright law, while his English friends and confreres were denied a reciprocal privilege in the United States. Always sensitive to the climate of literary opinion, James was fearful of becoming a target for English reprisal; therefore, he deliberately chose not to register copyrights for some of his work (especially nonfiction) that was first published in Great Britain. If piracy resulted, this was a relatively small price to pay for maintaining good relations with English publishers and men of letters. In 1884, for example, "The Art of Fiction" was promptly bound up with Walter Besant's address by the marauding Boston firm of Cupples, Upham & Company; but James was unperturbed. "I lately published an article (The Art of Fiction) in *Longman,*" he told Benjamin Ticknor, "without appending a warning as to the U.S. copyright. But I did this on purpose, as the paper was not a story. I don't like to flaunt that American claim here for anything but stories, & consider that the reproduction (partial or entire) of that article in the U.S. will have done me more good than harm—as it will have advertised my fictions!"[2]

Later in the decade, Robert Underwood Johnson, the secretary of the American Copyright League, asked James for a letter of support that could be read before the League's assembled membership. The novelist gladly accepted the assignment, and, when it was completed, urged Johnson to circulate it as widely as possible:

> I much doubted of the fitness of my letter for public perusal—& yet I can't help wishing that as the only utterance on the subject I have ever had a chance to make (& my position here makes it becoming that I should have uttered *something,* at some time) it should be reproduced or reported somewhere. Could the *Century* ever find a place for it in those miscellaneous last pages?

The *Century* was crowded, but Johnson would find room for James's remarks in the *Critic.* "I . . . rejoice in the thought that they are printed," James confided.[3] As his eloquent letter testified, in London the novelist felt even more acutely the "particular humiliation of seeing the right thing done and not being able to feel that it is *we* who do it—being condemned to feel, on the contrary, that it is we who have refused to do it,—erratically, perversely, and so incongruously that it would be grotesque if it were not lamentable."[4] Johnson also forwarded James's letter to Senator Jonathan Chace, whose legislative efforts (and shrewd parliamentary tactics) were eventually successful in securing passage of a copyright bill in 1891.[5]

In the meantime, however, Senator Chace sponsored a number of unsuccessful measures, each one prematurely hailed by optimistic literati as the instrument of deliverance. A particularly egregious result of this misplaced trust was a lavish banquet sponsored by the Society of Authors in July 1888 to celebrate the anticipated passage of a copyright agreement.

Eminent American authors were to be the guests of honor, and Edmund Gosse pressed his good friend Henry James to attend. James's refusal was motivated by a shrewdly political sense of the Society's ill-timed action. What was there, after all, to celebrate? No legislation had been approved; the Society's leaders had inflated their hopes on empty newspaper rumors and reverberations. "Let me say brutally," James concluded, "and for your private ear, that I don't see how we—the 'American authors'—can accept the generous & ill-judged invitation without making fools of ourselves. . . . My dear Gosse, if such a manifestation takes place *now,* what would be left for the day our national shame is quenched?"[6] His confidence obviously shaken, Gosse immediately informed Walter Besant, the Society's president, that "Henry James has declined our invitation in a letter of 20 pp. in which he vehemently attempts to dissuade us from having the dinner at all. He thinks it impolitic & highly undesirable." The list of honored guests was rapidly diminishing: "If [James Russell] Lowell & H. James abstain," Gosse warned, "the only other remarkable American to be invited is Bret Harte. The rest are bores or mediocrities or both. Do you not think this is very serious?"[7] James tried to prevent Lowell (America's ambassador to the Court of St. James) from "tumbling into a (however well-intentioned) trap for fatuity,"[8] and advised him not to go. Again to Gosse and Besant he repeated his own refusal—this time more apologetically, in case the Society desired an explanation for his absence.[9] Unpersuaded, Besant and Gosse plunged ahead with their plans. The dinner was served; the champagne was poured; and the copyright bill died in committee. As James wryly noted to Robert Louis Stevenson, "The incorporated society of authors (I belong to it, and so do you, I think, but I don't know what it is) gave a dinner the other night to American literati to thank them for praying for international copyright. I carefully forbore to go, thinking the gratulation premature, and I see by this morning's *Times* that the banquetted boon is further off than ever."[10]

The Society's impolitic actions simply confirmed James's deepest and most instinctive feelings about the prospects for developing a meaningful cultural bond between the two countries:

> I feel strongly that in the present state of Anglo-American relations all international *festive* manifestations, all speechifying & palaver, all effusion and intercompliments in the heat of the moment are most short-sighted and dangerous—provocative of inevitable reaction—later-coming irony & acrimony. Such things will never make the least difference—the least real difference—when a strain comes up: whereas other things, the quiet work & the quiet forbearance of individuals, may & does. All that sort of thing seems to me good only for advertising American Exchanges & international newspapers & cables & telephones & other unliterary enterprises. The sweet flower of esteem between country & country can only be crushed by such ponderous machinery. Moreover, we men of letters are the people in the world who have

least need of it; for we have each of us a far more effective instrument of our own for working exquisite & magical results. We have only to go about our business with tact & taste writing better books for perusal *de part & d'autre,* & the trick is played. *That,* it seems to me, will be the only good way, the only way not vulgar & small, of celebrating the establishment of international copyright when it *does* come.

The dearest wish of my heart—it is really what, as a literary man, I live for—is the coming to pass of such relations between the two countries as that the copyright matter shall be but a drop in the deep bucket of their harmony. This is one of the things that will make most in the world for civilization, & the whole programme of my existence (I think I sufficiently show it) is to contribute my mite to such a consummation. I work only for that—as one must work only to work well—in the long run. Nothing at this hour would give me more pleasure than if an intelligent stranger, deigning to cast a glance on my productions, should say that he was mystified—couldn't tell whether they are the work of an American writing about England or of an Englishman writing about America. I think that even *now* such a stranger might be a little mystified & I believe he will be still more so in the future. *That* I should regard as a practical contribution—as success![11]

Appendix B
Henry James's Literary Income

No man but a blockhead ever wrote, except for money.

Samuel Johnson, Boswell's *Life* (1776)

I am getting to perceive that I *can* make money, very considerably, if I only set about it right, and the idea has an undeniable fascination.

Henry James, to his mother, 2 February [1880]

There had always been—let us face it—a suspicion of vulgarity about the Old Master.

Graham Greene, *The Lost Childhood and Other Essays* (1951)

Henry James certainly agreed with Dr. Johnson that only a blockhead would write without pay, but, as in Johnson's case, this dictum characteristically evades the complexities of the artist's motives and offers only a simplified and defensive rationale of his behavior in the marketplace.[1] Almost from the beginning, critics have noticed that money plays an important role in James's work; its role in James's life has remained relatively obscure. Henry Nash Smith has recently complained that an exact computation of James's income has never been published;[2] unfortunately, no exact computation is possible: too many documents have been destroyed (many by the novelist himself). An informed estimate, however, is not beyond the grasp of the literary historian.

Throughout his professional career, James's literary income derived from two principal sources: the sale of serial rights to magazines and earnings from his published books. Accustomed as we are to a literary marketplace in which the best-seller seems to tower above everything else—

so much so that a spate of books assailing the "blockbuster" complex have recently appeared[3]—it is difficult to imagine a time when readers preferred to follow a novel through leisurely installments of a monthly magazine. Nevertheless, this habit prevailed among the Anglo-American public for most of Henry James's productive life.[4] All but a handful of his stories and novels appeared first in magazines, from which he derived the better part of his income. To be sure, blockbusters and best-sellers were written in James's day; indeed, his letters are filled with anguished resentments against them. But by focusing almost exclusively on examples of far-reaching popularity, historians of the book trade have tended to slight the more representative, if less spectacular, careers of writers (like James) who worked diligently and depended on more precarious ventures of the imagination to earn their bread. For these men and women, by far the majority, serialization of their work in English and American periodicals was much more significant, financially, than returns from published volumes.[5] Until very late in the century, most publishers were unwilling to speculate on future sales of a book by advancing lump sums of cash to their authors. Unavoidable delays in the accounting of sales meant that a writer might not receive any return from a book until a year or so after publication. Successful entry into the serial market was the key to his survival.

This fact was certainly no secret to men of letters in the nineteenth century. Publishers themselves testified to it. "It is impossible to make the books of most American authors pay, unless they are first published and acquire recognition through the columns of the magazines," one publisher told a Congressional committee studying the question of international copyright in 1885. "If it were not for that one saving opportunity of the great American magazines, which are now the leading ones of the world and have an international reputation and circulation," he continued, "American authorship would be at a still lower ebb than at present."[6] Indeed, William Dean Howells wondered how earlier American writers (like Hawthorne) managed to survive without a serial market for their work. Howells conceded that some antebellum authors "must have made money by their books," but he doubted "whether any one could have lived, even very simply, upon the money his books brought him. No one could do that now, unless he wrote a book that we could not recognize as a work of literature."[7]

Henry James couldn't, as the record of his earnings amply demonstrates. Excepting the years of his active engagement with the theatre (1893–95), only twice before 1900 did James's income from book sales and advances exceed his receipts from periodicals, and both of these instances were exceptional. In 1882 royalties from sales of *The Portrait of a Lady* were slightly higher than James's income from the magazines, but he produced very little salable work that year owing to the death of his father. And in 1885 his small return from periodicals reflects the fact that he was not paid for the serialization of *The Bostonians,* because of the bankruptcy of his American publisher. After the turn of the century, both English and American publishers more frequently agreed to make sizable advances on future royalties of James's work, but he was still anxious to reap the considerable benefits of serialization whenever possible. Fastidious artist that he was, James nevertheless was willing to carve up even *The Golden Bowl* into acceptable installments, when the prospect of a large return from an American magazine seemed likely:

> I should be delighted indeed that you shld. be able to arrange for the serialization of *The Golden Bowl* [he told James B. Pinker, his literary agent]; it would be a dream of bliss, & I should bless your name forever! But I should have artfully to *divide,* & in some degree heroically *cut* it, for this purpose (it is, alas, too long!) for I shld. wish it to lend itself thereto very completely & perfectly. This would take ten days or a fortnight. The being able to *realize* upon it has become, I am obliged to say, in view of my going to America, a very important thing for me.[8]

The novelist's scissors flew as he made "various heartbreaking excisions" (including "three priceless gems of chapters"), but at the eleventh hour Pinker's negotiations with the *Century* fell through. "Oh, if I could only [have] known in *advance* that this question of serialization wd. come up," James lamented, "I could have arranged so as to capture them to a certainty."[9] Throughout his professional career, the market for serial rights was James's primary concern.

Unfortunately, records of payments to James from magazines are hard to come by. Nevertheless, extrapolation from letters and receipts that have survived does offer a fairly reliable means of estimating James's income from the serial marketplace.

Not surprisingly, explicit documentation is almost nonexistent for the earliest years of James's career. In his *Autobiography,* the novelist describes his elation at receiving a cheque for twelve dollars from the *North American Review* for his first piece of criticism. That was in 1864, but for another nine years the record is virtually silent. Almost all of James's contributions to the magazines have been identified, however; and in most cases their average rates of pay have been determined. For each contribution, a simple multiplication of rate times length yields an admittedly hypothetical, but probably not a grossly inaccurate, figure of James's likely return. Whenever possible, I have measured the length of James's contributions in their original serial formats; fractions of pages have not been rounded. Information about rates of payment has been gathered from a variety of sources and is summarized here.

The North American Review (NAR): Edel reports that the NAR paid James at the rate of $2.50 per page for his early contributions (*Henry*

James, I, 209). This figure has been used in calculations through 1873, when data from the family correspondence suggest that James was receiving a slightly higher rate of $3.33 per page. In the 1860s Charles Eliot Norton, co-editor of the NAR, received $3.00 per page for his contributions,[10] which suggests that James's early rate of $2.50 was decently comparable.

The Atlantic Monthly (AM): Until the success of *The Portrait of a Lady,* the AM paid James its standard rate of $10 per page for his contributions. The price for short stories, regardless of length, was $100. These sums are documented in family correspondence during the early 1870s and have been used to extrapolate payments for earlier contributions. After the *Portrait,* James demanded better terms and the AM paid him $15 per page for all his work. This was the highest rate offered, according to Thomas Bailey Aldrich (who edited the magazine), and was comparable to the top rates of $20 per page at some other American periodicals (*The Century,* for example), owing to the AM's smaller page format.[11]

The Nation (N): After 1873 actual payments for James's contributions can be followed in the magazine's account book (NAB), carefully kept by Wendell Phillips Garrison, and since preserved in the New York Public Library. These extensive records show that James was paid at the rate of $20 per page. This figure has been used to extrapolate his income from earlier contributions, with one exception: for a specially commissioned series of travel sketches ("A European Summer," 1872–73), James received $50 per article regardless of length.[12]

The Galaxy (G): The irregular fortunes of this periodical have been ably traced by Justus R. Pearson, Jr., who reports that $8 per page was its standard rate for contributions.[13] This figure has been used to estimate payments for James's occasional travel writing and criticism. The novelist's letters suggest, however, that (like the *Atlantic*) the *Galaxy* had a piece rate for fiction, though the New York magazine apparently paid more—$150 per story.[14] This amount possibly is generous with respect to James's earliest contributions of fiction in the 1860s; but, in the absence of more reliable information, it has been used to estimate payments for these as well.

References to James's receipts and expenses became much more prominent in the family's correspondence when he began his extensive European travels in the early 1870s and especially after he took up residence in Paris in the winter of 1875–76. While the writer was abroad, James's father handled much of his business with the American magazines, to which he contributed a prodigious number of travel articles, reviews, and occasional short stories. In fact, James wrote much more than his usual serial publishers could handle; consequently, he was forced to diversify and expand his market—first in America and, eventually, in England.

Although James deprecated the vulgarity of the second string of American literary monthlies, he appreciated the comparatively generous rates they paid for his contributions. *Scribner's Monthly,* for example, consistently paid James $150 for short fiction and $250 for each installment of *Confidence. Lippincott's* (L), however, offered the same rate as the *Atlantic:* $10 per page.[15] Only a handful of shorter pieces were placed there from 1877 to 1879.

James established a more lasting relationship with the house of Harper after he gave them "Daisy Miller," which was an overnight success in their cheaply priced Half Hour Series. The Harpers published a variety of magazines, each aimed at a slightly different segment of the reading public. *Harper's Monthly* was the literary flagship, comparable in style and content to the *Atlantic, Scribner's,* or the *Century. Harper's Weekly* was published in tabloid form, its folio-size pages grotesquely broken up by profuse illustration. *Harper's Bazar* and *Harper's Young People* were aimed at feminine and juvenile readers, respectively. Frank Luther Mott reports that in the 1870s the Harpers paid for contributions at a standard rate of a penny a word ($8 per page in the *Monthly,* $40 in the oversized *Weekly*); in the 1890s the same rate applied to their more "popular" magazines, but the *Monthly* offered its contributors two cents a word.[16]

Estimating payments from the Harpers is difficult, however, because they often gave certain writers preferential treatment. Surviving records show that James was paid slightly more than a penny a word for his earliest contributions to *Harper's Monthly* in 1879–80. *Washington Square,* for example, earned him $10 per page.[17] Given James's aggressive attitude toward the *Atlantic* after the success of *The Portrait of a Lady,* it seems likely that he also pressured the Harpers for a better scale of pay in the 1880s. I have therefore assumed a comparable rate of $15 per page for his contributions to *Harper's Monthly* and $75 per page for *Harper's Weekly* (HP). The Harpers must have paid him well, for, as James told his brother William in 1894, he made it a rule "not to say 'No'" to them.[18] After 1900, payments from the firm are more explicitly recorded in surviving correspondence.

James's income from these and other magazines is summarized in the tables that follow, together with a list of abbreviations that has been used to simplify references. Entries are identified by the numbers (prefixed by the letter *D*) assigned to them in the third edition of *A Bibliography of Henry James.* The exact amount paid for a contribution is listed only if a source has been found to verify it. Extrapolations from confirmed sources are given in brackets; estimates made without other directly comparable evidence are marked with a single question mark. An entry followed by a double question mark is an admitted guess—these, fortunately, are few in number.

James's earnings from sales and advances on published books have been tabulated from numerous sources, especially publishers' archives and the novelist's unpublished letters and diaries. A certain measure of distortion is inevitable in dealing with publishers' records, because few firms balanced their books in tandem with the calendar year. Houghton Mifflin Company and its predecessors, for example, occasionally inventoried stock in May and November, at other times in April and October; therefore, it is almost impossible to say exactly how many copies of a particular book were sold in a given calendar year. It *is* possible, however, to determine how many copies were sold in a given twelve-month period. Royalty income from each title can then be extrapolated by multiplying the sales figure by James's rate of royalty and the volume's retail price. In the following tables, I have incorporated the results of these calculations into the most proximate calendar group. Thus, James's income from sales tallied in April and October 1880 (i.e., books sold from November 1879 to October 1880) has been added to the total for the calendar year 1880.

In other instances, averages and estimates have had to suffice. Literary historians around the world exhaled a collective sigh of relief when the massive archives of the Macmillan Company were saved from destruction in 1968 and deposited in the British Library. The firm's financial records, however, were not included. Roger Gard apparently had access to them before the transfer to the Library was effected, for he reports that the "Macmillan records show, after 1896, exactly how well James's novels continued to sell. . . . The average annual payment until 1909 (when the records stop) was £12.4.9, the total payment £171.6.8."[19] Unfortunately, Mr. Gard took no more detailed notes from these records,[20] which have since been destroyed. Therefore, I have included his calculated average ($60) in my tabulation of James's income from the English market during each of these years. After 1909, payments from Macmillan are recorded in James's manuscript diaries.

It should be kept in mind that the figures tallied in these tables represent James's *literary* income. His earnings from the family's Syracuse properties, which were considerable, are excluded. (See note 1 to Chapter V.) The amounts indicated are also "net": transactions handled by James's literary agents were subject to a 10 percent commission, which has been subtracted from all appropriate items. Almost no records have survived to document James's dealings with A. P. Watt in the late 1880s and early 1890s; it is therefore impossible to know whether the agent took a cut from James's serial earnings during this period. (Watt did pocket 10 percent [£25] of the sum James received from Macmillan for a five-year lease on English rights to *The Tragic Muse.*) On the other hand, almost all of the details of James's more important relation with James B. Pinker (dating from 1898) are preserved in a remarkable collection of letters in the Beinecke Library at Yale.[21] From these I have gleaned the most explicit information about James's later activity in the literary marketplace.

Despite these reservations and qualifications, I am confident that the totals I have arrived at truthfully represent the overall pattern of James's income from his writing. To be sure, additional research will uncover new evidence and occasionally may supply a definite figure where an approximate one has had to suffice in the present study; but the particular fluctuations revealed by the following data will probably not be much altered.

All figures are given in dollars. In light of recent economic history, it is perhaps difficult to imagine an era in which the international monetary system was not subject to violent dislocations. Throughout James's lifetime, however, the pound sterling was consistently valued at $4.85—the rate I have used for all currency conversions. Indexed for inflation, the annual sums listed would have to be multiplied by a factor of at least eight to arrive at an estimate of the 1986 purchasing power of James's income.[22] By any standard, the Master was decently well off.

Unless otherwise indicated, all unpublished letters cited in the tables are deposited in the Houghton Library. All dates are given as they appear in the original documents; brackets have been added whenever an emendation has been made for the sake of clarity (e.g., dating a letter from its envelope's postmark). Complete bibliographical information for published works is included in the Notes section that follows the tables.

LIST OF ABBREVIATIONS

AJ	Alice James
AM	*Atlantic Monthly* rate
BL	Macmillan Archive, British Library
Edel	Leon Edel, *Henry James,* 5 vols.
FM	Frederick Macmillan
Gal	*Galaxy* rate
HA	*Archives of Harper and Brothers, 1817–1914* (microfilm edition)
HJ	Henry James
HJD	Henry James Diaries, 1909–15 (Harvard)
HJL	*Henry James Letters,* 4 vols.
HJSr	Henry James, Senior
HMC	Houghton, Mifflin & Company
HP	Harper periodical rate
JBP	James B. Pinker
L	*Lippincott's* rate
LC	Manuscript Division, Library of Congress
MLB	Macmillan Letter Books, Macmillan Archive, British Library
Mrs. HJSr	Mrs. Henry James, Senior
N	*Nation* rate
NAB	*Nation* Account Books, Manuscript Division, New York Public Library
NAR	*North American Review* rate
P	Scribner Archive, Firestone Library, Princeton University
PS	Henry James, *Parisian Sketches,* ed. Leon Edel and Ilse Dusoir Lind
T	Payment from Tauchnitz' Library of English and American Authors
UK	English market
US	American market
UVA	Clifton Waller Barrett Collection, Alderman Library, University of Virginia
WJ	William James
Y	Collection of American Literature, Beinecke Rare Book and Manuscript Library, Yale University

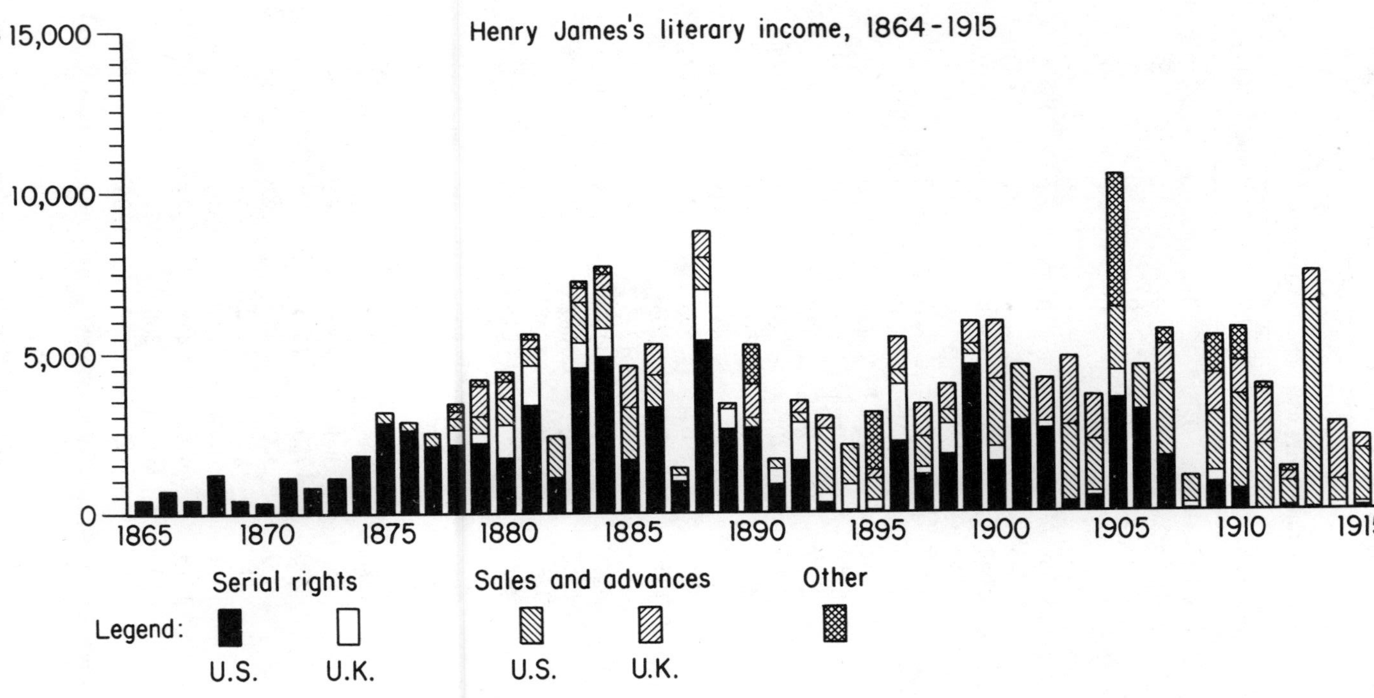
Henry James's literary income, 1864-1915
$ 15,000
10,000
5,000
0
1865
1870
1875
1880
1885
1890
1895
1900
1905
1910
1915
Serial rights
Sales and advances
Other
Legend:
U.S.
U.K.
U.S.
U.K.

Table 1. HENRY JAMES'S LITERARY INCOME, 1864–1915 (in dollars)

	Serial Rights		Sales and Advances			
Year	U.S.	U.K.	U.S.	U.K.	Other	Total
1864	12	0	0	0	0	12
1865	365	0	0	0	0	365
1866	621	0	0	0	0	621
1867	365	0	0	0	0	365
1868	1134	0	0	0	0	1134
1869	350	0	0	0	0	350
1870	265	0	0	0	0	265
1871	1042	0	0	0	0	1042
1872	757	0	0	0	0	757
1873	1035	0	0	0	0	1035
1874	1725	0	0	0	0	1725
1875	2814	0	285	0	0	2644[1]
1876	2579	0	197	0	0	2776
1877	2057	0	385	0	0	2442
1878	2063	520	337	243	194T	3357
1879	2092	370	509	978	194T	4143
1880	1650	1050	835	535	291T	4361
1881	3300	1280	598	250	97T	5525
1882	1055	0	1203	0	97T	2355
1883	4497	800	1275	407	194T	7173
1884	4815	950	1160	485	194T	7604
1885	1550	0	1682[2]	1213	97T	4542
1886	3265	0	1038[3]	970	0	5273
1887	925	150	245	0	0	1320
1888	5330[4]	1607	973[5]	788	0	8698
1889	2550	680	106	0	0	3336
1890	2560	15	315	1091	1213[6]	5194
1891	820	493	266	0	0	1579
1892	1560	1205	293[7]	379	0	3437
1893	250	300	2009	364[8]	0	2923
1894	40	780	1195	0	0	2015
1895	0	320	686	243	1785[9]	3034
1896	2126	1835	434	1030	0	5425
1897	1114	198	987	1030	0	3329
1898	1710	990	438	788	0	3926
1899	4558	345	308	715	0	5926
1900	1512	445	2159	1806	0	5922
1901	2727[10]	90	1668	60	0	4545
1902	2528[11]	20	199	1370	0	4117
1903	225	0	2407[12]	2146	0	4778
1904	437	125	1630	1370	0	3562

Year	Serial Rights U.S.	Serial Rights U.K.	Sales and Advances U.S.	Sales and Advances U.K.	Other	Total
1905	3500[13]	873[14]	1937	60	4050[15]	9520
1906	3100[16]	0	1380	60	0	4540
1907	1600[17]	0	2395	1191	437[18]	5623
1908	0	204	733	60	0	997
1909	777	380	1860	1273[19]	1147[20]	5437
1910	488	97	3012	1075	982[21]	5654
1911	0	0	2005	1762	130[22]	3897
1912	0	102	766	270	109T	1247
1913	0	63	6435[23]	900	0	7398
1914	0	205	664	1766[24]	0	2635
1915	110[25]	110	1612[26]	394	0	2226

[1]HJ paid for the stereotype plates of *Transatlantic Sketches,* and the cost of these ($555) has been subtracted from his gross literary income for 1875.

[2]For books issued by the Macmillan Company in both the United States and England, HJ's advances on royalties have been divided equally between the two countries. Of the sum advanced on *The Bostonians* in 1885, $1212 has been credited to the U.S. column, $1213 to the U.K. column.

[3]Includes one-half ($970) of Macmillan's advance on *The Princess Casamassima.*

[4]Includes $2200 advanced by Houghton, Mifflin & Company on serial rights to *The Tragic Muse.*

[5]Includes one-half ($788) of Macmillan's collective advance on *Partial Portraits, The Reverberator, The Aspern Papers, A London Life,* and a projected volume of short stories (*The Lesson of the Master,* 1892).

[6]Royalties earned by the dramatic production of *The American.*

[7]Includes one-half ($121) of Macmillan's advance on *The Real Thing.*

[8]Represents one-half of the Harpers' advance on *The Private Life* and *Essays in London and Elsewhere,* which were distributed in England by James R. Osgood, McIlvaine & Co., a Harper affiliate.

[9]Includes $485 forfeited by the actress Ellen Terry on the dramatic rights to *Covering End* and $1300 in royalties earned by the production of *Guy Domville.*

[10]Includes one-half ($2182) of the Harpers' payment for serial rights to *The Ambassadors,* published in the *North American Review* in 1903.

[11]Includes the remaining half ($2183) of the Harpers' payment for serial rights to *The Ambassadors.*

[12]Includes one-half ($606) of William Blackwood's payment for the copyright in the first 7000 copies of *William Wetmore Story and His Friends,* which was distributed in the United States by Houghton, Mifflin.

[13]Includes advance payment of $1400 for serial rights to four installments of *The American Scene* that appeared in *Harper's Magazine* in 1906.

[14]Represents Chapman & Hall's payment for serial rights to *The American Scene,* four installments of which appeared in the *Fortnightly Review* in 1906.

[15]Fees from HJ's American lecture tour.

[16]Includes the Harpers' payment of $450 for serial rights to "Julia Bride," which was not published in *Harper's Magazine* until 1908.
[17]Includes the Harpers' payment of $350 for serial rights to the chapter from *The American Scene* on "Charleston" (never published in a Harper periodical), and $350 for HJ's contribution to *The Whole Family*, which appeared in *Harper's Bazar* in 1908.
[18]Royalties advanced on English dramatic rights to *The High Bid.*
[19]Includes $485 paid by William Heinemann as half-profits on *A Little Tour in France* (1900) and *English Hours* (1905), and $655 advanced by Thomas Nelson on royalties of his reprint of *The American.*
[20]Includes $273 in royalties earned by the English production of *The High Bid*, $437 forfeited on the American rights to the same play, and $437 advanced on English dramatic rights to *The Other House*, which was never produced.
[21]Includes $109 paid by Tauchnitz for foreign rights to *The Finer Grain*, and $873 in royalties advanced on English dramatic rights to *The Outcry*, which was never produced.
[22]Royalties earned by the English production of *The Saloon.*
[23]Includes one-half ($3600) of an advance from Charles Scribner's Sons for an American novel still to be written by HJ. The money was funneled through the publisher by Edith Wharton, who wanted to relieve HJ's persistent anxiety about his financial affairs. The other half was to be paid on delivery of the manuscript, but HJ did not live to complete it.
[24]Includes $873 paid by J. M. Dent in exchange for a seven-year lease on the copyright to *Notes on Novelists.*
[25]Payment for the serial rights to "Mr. & Mrs. James T. Fields" has been divided between both countries.
[26]Includes $1125 advanced by Charles Scribner's Sons on royalties for *Notes on Novelists*, published in 1914.

Table 2. HENRY JAMES'S INCOME FROM PERIODICALS, 1864–1915 (in dollars)

Entry	Amount	Notes
1864		
D1	[gratis??]	
D2	12	HJ, *Autobiography*
1865		
D3	[40]	NAR (D3–5)
D4		
D5		
D6	[100]	AM
D7	[18]	NAR
D8	[23]	NAR (D8–9)
D9		
D10	[25]	N
D11	[25]	N
D12	[16]	N
D13	[20]	N
D14	[7]	NAR

Entry	Amount	Notes
D15	[24]	N
D16	[23]	N
D17	[20]	N
D18	[24]	N
1866		
D19	[20]	N
D20	[18]	N
D21	[17]	N
D22	[100]	AM (story)
D23	[18]	N
D24	[20]	N
D25	[16]	N
D26	[15]	N
D27	[20]	NAR
D28	[32]	N
D29	[150]	Gal (story)
D30	[25]	N
D31	[25]	N
D32	[120]	AM
D33	[25]	N
1867		
D34	[100]	AM (story)
D35	[25]	N
D36	[6]	NAR
D37	[100]	AM (story)
D38	[24]	N
D39	[24]	N
D40	[10]	NAR
D41	[16]	N
D42	[20]	N
D43	[20]	N
D44	[20]	N
1868		
D45	[150]	Gal (story)
D46	[9]	NAR
D47	[30]	N
D48	[35]	N
D49	[100]	AM (story)
D50	[100]	AM (story)
D51	[19]	NAR
D52	[25]	N

Table 2. HENRY JAMES'S INCOME FROM PERIODICALS, 1864–1915

Entry	Amount	Notes
D53	[150]	Gal (story)
D54	[20]	N
D55	[20]	N
D56	[100]	AM (story)
D57	[150]	Gal (story)
D58	[14]	NAR
D59	[8]	NAR
D60	[35]	N
D61	[25]	N
D62	[25]	N
D63	[25]	N
D64	[39]	NAR
D65	[30]	N
D66	[25]	N
1869		
D67	[100?]	Gal (play)
D68	[150]	Gal (story)
D69	[100]	AM (story)
1870		
D70	[25]	AM
D71	[42]	N
D72	[25]	N
D73	[20]	AM
D74	[15]	N
D75	[38]	N
D76	[100]	AM (story)
1871		
D77	[100]	AM (story)
D78	[gratis?]	Charity
D79	[500?]	AM (serial in 5 installments)
D80	[30]	AM
D81	[150]	Gal (story)
D82	[42]	N
D83	[40]	N
D84	[30]	AM
D85	[150]	Gal (story)
1872		
D86	[100?]	AM (play)
D87	[32]	AM

(in dollars) (*Continued*)

Entry	Amount	Notes
D88	[40]	N
D89	[10]	N
D90	[15]	AM
D91	[25]	AM
D92	[30]	N
D93	[40]	AM
D94	[65]	AM
D95	50	HJ to Mrs. HJSr, 28 Feb. [1873] (D95–100, D108)
D96	50	
D97	50	
D98	50	
D99	50	
D100	50	
D101	[100]	AM (story)
1873		
D102	60	HJL, 1:378
D103	75	HJSr to HJ, 18 March [1873] (D103–5)
D104		
D105		
D106	[100]	AM (story)
D107	30	Mrs. HJSr to HJ, 1 April [1873]
D108	50	See D95
D109	65	Mrs. HJSr to HJ, 27 April [1873]
D110	[150]	HJL, 1:378
D111	[40]	N
D112	100	Mrs. HJSr to HJ, 25 May [1873] (D112–13)
D113	60	
D114	40	NAB
D115	25	Aziz, *Tales of Henry James,* 2:xlv
D116	40	NAB
D117	30	NAB
D118	75	HJL, 1:411
D119	[95]	AM
1874		
D120	30	NAB
D121	[100]	HJL, 1:378
D122	[10?]	Extrapolated from D140
D123	[70]	AM
D124	[300?]	Gal (story, 2 installments)
D125	10	NAB
D126	15	NAB

Table 2. HENRY JAMES'S INCOME FROM PERIODICALS, 1864–1915

Entry	Amount	Notes
D127	65	WJ to HJ, 22 March 1874
D128	[103]	NAR
D129	[15]	See D140
D130	25	NAB
D131	[15]	See D140
D132	[15]	See D140
D133	150	Aziz, *Tales of Henry James,* 2:xlvii
D134	[15]	See D140
D135	[15]	See D140
D136	30	NAB
D137	[60]	AM
D138	25	NAB
D139	[15]	See D140
D140	15	WJ to HJ, 25 June 1874; the *Independent* apparently paid HJ $15 for each of his brief travel sketches
D141	[15]	See D140
D142	[15]	See D140
D143	35	NAB
D144	10	NAB
D145	[150]	Gal (story)
D146	[15]	See D140
D147	30	NAB
D148	30	NAB
D149	25	NAB
D150	[20]	NAR
D151	[18]	NAR
D152	[100]	AM (story)
D153	20	NAB
D154	[37]	AM
D155	12	NAB
D156	[30]	AM
D157	[25]	AM
D158	23	NAB
D159	12	NAB
1875		
D160	[18]	NAR
D161	[23]	NAR
D162	[20]	AM
D163	1200	HJL, 1:437
D164	20	NAB (D164–72)
D165	35	
D166	23	

(in dollars) (*Continued*)

Entry	Amount	Notes
D167	54	(D167–69)
D168		
D169		
D170	20	
D171	43	(D171–72)
D172		
D173	[30]	AM
D174	23	NAB (D174–97)
D175	42	(D175–76)
D176		
D177	22	(D177–78)
D178		
D179	33	(D179–81)
D180		
D181		
D182	22	
D183	22	
D184	22	
D185	22	
D186	16	
D187	8	
D188	7	
D189	30	(D189–91)
D190		
D191		
D192	16	(D192–93)
D193		
D194	33	(D194–95)
D195		
D196	22	(D196–97)
D197		
D198	[72]	Gal
D199	20	NAB (D199–200)
D200		
D201	12	NAB
D202	10	NAB
D203	10	NAB
D204	23	NAB
D205	[150]	Gal (story)
D206	[30]	Gal
D207	7	NAB
D208	10	NAB
D209	12	NAB

Table 2. HENRY JAMES'S INCOME FROM PERIODICALS, 1864–1915

Entry	Amount	Notes
D210	[80]	Gal
D211	10	NAB (D211–12)
D212		
D213	35	NAB
D214	15	NAB
D215	[85]	Gal
D216	23	NAB
D217	10	NAB
D218	15	NAB
D219	[100]	Gal
D220	18	NAB
D221	19	NAB (D221–22)
D222		
D223	125	HJL, 2:16
D224	10	NAB
D225	15	NAB
D226	20	PS
D227	17	NAB
D228	20	PS
D229	25	NAB (D229–31)
D230		
D231		
1876		
D232	10	NAB (D232–33)
D233		
D234	20	PS
D235	41	NAB
D236	18	NAB
D237	20	PS
D238	35	NAB (D238–39)
D239		
D240	20	PS
D241	[120]	Gal
D242	16	NAB
D243	20	PS
D244	20	PS
D245	6	NAB
D246	20	PS
D247	12	NAB
D248	20	PS
D249	15	NAB
D250	[24]	Gal

(in dollars) (*Continued*)

Entry	Amount	Notes
D251	20	PS
D252	18	NAB
D253	20	PS
D254	29	NAB
D255	20	PS
D256	10	NAB
D257	20	PS
D258	20	PS
D259	1350	HJL, 2:22, 31, 51
D260	20	PS
D261	20	PS
D262	9	NAB
D263	14	NAB
D264	20	PS
D265	24	NAB
D266	20	PS
D267	10	NAB
D268	150	Edel, 2:247
D269	20	PS
D270	20	PS
D271	150	Edel, 2:247
D272	3	NAB
D273	6	NAB
D274	6	NAB
D275	100	HJ to HMC, 17 Dec. 1876
D276	23	NAB
D277	20	NAB
1877		
D278	*	Payments from the *Galaxy* in 1877 totaled $1200, according to HJL, 2:155, and are indicated by asterisks in the middle column
D279	9	NAB (D279–83)
D280	7	
D281	23	
D282	30	(D282–83)
D283		
D284	*	
D285	30	NAB (D285–86)
D286		
D287	13	NAB (D287–95)
D288	21	
D289	25	

Table 2. HENRY JAMES'S INCOME FROM PERIODICALS, 1864–1915

Entry	Amount	Notes
D290	38	(D290–91)
D291		
D292	10	(D292–93)
D293		
D294	20	(D294–95)
D295		
D296	*	
D297	24	NAB (D297–300)
D298	10	
D299	38	(D299–300)
D300		
D301	*	
D302	20	NAB (D302–3)
D303		
D304	8	NAB (D304–6)
D305	13	
D306	23	
D307	*	
D308	10	NAB
D309	10	NAB
D310	*	
D311	[100]	L
D312	*	
D313	*	
D314	[80]	L
D315	28	NAB (D315–16)
D316		
D317	9	NAB
D318	[80]	L
D319	*	
D320	150	HJL, 2:130, 155
D321	10	NAB
D322	[20]	L
D323	*	
1878		
D324	[80]	Gal
D325	100	HJ to Mrs. HJSr, 13 Jan. [1878]
D326	24	NAB (D326–28)
D327	22	
D328	10	
D329	[70]	AM
D330	7	NAB

(in dollars) (*Continued*)

Entry	Amount	Notes
D331	7	NAB
D332	[70]	AM
D333	[100]	L
D334	24	NAB
D335	21	NAB (D335–36)
D336		
D337	[220]	HJL, 2:187–88; James's letter suggests that at this time the *Cornhill* paid approximately £1 per page for fiction.
D338	35	NAB (D338–29)
D339		
D340	7	NAB
D341	17	NAB
D342	16	NAB (D342–43)
D343		
D344	1000	HJL, 2:252
D345	[80]	L
D346	150	HJL, 2:130, 155
D347	23	NAB (D347–50)
D348	29	
D349	47	
D350	28	
D351	300	HJL, 2:187–88
D352	13	NAB (D352–63)
D353	40	(D353–57)
D354		
D355		
D356		
D357	6	
D358	43	(D358–59)
D359		
1879		
D360	26	
D361	30	(D361–62)
D362		
D363	27	
D364	[80]	L
D365	[100?]	HJL, 2:215: "I have lately been induced by lucrative offers to write a couple of articles for the *North American Review* . . ."
D366	[100]	AM (story)
D367	24	NAB (D367–69)
D368	28	

Table 2. HENRY JAMES'S INCOME FROM PERIODICALS, 1864–1915

Entry	Amount	Notes
D369	24	
D370	125	From *Harper's;* HJL, 2:226
	170	From *Macmillan's;* HJ to FM, [17 Feb. 1879] (BL)
D371	28	NAB
D372	1500	HJL, 2:225
D373	[200?]	HJ to HJSr, 16 Dec. [1879]: "a handsome reward was offered (& paid)"
1880		
D374	[200?]	See D365
D375	[100?]	See D373
D376	[150?]	Assumes standard American periodical rate of $10 per page
D377	800	From *Harper's Monthly;* Harper Memorandum Book, 5:402 (HA)
	650	From the *Cornhill;* see D337
D378	3500	From the *Atlantic;* HJL, 2:252
	1580	From *Macmillan's;* HJ to FM, 28 Sept. [1879] (BL). When James began *The Portrait of a Lady,* he contracted with *Macmillan's* and the *Atlantic* for a twelve-part serial. He eventually found it impossible to foreshorten the conclusion, however, and asked both magazines for additional space. What editor could refuse? The *Atlantic* probably paid James his established rate of $250 a number for the two extra installments (as it later did when *The Princess Casamassima* exceeded its planned dimensions); Macmillan paid James at a rate of £2 per page for everything beyond the first twelve installments, which were covered by their original payment of £250. The extra pages numbered 38; thus, James received a total of £326 ($1580) for the English serial rights. See HJ to FM, 14 Oct. [1881] (BL): a marginal notation in Macmillan's hand—"19 pp. @ £2 = £38"—confirms the additional payments. The last installment of the *Portrait* (Dec. 1881) was 19 pages long.
1881		
D379	300	R. W. Gilder to R. U. Johnson, 27 March 1880 (Johnson Papers, New York Public Library)
1882		
D380	[90]	AM; after *The Portrait of a Lady* was serialized, HJ commanded a higher than average rate of $15 per page from the *Atlantic.*

(in dollars) (*Continued*)

Entry	Amount	Notes
D381	[165]	AM
D382	[300]	HJ to HJSr, 31 July [1882]: "I have engaged to do considerable work for the [*Century*] for the coming year—it is the best paid thing, & it is tantamount to publishing in England, as [it] has a large circulation here." Gilder paid James $300 for a nonfiction piece the year before (see D379); James received a similar amount in 1888 for an article on London (see D430). It seems likely that $300 was his typical asking price for *Century* work.
D383	500	HJ to James R. Osgood, 8 April 1883 (LC)
1883		
D384	750	HJ to James R. Osgood, 8 April 1883 (LC)
D385	150	HJ to HMC, 2 March 1883
D386	1000	HJ to James R. Osgood, 27 Aug. [1882] (UVA)
D387	[300]	Extrapolated from D382
D388	[300]	Extrapolated from D382
D389	[300]	Extrapolated from D382
D390	[1700]	AM; $1235 was paid in 1883, $465 in 1884: HJ to HMC, 16 June [1883], 7 Feb. & 28 April [1884]
D391	[300]	Extrapolated from D382
D392	[112]	AM
D393	[50??]	
D394	500	Contract between HJ and James R. Osgood, 13 April 1883, (Houghton Mifflin Archive, Harvard)
D395	[300]	Extrapolated from D382
D396	[200]	AM
1884		
D397	[100]	Extrapolated from D400
D398	[50??]	
D399	1000	HJ to James R. Osgood, 29 Jan. 1884 (Duke University)
D400	388	FM to HJ, 14 May 1884, MLB, MS 55417, p. 1280 (BL). To compete with lavishly illustrated American periodicals like the *Century,* the Macmillans launched the *English Illustrated Magazine* and paid higher fees for contributions, slightly under £4 per page in HJ's case.
D401	1150	Charles A. Dana to William Dean Howells, 9 June 1884, in Ballou, *Building of the House,* p. 376
D402	[1500]	Extrapolated from D401, the payment for which was six cents per word
D403	500	See D394

Table 2. HENRY JAMES'S INCOME FROM PERIODICALS, 1864–1915

Entry	Amount	Notes
D404	[97]	Extrapolated from D420
D405	[315]	Extrapolated from D400
1885		
D406	0	James was to receive $4000 from his publisher when the serial run of *The Bostonians* was completed, but James R. Osgood filed for bankruptcy the month prior to its termination in the *Century*, and no payment was ever made.
D407	[150]	AM
D408	4550	AM; HJL, 3:89. The bulk of this ($3150) was paid in 1886.
1886		
D409	[60]	HP
D410	[55]	HP
1887		
D411	[150?]	Extrapolated from D430
D412	[75]	HP
D413	[250]	HP
D414	[100]	HP
D415	[150]	Extrapolated from D419
D416	[50?]	Extrapolated from D430
D417	[gratis]	
1888		
D418	[270]	HP
D419	1000	FM to HJ, 30 Nov. [188]7, MLB, MS 55425, p. 480 (BL). FM agreed to pay HJ a competitive rate of £2.10 per page for fiction.
D420	112	HJL, 3:229, James writes that £1 per page is now the going rate for nonfiction in English periodicals.
D421	[900]	AM
D422	[300]	Extrapolated from D382
D423	[95]	Extrapolated from D420
D424	[300]	Extrapolated from D382
D425	[460]	HP
D426	[900?]	Assumes competitive American periodical rate of $15 per page
D427	[300?]	Extrapolated from D443
D428	364	FM to HJ, 25 May [188]8, MLB MS 55426, p. 608 (BL). Macmillan continued to pay more for HJ's contributions to the firm's illustrated magazine, but the premium rates offered during the first year of its publication were subsequently scaled back.

(in dollars) (*Continued*)

Entry	Amount	Notes
D429	[100]	Extrapolated from D420
D430	300	Paid in 1887; HJ to R. U. Johnson, 11 April 1887
1889		
D431	4950	AM; $2200 was paid in 1888, $2100 in 1889, and $650 in 1890
D432	[250]	Extrapolated from D461
D433	[160]	HP
D434	[80]	Extrapolated from D420
D435	[gratis]	
D436	[40]	HP
D437	[600]	Assumes competitive English periodical rate of £2.10 per page for fiction
D438	[gratis]	
1890		
D439	[150?]	Extrapolated from D430
D440	[15]	Extrapolated from D420
D441	[60]	HP
D442	1700	HJ to Harper and Brothers, 18 Feb. 1890 (Morgan Library)
1891		
D443	243	HJ to JBP, 25 Feb. 1900 (Y)
D444	[25]	Extrapolated from D420
D445	[130]	From *Harper's Weekly;* HP
	[65]	From *Black & White;* extrapolated from D510
D446	[60]	Extrapolated from D420
D447	[300]	AM
D448	[390]	AM
D449	[100]	Extrapolated from D510
1892		
D450	[225]	AM
D451	[30]	Extrapolated from D428
D452	[250]	Extrapolated from D428
D453	[300]	AM
D454	[100]	Extrapolated from D510
D455	[400]	Extrapolated from D419
D456	[65?]	Howells's editorship of *Cosmopolitan* probably ensured that James was paid at least two cents per word for his contributions.
D457	[60]	Extrapolated from D510
D458	[400?]	See D456

Table 2. HENRY JAMES'S INCOME FROM PERIODICALS, 1864–1915

Entry	Amount	Notes
D459	[165]	Extrapolated from D428
D460	[70?]	Assumes a rate competitive with *Black & White*
D461	250	Edward L. Burlingame to HJ, 17 May 1892, Burlingame Letter Books, 14:123 (P)
D462	[320?]	See D456
D463	[130?]	See D460
1893		
D464	[50??]	
D465	[140]	Extrapolated from D419
D466	[110]	Extrapolated from D420
D467	[250]	Extrapolated from D461
1894		
D468	[300?]	Assumes the comparatively generous rate for an English periodical of two cents a word; see HJ to WJ, 28 May 1894: "I haven't sent you 'The Yellow Book'—on purpose; and indeed I have been weeks and weeks receiving a copy of it myself. I say on purpose because although my little tale which ushers it in ('The Death of the Lion') appears to have had, for a thing of mine, an unusual success, I hate too much the horrid aspect and company of the whole publication. And yet I am again to be intimately—conspicuously—associated with the second number. It is for gold and to oblige the worshipful [Henry] Harland (the editor)." HJL, 3:482
D469	[40]	HP
D470	[480?]	See D468
1895		
D471	[320?]	See D468
1896		
D472	[310?]	Assumes the comparatively generous rate for an English periodical of two cents per word; HJ later told Violet Hunt that the editor "published 2 longish things of mine in *Cosmopolis,* [and] paid me decently well for them. . . ." HJ to Violet Hunt, 8 Jan. 1902 (UVA)
D473	[435]	AM
D474	[75]	Extrapolated from D420
D475	[1500]	AM
D476	166	Robert McClure to Stone & Kimball, 10 April 1896 (Univ. of Iowa); HJ to E. L. Godkin, 17 April 1896

(in dollars) (*Continued*)

Entry	Amount	Notes
D477	1450	James, *Letters to an Editor,* p. 6
D478	[25]	HP
1897		
D479	[150?]	See D468
D480	365	From both the *Chap Book* and the *New Review;* see Sidney Kramer, *A History of Stone & Kimball and Herbert S. Stone & Co., With a Bibliography of Their Publications, 1893–1905* (Chicago: Univ. of Chicago Press, 1940), p. 271
D481	[50]	HP (D481–91)
D482	[50]	
D483	[50]	
D484	[50]	
D485	[50]	
D486	[50]	
D487	[50]	
D488	[50]	
D489	[50]	
D490	[230]	
D491	[63]	
D492	[50]	Extrapolated from D495
1898		
D493	[270?]	See D472
D494	[900?]	Assumes the comparatively modest rate for an American periodical of two cents a word. HJ described "The Turn of the Screw" to Howells as "the most abject, down-on-all-fours pot-boiler, pure & simple, that a proud man brought low ever perpetrated. He will do it again & again, too, even for the same scant fee: it's only a question of a chance!" HJ to W. D. Howells, 4 May 1898
D495	50	HJ to W. D. Howells, 4 May 1898
D496	[24]	Extrapolated from D420
D497	[24??]	
D498	50	See D495 (D498–508)
D499	50	
D500	50	
D501	50	
D502	50	
D503	50	
D504	50	
D505	50	
D506	50	

Table 2. HENRY JAMES'S INCOME FROM PERIODICALS, 1864–1915

Entry	Amount	Notes
D507	50	
D508	[50]	
D509	2910	Paid in 1899; Harper Contract Books, 10:274 (HA)
D510	[360?]	From *Collier's Weekly;* extrapolated from D515
	90	From *Black & White;* HJ to JBP, 10 May 1899 (Y). This serial appearance of "The Given Case" is not recorded by *A Bibliography of Henry James,* but the story was published in the issues of 11 & 18 March 1899, pp. 302–4, 334–36, and was illustrated by Lester Ralph. The payment documented in HJ's letter to his agent suggests that he was paid a penny a word for his contribution.
1899		
D511	255	HJ to JBP, 24 July 1899 (Y)
D512	225	Paid in 1898; HJ to JBP, 21 Nov. 1898 (Y)
D513	365	HJ to Edward L. Burlingame, 7 Sept. 1899 (P); to show what his work was commanding from other magazines, HJ told Burlingame that the *North American Review* had recently agreed to purchase four critical papers from him at £75 each.
D514	230	HJ to JBP, 2 Sept. 1899 (Y)
1900		
D515	175	HJ to JBP, 6 July 1899 (Y)
D516	225	Paid in 1898; HJ to JBP, 23 Nov. 1898 (Y)
D517	365	See D513
D518	203	Paid in 1899; Bliss Perry to JBP, 3 & 23 Oct. 1899, HMC Letter Books, 24:558, 682 (Harvard)
D519	[245?]	From *Truth;* extrapolated from HJ to JBP, 27 Feb. 1900 (Y)
	60	From the *Cornhill;* HJ to JBP, 7 June 1900 (Y). The declining fortunes of the magazine (and HJ!) are reflected in its relatively uncompetitive rate of £1 per page for fiction.
D520	270	HJ to JBP, 7 June 1900 (Y)
D521	[225]	Extrapolated from D516
D522	270	Paid in 1899; HJ to JBP, 23 Nov. 1899 (Y)
D523	182	From *Harper's Bazar;* HJ to JBP, 12 April 1900 (Y)
	[65]	From the *Cornhill;* extrapolated from D519
1901		
D524	130	Paid in 1899; HJ to JBP, 26 Oct. 1899 (Y)
D525	365	See D513
D526	320	Paid in 1900; HJ to JBP, 6 Feb. 1900 (Y)

(in dollars) (*Continued*)

Entry	Amount	Notes
D527	275	Paid in 1899; HJ to JBP, 7 Dec. 1899 (Y)
D528	[180]	From the *Critic;* assumes a competitive American periodical rate of $15 per page
	[90]	From the *Cornhill;* extrapolated from D519
D529	gratis	HJ to JBP, 6 Nov. 1901 (Y)
1902		
D530	[40]	From the *Critic;* see D528
	[20]	From the *Cornhill;* extrapolated from D519
D531	225	Paid in 1900; HJ to JBP, 29 Sept. 1900 (Y)
D532	365	See D513
1903		
D533	4365	Half paid in 1901, half in 1902; "Correspondence Relating to Contracts," 1 May 1901 (HA)
D534	[225]	AM
1904		
D535	[125]	Extrapolated from D420
D536	437	HJ to JBP, 12 Dec. 1904 (Y)
1905		
D537	1050	HJ to JBP, 6 March 1905 (Y)
D538	450	HJ to JBP, 7 Aug. 1905 (Y)
D539	250	HJ to Bliss Perry, 23 May 1905
D540	350	*North American Review* to JBP, 3 March 1906 (Berg Collection, New York Public Library)
1906		
D541	175	From the *North American Review;* the magazine divided HJ's article into two installments (D541–42) but paid him as if it were one. HJ to JBP, 9 March 1906 (Y)
	218	From the *Fortnightly Review;* Chapman & Hall paid HJ £180 ($873) for the serial rights to *The American Scene* and eventually published four installments from the book. The total sum has been divided among the appropriate entries.
D542	175	See D541
D543	1050	Paid in 1905; HJ to JBP, 9 Nov. 1905 (Y)
D544	350	From the *North American Review;* HJ to JBP, 9 March 1906 (Y)
	218	From the *Fortnightly Review;* see D541
D545	350	From the *North American Review;* HJ to JBP, 9 March 1906 (Y)

Table 2. HENRY JAMES'S INCOME FROM PERIODICALS, 1864–1915

Entry	Amount	Notes
	218	From the *Fortnightly Review;* see D541
D546	350	HJ to JBP, 10 June 1906 (Y)
D547	350	Paid in 1905; HJ to JBP, 9 Nov. 1905 (Y)
D548	350	HJ to JBP, 10 June 1906 (Y)
D549	218	See D541
D550	900	HJ to JBP, 25 June 1906 (Y)
1907		
D551	900	HJ to JBP, 31 July 1906 (Y)
1908		
D552	450	Paid in 1906; HJ to JBP, 6 Dec. 1906 (Y)
D553	350	Paid in 1907; HJ to JBP, 2 May 1907 (Y)
D554	204	HJ to JBP, 23 Sept. 1908 (Y)
1909		
D555	[50??]	
D556	[147]	Extrapolated from HJD
D557	183	HJ to JBP, 19 Aug. 1909 (Y)
D558	450	HJ to JBP, 18 June 1909 (Y)
D559	327	HJ to JBP, 21 July 1909 (Y)
1910		
D560	270	HJ to Elizabeth Jordan, 2 June & 8 July 1909 (UVA)
D561	97	From the *English Review;* F. Chalmers Dixon to JBP, 31 May 1910 (Berg Collection, New York Public Library)
	218	Paid by *Putnam's Magazine* before it folded (HJD); the story never appeared serially in America.
[No serial publications in 1911]		
1912		
D562	gratis	
D563	[gratis?]	
D564	102	HJD
1913		
D565	63	HJD
1914		
D566	[84]	Extrapolated from D565
D567	121	HJD

(in dollars) (*Continued*)

Entry	Amount	Notes
1915		
D568	gratis	
D569	gratis	
D570	gratis	
D571	220	From both the *Atlantic* and the *Cornhill;* HJD
D572	[gratis?]	
D573	gratis	
D574	gratis	
D575	gratis	
D576	gratis	

Notes

CHAPTER I

1. For a trenchant review of the completed biography, see Millicent Bell, "Henry James: The Man Who Lived," *Massachusetts Review,* 14 (1973), 391–414.
2. A simple listing of secondary sources published as of 1981 fills four volumes. See Linda J. Taylor, *Henry James, 1866–1916: A Reference Guide,* Kristin Pruitt McColgan, *Henry James, 1917–1959: A Reference Guide,* Dorothy McInnis Scura, *Henry James, 1960–1974: A Reference Guide* (Boston: G. K. Hall, 1979–82), and John Budd, *Henry James: A Bibliography of Criticism, 1975–1981* (Westport, Conn.: Greenwood Press, 1983).
3. H[erbert] Butterfield, *The Whig Interpretation of History* (New York: Charles Scribner's Sons, 1951), and "The History of Historiography" in *Man on His Past: The Study of the History of Historical Scholarship* (Cambridge: Cambridge Univ. Press, 1955), pp. 1–31.
4. Henry James, *The Sense of the Past* (London: W. Collins Sons, [1917]), p. 48.
5. Henry James to William Dean Howells, 17 Aug. 1908, *The Letters of Henry James,* 2 vols., ed. Percy Lubbock (New York: Charles Scribner's Sons, 1920), II, 99.
6. Morton Fullerton, "The Art of Henry James," *Quarterly Review,* 212 (April 1910), 393.
7. *The Lesson of the Master,* comp. Simon Nowell-Smith (London: Constable, 1947).
8. Henry James III to Percy Lubbock, 20 May 1919 (Brotherton Collection, Univ. of Leeds).
9. See *Letters of Henry James,* I, 144–45.
10. Percy Lubbock, *The Craft of Fiction* (1921; rpt. London: Jonathan Cape, 1954), p. v.
11. Theodora Bosanquet, *Henry James at Work* (London: The Hogarth Press,

1924), p. 14. Also relevant is her earlier article, "Henry James," *Fortnightly Review,* 107 (June 1917), 995–1009, in which she asserted that James's "fundamental economic independence of his work enabled him to fashion it in the mould he desired, irrespective of the demands of the market" (p. 1008).

12. Henry James to Hendrik Anderson, 6 Aug. 1905, *Henry James Letters,* 4 vols., ed. Leon Edel (Cambridge, Mass.: Belknap-Harvard Univ. Press, 1972–84), IV, 369; and James to Anderson, [18 Oct.] & 25 Nov. 1906 (James Papers, Univ. of Virginia).
13. As a corollary to Butterfield's analysis of trends in historiography, each phase of interpretation often is shadowed by its antithesis: an antiheroic view is developed to counter the heroic, and so forth. Brooks's *The Pilgrimage of Henry James* (New York: E. P. Dutton, 1925), and Parrington's meager two-page obituary of James in his otherwise magisterial *Main Currents in American Thought,* 3 vols. in 1 (New York: Harcourt, Brace, 1930), III, 239–41, are good examples of this phenomenon. Similarly, Maxwell Geismar's *Henry James and Jacobites* (Boston: Houghton Mifflin, 1963) attempted to deflate the interest in James that was sparked by the modernist critics of the succeeding generation.
14. Edmund Wilson, "New Documents on the Jameses," *New Yorker,* 23 (13 Dec. 1947), 133.
15. Leon Edel, *Henry James: The Untried Years, 1843–1870* (Philadelphia: J. B. Lippincott, 1953), pp. 11–12. Other titles in the series are vol. II: *The Conquest of London, 1870–1881;* vol. III: *The Middle Years, 1882–1895;* vol. IV: *The Treacherous Years, 1895–1901;* and vol. V: *The Master, 1901–1916* (Philadelphia: J. B. Lippincott, 1962–72).
16. A typical example of this biographic distortion is Ferner Nuhn's description of James's circumstances at the time he settled in England: "If he was not exactly a visiting prince to his enchanted realm, he was at least a well-provided-for baronet." See *The Wind Blew from the East* (New York: Harper and Brothers, 1942), p. 143.
17. Leon Edel and Dan H. Laurence, *A Bibliography of Henry James* (London: Rupert Hart-Davis, 1957), p. 12. This statement reappears in the new third edition, revised with the assistance of James Rambeau (New York: Oxford Univ. Press, 1982), p. 12.
18. See Leon Edel, *Henry James: The Conquest of London,* pp. 237–45; *Henry James: The Middle Years,* pp. 264–65; and *Henry James: The Treacherous Years,* pp. 72–80.
19. William Charvat, "Literary Economics and Literary History" [1950], in *The Profession of Authorship in America, 1800–1870* ([Columbus]: Ohio State Univ. Press, 1968), pp. 284, 285, 292.
20. See, for example, Richard Nicholas Foley, *Criticism in American Periodicals of the Works of Henry James from 1866 to 1916* (Washington, D.C.: Catholic Univ. of America Press, 1944); Donald M. Murray, "The Critical Reception of Henry James in English Periodicals, 1875–1916," Diss. New York University, 1950; Murray's article, "Henry James and the English Reviewers, 1882–1890," *American Literature,* 24 (March 1952), 1–20; William T. Stafford, "The American Critics of Henry James: 1864–1943," Diss. University of Kentucky, 1956; and Akilah Mohamed El-Metwalli Ramadan, "The

Reception of Henry James's Fiction in the Main English Periodicals Between 1875 and 1890," Diss. University of London, 1960.

21. See Roger Gard, ed., *Henry James: The Critical Heritage* (New York: Barnes & Noble, 1968).
22. Henry Nash Smith, *Democracy and the Novel: Popular Resistance to Classic American Writers* (New York: Oxford Univ. Press, 1978), p. 4. In a sense, Smith simply inverts Brooks's argument about James's presumably failed potential by shifting the burden of responsibility away from the novelist and onto his audience.
23. Henry James, "Dumas the Younger, 1895," in *Notes on Novelists* (New York: Charles Scribner's Sons, 1914), p. 366; and James to Geoffrey Keynes, 29 March 1909, in Keynes's *Henry James in Cambridge* (Cambridge: W. Heffer & Sons, 1967), p. 12.

CHAPTER II

1. Stephen Spender, *The Destructive Element: A Study of Modern Writers and Beliefs* (London: Jonathan Cape, 1935), p. 47.
2. Edith Wharton, *A Backward Glance* (New York: D. Appleton-Century Co., 1934), p. 191.
3. Henry James to William Morton Fullerton, 25 Jan. 1895 (James Papers, Harvard).
4. Henry James, preface to *The Portrait of a Lady,* in *The Art of the Novel,* ed. R. P. Blackmur (New York: Charles Scribner's Sons, 1934), p. 48.
5. Richard Poirier, *The Comic Sense of Henry James* (New York: Oxford Univ. Press, 1960), p. 188. James told his audience at Deerfield, Massachusetts,

> Oh, do something from your point of view; an ounce of example is worth a ton of generalities; do something with the great art and the great form; do something with life. You each have an impression colored by your individual conditions; make that into a picture, a picture framed by your own personal wisdom, your glimpse of the American world. The field is vast for freedom, for study, for observation, for satire, for truth. . . . I have only two little words for the matter remotely approaching to rule or doctrine; one is life and the other freedom. . . . If [the novel] is in a bad way, and the English novel is, I think, nothing but absolute freedom can restore its self-respect.

As Poirier makes clear, "Assertions which tell us that Isabel has 'an immense curiosity about life,' or that, as against Osmond, she pleads 'the cause of freedom,' or other uses of words like 'freedom,' 'liberty,' and 'knowledge' are so frequent in [*The Portrait*] that there is no need to collect them." The full text of James's letter is reprinted in *Henry James Letters,* III, 257–58.

6. Henry James, *Autobiography: A Small Boy and Others, Notes of a Son and Brother,* and *The Middle Years,* ed. F. W. Dupee (New York: Criterion Books, 1956), p. 7.
7. *The Portrait of a Lady* (Boston: Houghton, Mifflin, 1881), p. 19.
8. Ralph Waldo Emerson, *Nature,* in *Selections from Ralph Waldo Emerson,* ed. Stephen E. Whicher (Boston: Houghton Mifflin, 1957), p. 21. Hawthorne explores his professional problem in the 1851 preface to *Twice-Told Tales,*

Vol. IX of the Centenary Edition of the Works of Nathaniel Hawthorne ([Columbus]: Ohio State Univ. Press, 1974), pp. 3–7.

9. The best analysis of these motives in the shaping of James's career is still Alfred R. Ferguson's "The Triple Quest of Henry James: Fame, Art, and Fortune," *American Literature,* 27 (Jan. 1956), 475–98. A largely derivative, and not entirely accurate, survey of James's personal economic situation is also given by Jan W. Dietrichson in *The Image of Money in the American Novel of the Gilded Age* (New York: Humanities Press, 1969), pp. 40–50.
10. Edith Wharton, *A Backward Glance,* p. 366.
11. John Rodenbeck, "The Bolted Door in James's *Portrait of a Lady,*" *Modern Fiction Studies,* 10 (Winter 1964–65), 330–40.
12. Henry James to Charles Eliot Norton, 6 May [1872], *Henry James Letters,* I, 275–76.
13. *The Portrait of a Lady,* p. 375.
14. *The Art of the Novel,* p. 57.
15. Henry James, *Autobiography,* p. 196. In the remainder of this chapter, references to this edition appear parenthetically in the text.
16. Probably most familiar is Edel's wholly speculative reading of the nightmare as a reflection of "the fears and terrors of a 'mere junior' threatened by elders and largely by his elder brother" (*Henry James: The Untried Years,* p. 75), although more recent criticism has dismissed this interpretation as "the least interesting way of understanding James's remarks" (Stephen Donadio, *Nietzsche, Henry James, and the Artistic Will* [New York: Oxford Univ. Press, 1978], p. 257). Millicent Bell also departs from Edel's reading by suggesting that, rather than defying some wholly external agent in the dream, James is confronting some aspect of himself. Taking her cue from "The Jolly Corner," Bell asserts that James is "seeing his own possibilities in the face at last turned towards him—which suggests another set of anxieties altogether" ("Henry James: The Man Who Lived," p. 398). As the title of his book suggests, Donadio reads the dream-adventure as a Nietzschean parable of the will to power, emanating from a writer who, "far from being a man who failed to come to terms with the ordinary life of his own time (as the stereotype of James would have it), is a man actively and unequivocally engaged in what he sees as a continual combat against the disheartening limitations of the actuality he faces daily" (pp. 103–4).
17. After James had delivered "The Lesson of Balzac" to several American audiences during his tour of 1904–5, he boasted to a friend, "meanwhile I am *lecturing* a little to pay the Piper, as I go—for high fees (of course) and as yet but three or four times. But they give me gladly £50 for fifty minutes (a pound a minute—like Patti!)—and always the same lecture. . . . I do it beautifully—feel as if I had discovered my vocation—at any rate amaze myself" (Henry James to Mrs. W. K. Clifford, 21 Feb. [19]05, *Letters of Henry James,* II, 30). Significantly, the thrill of hearing "vast, high-piled auditory thundering applause" was now augmented by the prospect of large financial returns.

    Two weeks later James told his agent that the proceeds from his lecture "boom" were exceeding his wildest dreams:

> They seem positively to *rejoice* to give me *£50* for 50 minutes (20/ a minute,) & Indianapolis gives me on the 16th next *£80* for the same (almost as if I were Patti!) I gave the "Lesson of Balzac" at St. Louis on the 7th, & then . . . *4* times in all at Chicago (to different associations), making £200 for the 4 hours. If I had only known this in advance—that is more about it, & realized that I *can* lecture, very prettily, & could have taken more time to prepare a more popular subject &c.—if I could have done all this I might be doing it to very "big business" indeed. . . . But what greedy talk! However, you will understand! (Henry James to James B. Pinker 6 March 1905 [Collection of American Literature, Yale])

James wrote to another correspondent that he "was positively & preposterously *caressed* by the people" at St. Louis; and in Chicago "the kindness of every one [was] overwhelming; I've sung my little song again twice, & I fairly blush for the consequences. The appetite for culture careers along on the arm of the hunger for millions like a pair [of] mismated fantastics at a Bal de l'Opera" (Henry James to Mrs. [James] Sullivan, 11 March 1905 [James Papers, Morgan Library]).

William Dean Howells, who first proposed the lecture-circuit idea to James as a means of financing his trip to America, confidentially had informed the American sponsors that the novelist "ought to lecture very few times, and *not* on any tours of public vastness." Remembering the fiasco of *Guy Domville* and James's anxiety about personal publicity, Howells urged that "he should read . . . in drawing-rooms, country-club-rooms, and the like, and the audience should be more or less cultivated, and made to feel itself privileged." Howells's reservations were gathered firsthand: this letter was written under James's roof and posted from Rye, Sussex, to Elizabeth Jordan, 1 June 1904 (*Selected Letters,* ed. George Arms et al., 6 vols. [Boston: Twayne Publishers, 1979–83], V, 103). But James's experience the following spring was a triumphant reversal of his earlier intercourse with an audience. The gallery jeered at him in London after *Guy Domville;* in America he was "caressed by the people." Marie P. Harris discusses James's American speaking engagements in her article, "Henry James, Lecturer," *American Literature,* 23 (Nov. 1951), 302–14.

18. Henry James, "The Turning Point of My Life" in Carol Holly's article, "Henry James's Autobiographical Fragment: 'The Turning Point of My Life,'" *Harvard Library Bulletin,* 31 (Winter 1983), 42.
19. Henry James to Mrs. Edward Compton, 15 March [1895]; Henry James to William James, 9 Jan. 1895, *Henry James Letters,* III, 521, 508. See also Edel, *Henry James: The Treacherous Years,* pp. 72–80.
20. Henry James to William James, 23 July 1890, *Henry James Letters,* III, 300.
21. Leon Edel, "Henry James: The Dramatic Years," *The Complete Plays of Henry James* (Philadelphia: J. B. Lippincott, 1949), pp. 43, 51. See also Edel, *Henry James: The Middle Years,* pp. 262–67, 335–40.
22. Henry James to William Dean Howells, 2 Jan. 1888, *Henry James Letters,* III, 209.
23. Henry James to William Dean Howells, 6 May [1878] (Howells Papers, Harvard).
24. Edel, *Henry James: The Middle Years,* p. 40.
25. James's article appeared in the *Atlantic Monthly,* 50 (Aug. 1882), 253–63. The

latter half was reprinted as "London Plays, 1882" in *The Scenic Art,* ed. Alan Wade (New Brunswick, N.J.: Rutgers Univ. Press, 1948), cited here, p. 162.

26. Henry James to Thomas Bailey Aldrich, 1 June [1882] (Aldrich Papers, Harvard).
27. Henry James to Thomas Bailey Aldrich, 22 Aug. [1882] (Aldrich Papers, Harvard).
28. Herbert F. Smith, *Richard Watson Gilder* (New York: Twayne Publishers, 1970), pp. 81–82. Gilder edited the *Century* at this time.
29. Henry James to James R. Osgood, 27 Aug. [1882] (James Papers, Univ. of Virginia). The comparatively high fee James received for the play apparently soured the parsimonious Yankees of Houghton, Mifflin, & Company who published the magazine. When Howells offered one of his dramatic sketches to the *Atlantic* in 1884, Aldrich refused it, remarking that "stories in dramatic form haven't been popular downstairs [i.e., in the business office] since James's Daisy Miller" (Aldrich to Howells, 10 May 1884 [Howells Papers, Harvard]). Houghton, Mifflin's displeasure was revealed to James when they declined to publish his play in book form, an otherwise standard practice for *Atlantic* serials. Thus freed from further obligation to the firm, James offered the book rights to Osgood, who promptly issued *Daisy Miller: A Comedy,* conforming to the author's absolute condition "that it be printed in the manner of the French comedies—that is, with the names of the characters *above* the speeches, & not on a line with them" (James to Osgood, 5 May [1883], *Henry James Letters,* II, 45). James also demanded better terms than Houghton, Mifflin's usual 10 percent royalty, and he signed a sliding-scale contract with Osgood that paid 10 percent royalty on the first 1500 copies and 20 percent thereafter (Ticknor & Co. Costbooks, XIII, 9 [Houghton Mifflin Archive, Harvard]). James's artistic standards in the theatre derived always from the French, but his business instincts were thoroughly American.
30. Entry for 11 Nov. [1882], *The Notebooks of Henry James,* ed. F. O. Matthiessen and Kenneth B. Murdock (New York: Oxford Univ. Press, 1947), p. 44.
31. Henry James to Lawrence Barrett, 11 Aug. [1884], quoted in Edel, *The Complete Plays,* p. 44. James rightly felt that the "descriptive, analytic, [and] psychological" aspects of *The Portrait* rendered it "inconvertible" into dramatic form. As James told Barrett, "These are elements which, to become popular with any English-speaking audience, a drama must possess—as you are no doubt still better aware than I—only in a barely perceptible degree." Still, James felt that his interest in the stage could be revived "in the presence of any prospect of (to put the matter in its homely crudity) pecuniary gain!" James to Barrett, 18 July [1884], *Henry James Letters,* III, 46–47.
32. Henry James to Julian Sturgis, 20 Sept. [1886], quoted in Edel, *The Complete Plays,* p. 44.
33. Henry James to William Dean Howells, 10 Jan. 1891 (Howells Papers, Harvard).
34. Henry James to Alice James and Katherine P. Loring, [4 Jan. 1891], *Henry James Letters,* III, 320. Henry's letter came on the heels of an equally remarkable telegram to Alice: "Unqualified triumphant magnificent success universal congratulations great ovation for author great future for play . . . writing Henry" (idem).

35. Walter Isle, *Experiments in Form: Henry James's Novels, 1896–1901,* (Cambridge, Mass.: Harvard Univ. Press, 1968), p. 34.
36. Cf. Edel, *The Complete Plays,* p. 37.
37. Isle, *Experiments in Form,* p. 34. An unfortunate result of Isle's critical point of view is his conclusion that James's desire for popular success ended after the failure of *Guy Domville.* Other critics, most recently Henry Nash Smith, have tended to echo his interpretation of James's stories of artist-failures (like "The Next Time," conceived and published in the same year as *Guy Domville*) as the novelist's swan-song to the marketplace. Unquestionably, the rejection of James's play chastened his expectations, but his hunger for success (however unsatisfied) persisted until the end of his career.
38. Henry James to William James, 3 Jan. [1891], *Henry James Letters,* III, 317–18.
39. Henry James to Mr. & Mrs. Hugh Bell, 8 Jan. [1891], *Henry James Letters,* III, 323.
40. Henry James to William James, 6 Feb. [1891], *Henry James Letters,* III, 329.
41. Meeting those conditions was largely a matter of confronting the theatre-going public. Quoting the masters of the French drama (to whom James also looked for the benefit of example), Francis Fergusson observes that "The great Sarcey wrote, 'The audience is the necessary and inevitable condition to which dramatic art must accommodate its means. . . . From this simple fact we derive all the laws of the theatre without a single exception.' When James set out to write his comedies he put the problem to himself in exactly these terms: to accept that audience and learn to obey the laws derived from its habits and its taste." See Francis Fergusson, "James's Idea of Dramatic Form," *Kenyon Review,* 5 (1943), 495–96. A useful study that demonstrates the extent to which James revised the texts of his plays to meet the demands of popular taste is Henry Popkin's article, "The Two Theatres of Henry James," *New England Quarterly,* 24 (1951), 69–83. Popkin concludes that

> James's principal motives in revising [*The American*] seem to have been economy (dropping superfluous characters, simplifying introductions), simplifying characterizations (making Madame and Urbain de Bellegarde more villainous, making Noemie Nioche relatively innocuous, making Newman less vigorous), clarifying motivation (giving the Bellegardes a more obvious and baser motive for rejecting Newman, giving Claire a more tangible reason for obeying her mother), introducing sensations (the affair between Madame de Bellegarde and the Count de Cintre), and providing a happy ending (the reunion of the lovers and, in the revised fourth act, Valentin's recovery). These changes are precisely calculated to destroy the peculiar values of the original novel. (pp. 76–77)

42. Henry James to William Morton Fullerton, 2 Jan. 1891 (James Papers, Harvard.
43. Henry James to Mr. & Mrs. William James, [5 Jan. 1895], *Henry James Letters,* III, 507.
44. Henry James to William Morton Fullerton, 9 Jan. 1895, *Henry James Letters,* III, 510.
45. For the details of James's dispute with Daly, see Edel, *Henry James: The Middle Years,* pp. 340–45. James's letters to Daly and Miss Rehan appear in *Henry James Letters,* III, 368–69, 395–96, 444–49.

46. Henry James to William Dean Howells, 7 March 1902 (Howells Papers, Harvard).
47. Henry James to William Dean Howells, 11 Dec. 1902, *Henry James Letters,* IV, 250.
48. Entry for 23 Jan. 1895, *Notebooks,* p. 179.

CHAPTER III

1. Edel, *The Complete Plays,* p. 44.
2. Henry James, "Poor Richard" [1867], in *The Complete Tales of Henry James,* 12 vols., ed. Leon Edel (Philadelphia: J. B. Lippincott, 1961–64), I, 203.
3. Henry James to William Dean Howells, 19 Feb. 1912, *Letters of Henry James,* II, 221–22.
4. James, *Autobiography,* p. 476. In the remainder of this chapter, references to this edition appear parenthetically in the text.
5. Donald L. Mull, *Henry James's 'Sublime Economy': Money as Symbolic Center in the Fiction* (Middletown, Conn.: Wesleyan Univ. Press, 1973), p. 3.
6. Mull, *'Sublime Economy',* pp. 4–5. This imaginative landscape corresponds as well to the scene from *The Portrait of a Lady* in which Isabel carries her books into the "office," a room also suffused with many-hued light, filtering through green-papered windows.
7. Austin Warren, *The Elder Henry James* (New York: Macmillan, 1934), p. 127.
8. It may be useful to recall Alice James's advice to her brother William on the education of his children: "What enrichment of mind & memory can children have without continuity & if they are torn up by the roots every little while as we were! Of all things don't make the mistake wh. brought about our rootless & accidental childhood. Leave Europe for them until they are old eno' to have the Grand Emotion, undiluted by vague memories." Alice James to William James, 4 Nov. 1888, in *The Death and Letters of Alice James,* ed. Ruth Bernard Yeazell (Berkeley: Univ. of California Press, 1981), p. 148.
9. *The Portrait of a Lady,* pp. 21, 27.
10. Hawthorne's ironically Puritanic self-examination of his vocation as a mere "writer of story-books" appears in "The Custom House" Introduction to *The Scarlet Letter,* Vol. I of the Centenary Edition of the Works of Nathaniel Hawthorne, p. 10.
11. *The Portrait of a Lady,* pp. 171–72.
12. Mull, *'Sublime Economy,'* pp. 90, 91.
13. *The Portrait of a Lady,* p. 506.
14. Donald Sheehan, *This Was Publishing: A Chronicle of the Book Trade in the Gilded Age* (Bloomington: Indiana Univ. Press, 1952), p. 90. Sheehan notes that, while Harper and Brothers included an exemption clause in their standard contract form until the 1890s, it was routinely struck out before the document was signed, suggesting that the recovery of production costs was

relatively insignificant to the publisher. But the trade as a whole was probably more fiscally conservative. As George Haven Putnam explained in 1883, under a royalty arrangement, "the publisher assumes the expenses of manufacture and publication, and in consideration of this outlay, which can, as a rule, not be reimbursed from a sale of less than one thousand copies, the first thousand copies sold are frequently exempted from copyright. In other words, the publisher and the author begin to make money out of the book at the same time." Putnam went on to say that, with the effects of postwar inflation, the conventional number of 1000 copies was no longer adequate to recover the expenses of "novels and other works of light literature," because of the very low prices at which they were published. See [George Haven Putnam], *Authors and Publishers: A Manual of Suggestions for Beginners in Literature* (New York: G. P. Putnam's Sons, 1883), p. 21. The most recent historian of the publishing industry claims that exemption clauses for the first 1000 copies were a standard feature of contracts even into the years of World War I. See John Tebbel, *A History of Book Publishing in the United States:* Vol. II, *The Expansion of an Industry, 1865–1919* (New York: R. R. Bowker, 1975), p. 134.

15. Henry James, Sr. to Henry James, 4 March [1873] (James Papers, Harvard). James printed the text of this letter in slightly altered form in *Notes of a Son and Brother.* See *Autobiography,* pp. 401–2.
16. Henry James to Mrs. Henry James, Sr., 24 March [18]73, *Henry James Letters,* I, 357.
17. Henry James to Henry James, Sr., 22 [Dec.] 1873, *Henry James Letters,* I, 422.
18. Ticknor & Fields; Fields, Osgood; and James R. Osgood Copyright Accounts, 1860–76, p. 333 (Houghton Mifflin Archive, Harvard).
19. Henry James to J. R. Osgood & Co., 18 Aug. [1875], *Henry James Letters,* I, 480.
20. At which point 1889 copies had been sold at full royalty and 212 at a 90 percent discount for total earnings of $573. Sales and royalty information were gathered from the Copyright Account Ledgers of Houghton Mifflin Company and its predecessors, 1860–76, p. 333; 1876–81, p. 165; 1881–91, p. 163; 1900–1908, p. 246. The volume for 1891–1900 apparently has not survived, but copies of the firm's semiannual royalty statements for this period are deposited at Harvard, and these have been checked for the relevant data. See Houghton Mifflin Copyright Statements, 33 vols., 1889–1915 (Houghton Mifflin Archive, Harvard).
21. Small wonder that in his memoir James equated his father's physical incapacity with his crippled stance in the marketplace. "The two acceptances melt together for me," James wrote of his father, "that of the limits of his material action, his doing and enjoying, set so narrowly, and that of his scant allowance of 'public recognition,' or of the support and encouragement that spring, and spring so naturally and rightly" from "a message, richly and sincerely urged" (*Autobiography,* p. 351).
22. *Autobiography,* p. 344; Henry James to William James, 2 Jan. 1885, *Henry James Letters,* III, 62.
23. See, for example, Francis Whiting Halsey, *Our Literary Deluge and Some of*

Its Deeper Waters (New York: Doubleday, Page & Co., 1902); [Walter Hines Page], *A Publisher's Confession* (New York: Doubleday, Page & Co., 1905); Henry Holt, "The Commercialization of Literature," *Atlantic Monthly,* 96 (Nov. 1905), 577–600; Holt, "The Commercialization of Literature: A Summing Up," *Putnam's Monthly,* 1 (Feb. 1907), 563–75; and Robert Sterling Yard, *The Publisher* (Boston: Houghton Mifflin, 1913).

24. Henry James, "Alphonse Daudet" [1883], in *Partial Portraits* (1888; rpt. Ann Arbor: Univ. of Michigan Press, 1970), p. 196.
25. John Gross, *The Rise and Fall of the Man of Letters: Aspects of English Literary Life Since 1800* (London: Weidenfeld and Nicolson, 1969), p. 199.
26. Carl Bode, *The Anatomy of Popular Culture, 1840–1861* (Berkeley: Univ. of California Press, 1959), p. x.
27. Frankly overwhelmed by the sheer quantity of periodical literature and commentary that poured forth from the presses, James asserted in 1905 that

> our huge Anglo-Saxon array of producers and readers—and especially our vast cis-Atlantic multitude—presents production uncontrolled, production untouched by criticism, unguided, unlighted, uninstructed, unashamed, on a scale that is really a new thing in the world. It is the biggest flock straying without shepherds, making its music without a sight of the classic crook, beribboned or other, without a sound of the sheepdog's bark—wholesome note, once in a way—that has ever found room for pasture. The very opposite has happened from what might have been expected to happen. The shepherds have diminished as the flock has increased—quite as if number and quantity had got beyond them, or even as if their charge had turned, by some uncanny process, to a pack of ravening wolves.

See "The Lesson of Balzac" in *The Question of Our Speech, The Lesson of Balzac: Two Lectures* (Boston: Houghton, Mifflin, 1905), pp. 56–57.

28. Sheehan, *This Was Publishing,* p. 27. A useful historical essay on the cyclical problems of the trade is offered by Lewis A. Coser, Charles Kadushin, and Walter W. Powell in their study of the contemporary publishing scene, *Books: The Culture and Commerce of Publishing* (New York: Basic Books, 1982), pp. 13–35.
29. See Sheehan, *This Was Publishing,* p. 15; Coser et al., *Books,* p. 35; and, most recently, Christopher P. Wilson, *The Labor of Words: Literary Professionalism in the Progressive Era* (Athens: Univ. of Georgia Press, 1985), esp. pp. 1–16, 63–91.
30. [Gerald Duckworth & Co.], *Fifty Years, 1898–1948* (London: Duckworth, 1948), p. 7.
31. Walter Besant, *The Pen and the Book* (London: Thomas Burleigh, 1899), p. 315.
32. [George Haven Putnam], *Authors and Publishers,* p. 2.
33. Michael Sadleir, *Authors and Publishers: A Study in Mutual Esteem* [The J. M. Dent Memorial Lectures, No. 2] (London: J. M. Dent, 1932), p. 9.
34. The Copyright Act of 1891 brought the United States to the point reached by France in 1810 and by Great Britain and most of the German states in 1837. "By the time America had decided to take its first step," writes Aubert J. Clark, "the rest of the civilized world had united in the Berne Convention (1877). Even today the United States cannot bring itself to take another step

and become signatory to the Berne Protocol." See *The Movement for International Copyright in Nineteenth Century America* (Washington, D.C.: Catholic Univ. Press, 1960), pp. 182–83.

35. *The American* was promptly issued in England by Ward, Lock & Company in 1877, before James had established himself with Macmillan, who eventually brought out an authorized edition in 1879; and the short story "A Bundle of Letters" (1879), which first appeared serially in France (as a favor to James's friend Theodore Child, who edited the English-language *Parisian*), was bundled up as a twenty-five cent pamphlet by A. K. Loring of Boston in 1880, James having sacrificed his American copyright by not publishing simultaneously in the United States. The tale was also reprinted that year in George Munro's Seaside Library, together with "Sweet Nelly, My Heart's Delight" by Walter Besant and James Rice. For complete bibliographical information about these editions, see *A Bibliography of Henry James,* 3rd ed., pp. 32–33, 47–49.
36. Henry James to William James, 22 Sept. [1872], *Henry James Letters,* I, 300–301.
37. William Dean Howells to Charles Eliot Norton, 10 Aug. 1867, *Selected Letters,* I, 283.
38. Royal Gettmann provides a useful summary of Victorian publishing agreements and practices in his history of the Bentley firm, *A Victorian Publisher: A Study of the Bentley Papers* (Cambridge: Cambridge Univ. Press, 1960), pp. 76–118. Typical arrangements were (1) the author's outright sale of copyright (preferred, for example, by Trollope); (2) the lease of copyright for a fixed term of years; (3) half-profits, by which author and publisher divided a book's receipts equally, after the costs of production had been recovered (though this system was subject to widespread abuse, since publishers themselves determined what the costs of production were); and, lastly, (4) the royalty system. Gettmann comments, "It is not clear when this kind of agreement first came into use in the trade: on this and some other important points, the writers on publishing are silent. . . . [A]n equitable royalty system seems to have developed very slowly out of experience with the earlier kinds of agreements" (pp. 16, 18). Bentley's first royalty contract was signed with Eliza Lynn Linton for the *Autobiography of Christopher Kirkland* (1885); but as late as 1882 British manuals for writers did not even list royalty payments as a recognized means of remuneration (see, for example, *The Search for a Publisher; or, Counsels for a Young Author,* 8th ed. [London: Provost & Co., 1882], pp. 7–12). In 1883, however, Henry James negotiated a royalty agreement with Macmillan for the Collective Edition of his works published that year. He received a royalty of 10 percent of the retail price on all copies sold, together with an advance of £100. See Frederick Macmillan to Henry James, 25 April 1883, Macmillan Letter Books, Add. MS 55415, pp. 1146–47 (Macmillan Archive, British Library). Subsequent references to the Macmillan Letter Books will be abbreviated MLB, followed by the British Library additional manuscript catalogue number and page numbers where appropriate. A fuller description of the archive is given in the List of Sources which follows the Notes.

39. Edmund Gosse, *Aspects and Impressions* (London: Cassell & Co., 1922), p. 23.
40. Mrs. Henry James, Sr. to Henry and Alice James, 26 July [1872]; Henry James to Henry James, Sr., 11 Aug. [1872] (James Papers, Harvard).
41. In 1873 James briefly considered submitting a travel article on Italian cities to the *Cornhill,* but patience ruled the day. "If it were a *newer* subject," he told his mother, "I am pretty sure I could get Leslie Stephen to put it into the *Cornhill:* but I had rather make a better beginning with the *C[ornhill]*. This I mean to do. I presume to be able to do *Cornhill* writing." See Henry James to Mrs. Henry James, Sr., [May 1873], *Henry James Letters,* I, 389.
42. Henry James to Mr. & Mrs. Henry James, Sr., 14 Aug. [1873] (James Papers, Harvard).
43. Henry James to Thomas Sergeant Perry, 12 Jan. [1877], in Virginia Harlow, *Thomas Sergeant Perry: A Biography* (Durham, N.C.: Duke Univ. Press, 1950), pp. 294–95.
44. Henry James to Mrs. Henry James, Sr., 13 Jan. [1878], quoted in *A Bibliography of Henry James,* 3rd ed., p. 33.
45. Henry James to Macmillan & Co., 7 Aug. [1877], *Henry James Letters,* II, 131–32.
46. Frederick Macmillan to Henry James, 22 Aug. 1877, MLB, MS 55403, pp. 496–97 (Macmillan Archive, British Library). How seriously the Macmillans were interested in James can be measured by the fact that they went ahead with *French Poets and Novelists* over the objections of one of their most respected readers, John Morley, who dismissed the manuscript as "prosaic to the last degree, and *as criticism* not at all interesting." Compared to Saint-Beuve, Morley wrote, James "must be called mediocre. On the other hand, though the criticism as such is not interesting, the subjects *are* particularly so. . . . When all is said, I feel that the book might have some slight sale, but it would certainly make no deep literary mark. There would be no harm in printing it, but neither to literature would there be any good. . . . It is honest scribble work and no more." Morley's report is preserved in the Macmillan Archive at the British Library, and Charles Morgan quotes from it liberally in his commemorative history of the firm, *The House of Macmillan (1843–1943)* (London: Macmillan, 1944), pp. 114–15. Edel also provides the relevant details in *Henry James: The Conquest of London,* pp. 299–300. Despite his first reservations about James's critical abilities, Morley would invite the American to contribute a volume to Macmillan's English Men of Letters series the following year.
47. Henry James to Frederick Macmillan, 27 Aug. [1877] (Macmillan Archive, British Library).
48. Henry James to Alice James, 29 Dec. [1877], *Henry James Letters,* II, 148.
49. A collective half-profits agreement for all four books was signed by James on that date and returned to Macmillan, probably the following day. It is preserved with James's letters to the firm at the British Library.
50. Henry James to William James, 28 Jan. [1878]; and to Mrs. Henry James, Sr., 17 Feb. [1878], *Henry James Letters,* II, 150–51, 156.
51. Henry James to Frederick Macmillan, 5 April [1878] (Macmillan Archive, British Library). The evidence of Grove's attitude toward *The American* is

curiously contradictory. While the tone of James's first letter to Macmillan about the "editorial imagination" is rather condescending, he wrote to his parents on 19 April that Grove had "been reading *The American* 'with great delight'" (Henry James to Henry James, Sr., 19 April [1878], *Henry James Letters,* II 168). Five days later, however, James responded rather bemusedly to Grove's invitation to discuss the prospects of serializing his next novel in *Macmillan's Magazine,* which Grove edited. "I shall be very happy to come and see you on Monday next," James wrote,

> and give you what information I can about my projected novel, of which Frederick Macmillan spoke to you. I say "what information I can" for I have not yet the MS. in any state to show. I can, however, tell you definitely what the thing is about and show you some of it some time hence. But I confess frankly that if you broke down in the middle of *The American* I fear that there is a danger of the present story finding little more favour with you. Still, I hasten to add that I think I may claim for it that it is a stronger work than *The American.* As regards the latter I venture to recommend you, since you express a disposition to do so, to have, as they say, another "try" at it. Perhaps it will go more smoothly.

Simon Nowell-Smith (who prints this note in his collection of *Letters to Macmillan* [New York: St. Martin's Press, 1967], p. 169) asserts that James is speaking here of *The Europeans,* which Frederick Macmillan had liked. But James had almost finished writing that short serial, and most, if not all, of it was in the hands of William Dean Howells by the time James wrote to Grove (cf. Henry James to Henry James, Sr., 25 March [1878], *Henry James Letters,* II, 161–62). Furthermore, *The Europeans* was a book of which James never thought highly, and it is unlikely that he would have claimed it "a stronger work than *The American.*" A month earlier James had told his mother that the novel he was working on would be to *The American* "as wine to water," his first reference to what would eventually become *The Portrait of a Lady* (Henry James to Mrs. Henry James, Sr., 15 March [1878], *The Selected Letters of Henry James,* ed. Leon Edel [New York: Farrar, Straus, & Cudahy, 1955], pp. 52–53). Hence James's doubts about Grove's appreciation: if the editor had broken down with Christopher Newman, what would he do with Isabel Archer?

52. See Henry James to William Dean Howells, 9 Jan. & 10 March [18]74, *Henry James Letters,* I, 424, 437; and Edel, *Henry James: The Conquest of London,* pp. 160–61, 245–47.
53. Henry James, "Mr. and Mrs. Fields" [1915], in *The American Essays of Henry James,* ed. Leon Edel (New York: Vintage Books, 1956), p. 265.
54. Whatever its benefits to American publishers, courtesy of the trade was derided by authors—especially British ones—as a kind of honor among thieves. After the passage of international copyright undermined the foundation of trade courtesy, William Dean Howells genially referred to the practice as "a comity among . . . amiable buccaneers, who agreed not to interfere with each other"; but in the earlier time, when foreign authors and publishers had no legal recourse, critics of the industry spoke more bluntly. "No sooner does a valuable English book reach their shores," one Britisher complained in 1879, "than one or other of them seizes upon it, and straight-

away the book becomes *his* property; and as a code of honour exists amongst them, this right which has obtained by might is usually respected." See William Dean Howells, "The Man of Letters as a Man of Business" [1893], in *Literature and Life* (New York: Harper and Brothers, 1902), p. 18; and E[dward] M[arston], *Copyright, National and International, from the Point of View of a Publisher* (London: Sampson Low, 1879), p. 37.

55. Henry Holt, "The Commercialization of Literature," p. 589.
56. Quoted in Sheehan, *This Was Publishing*, p. 68. The loving cup was emblazoned with five gilt panels, bearing the names of Appleton, Harper, Scribner, and Holt, who collectively inscribed their affection for Putnam. See Henry Holt, *Garrulities of an Octogenarian Editor* (Boston: Houghton Mifflin, 1923), p. 211; and Frederick A. Stokes, "A Publisher's Random Notes, 1880–1935" [1935], in *Bowker Lectures on Book Publishing* (New York: R. R. Bowker, 1957), pp. 8–9.
57. Holt apparently regretted his decision. In 1905 he wrote that "professional courtesy should not be carried as far as I once carried it in my young and quixotic days, when an eminent author brought me a work of his own accord, and I declined it because he would not assert that he had cause of complaint against his then publisher." While he does not mention the author by name, Holt's description of his publishing situation (in 1905) matches James's to a tee: "He now publishes 'all over the place,' and of course has no publisher with any abiding interest in him; and his books do not support each other as they would if tied together. Partly in consequence of this, his sales are small, though his fame is large." The identification was more explicit in a letter Holt sent to Charles Scribner in 1901, complaining of their mutual loss of William James's *Varieties of Religious Experience.* Scribner had declined to "go into auction for James's book," as had Holt; consequently, they had both lost it to Longmans, Green & Company. To make matters worse, William James and his wife charged that Holt deliberately had urged Charles Scribner not to bid for the manuscript, a suspicion that cost Holt his long personal friendship with the family. The episode reminded Holt of a lesson he had learned many years before from the actions of William's brother (though he had failed to apply it in William's case): "Since I bowed *Henry* James out of my office some thirty years ago, and he, instead of going back to Osgood went to Harper (as his brother went from you and me to Longmans) I have not been trying to send authors back to their old publishers when they spontaneously come to me." See Henry Holt, "The Commercialization of Literature," p. 590; Holt to Charles Scribner, 25 Oct. 1901 (Scribner Archive, Princeton); and Charles Madison, *Owl Among the Colophons: Henry Holt as Publisher and Editor* (New York: Holt, Rinehart and Winston, 1966), pp. 53–54.
58. Wondering why James did not sell the American serial rights to Howells at the *Atlantic,* some critics have concluded that James withheld the story because it did not have the kind of happy ending that Howells and his readers preferred (and had insisted upon in the case of *The Europeans*). A more convincing explanation is found, however, when we remember that James was anxious to achieve serial publication in both countries, a practice on which the *Atlantic*'s owners (Houghton, Osgood) habitually frowned. When

Macmillan expressed his desire to publish *The Europeans* simultaneously in *Macmillan's Magazine*, James declined by saying, "I am rather afraid that, for various reasons, it will be difficult for you to arrange putting it into Macmillan's, even should your own circumstances permit. I thank you very much, however, for the offer. I wish this might be, and perhaps it may [in the future]." Although James knew that the *Atlantic* would not agree to such terms, Macmillan's offer would prove useful in his future planning. As James confided to his sister, "[the Macmillans] have asked me to give them my projected tale in the *Atlantic* for simultaneous publication in their magazine; but this can in all probability not be arranged. I value the offer, however, as a sign of extension, and it will serve for the next time.—*(Mention this, please, to no one.)*" See Howells, *Selected Letters,* II, 154; Frederick Macmillan to Henry James, 10 Dec. 1877, MLB, MS 55404, p. 470; James to Macmillan, 12 Dec. [1877] (Macmillan Archive, British Library); and Henry James to Alice James, 29 Dec. [1877], *Henry James Letters,* II, 148.

59. *Henry James Letters,* II, 80–81.
60. Harper Contract Books, III, 75–76, *The Archives of Harper and Brothers, 1817–1914* (Teaneck, N.J.: Chadwyck-Healey Microfilm Edition, 1982). The exemption clause was struck from this and all of James's future contracts with the Harpers.
61. Henry James, preface to "Daisy Miller," in *The Art of the Novel,* p. 268.
62. Henry James to William James, 23 July [1878], *Henry James Letters,* II, 179. James's doubts about the intellectual refinement of the English were famously recorded in a letter written to his brother some years earlier:

> The English have such a mortal mistrust of anything like criticism or "keen analysis" (which they seem to regard as a kind of maudlin foreign flummery) that I rarely remember to have heard on English lips any other intellectual verdict (no matter under what provocation) than this broad synthesis—"So immensely clever." What exasperates you is not that they can't say more, but that they wouldn't if they could. (ibid., I, 209)

63. Frederick Macmillan to Henry James, 31 July 1878, MLB, MS 55406, p. 633 (Macmillan Archive, British Library).
64. Although *The Europeans* was printed in two volumes, James was afraid that their brevity would be a source of disappointment. "[I]t was a cruel wrong its being announced or spoken of as a 'novel,'" he confided to Thomas Sergeant Perry, "but I hope it will be thought neat as far as it goes. It is distinctly slight." Henry James to Thomas Sergeant Perry, 13 Sept. [1878], in Harlow, *Thomas Sergeant Perry,* p. 300.
65. Henry James to Frederick Macmillan, [1 Aug. 1878], in Nowell-Smith, *Letters to Macmillan,* pp. 169–70. The editor dates this letter "May 1878," but James clearly is responding to Macmillan's offer of 31 July. James began his letter by saying, "I meant to have written you yesterday . . . ," which suggests that 1 August is a more likely date for its composition. The Royal Mail made deliveries several times daily in London during this period, and many of James's other responses to his publishers were posted the same day that their letters to him were dated and received.
66. Henry James to W. E. Henley, 28 Aug. [1878], *Henry James Letters,* II, 183.

The Harpers purchased all rights to "An International Episode" for $200 in October 1878, but they decided to market the story directly as an addition to their inexpensive Half-Hour Series, in which "Daisy Miller" first appeared. See Henry James to Harper and Brothers, 2 Oct. 1878, Harper Contract Books, II, 154.

67. Henry James to Mrs. Henry James, Sr., 29 Sept. & 4 July [1878] (James Papers, Harvard).
68. Henry James to Mrs. Henry James, Sr., 27 Oct. [1878] (James Papers, Harvard).
69. Henry James to Frederick Macmillan, [17(?) Nov. 1878]; Macmillan to James, 18 Nov. 1878, MLB, MS 55407, p. 545 (Macmillan Archive, British Library).
70. Henry James to Frederick Macmillan, [17 Feb. 1879] (Macmillan Archive, British Library).
71. Macmillan printed *The Europeans* in three editions of 250 copies each and sold them briskly. Two editions of 250 were printed to satisfy the demand for *Daisy Miller,* but sales dropped off almost immediately after the first printing was exhausted. By the end of 1879 *Daisy Miller* had sold about 285 copies. Frederick Macmillan to Henry James, 10 Nov. 1879, MLB, MS 55409, p. 940 (Macmillan Archive, British Library).
72. J. A. Sutherland, *Victorian Novelists and Their Publishers* (Chicago: Univ. of Chicago Press, 1976), p. 12.
73. As one publisher explained in 1879,

> the three-volume form is the crucible by which the public tests, not always or specially the literary value of a work, but its suitability and adaptation to its shifting tastes. If a work takes well in three volumes, it does not always follow that it will sell in a cheap form, but it is *some* guide for a publisher; if a good book fails in three volumes, its chances in a cheap form are gone. On the other hand, this curious public will not buy an original novel, however good it may be, in a cheap form on its first appearance. . . . By the time a novel or any other expensive book has percolated through the circulating libraries, its character has become known: if it suits the public, it will demand and get it, in a cheap form; if not, it dies.

See Marston, *Copyright, National and International,* p. 29. The role of the circulating libraries in perpetuating the three-volume novel is ably explored by Guinevere L. Griest in her study of *Mudie's Circulating Library and the Victorian Novel* (Bloomington: Indiana Univ. Press, 1970).

74. Henry James to Thomas Sergeant Perry, 14 Sept. 1879, *Henry James Letters,* II, p. 255. The year before James remarked to his father, "The way the busy people here [in London] find time to read novels, & the serious consideration they give them is to me a constant surprise; though I suppose it ought to be a gratification." Henry James to Henry James, Sr., 24 Nov. [1878] (James Papers, Harvard). Later comparisons only sustain James's impression. See for example, Oliver B. Bunce, "English and American Book Markets," *North American Review,* 150 (1890), 470–79, esp. 473.
75. Sutherland, *Victorian Novelists and Publishers,* p. 17. While Sutherland does not analyze Henry James's career to support this claim, James is the American exception that proves the rule, for much of his remarkable invention and productivity can be attributed to his status as a transatlantic author.

76. For a useful analysis of the differences between English and American production methods, see Simon Nowell-Smith, *International Copyright Law and the Publisher in the Reign of Queen Victoria* (Oxford: Oxford Univ. Press, 1968), p. 78.
77. Henry James to William Dean Howells, 17 June [1879], *Henry James Letters,* II, 244.
78. Henry James to William Dean Howells, 17 June [1879], *Henry James Letters,* II, 243.
79. Henry James to William James, 15 June [1879] (James Papers, Harvard).
80. Frederick Macmillan to Henry James, 3 Dec. 1878, MLB, MS 55407, p. 706 (Macmillan Archive, British Library).
81. Frederick Macmillan to Henry James, 20 Jan. 1879, MLB, MS 55407, pp. 1187–88 (Macmillan Archive, British Library).
82. Henry James to Frederick Macmillan, 14 July [1879], *Henry James Letters,* II, 251.
83. Henry James to Frederick Macmillan, 15 July [1879] (Macmillan Archive, British Library).
84. Henry James to Thomas Sergeant Perry, 14 Sept. 1879, *Henry James Letters,* II, 255.
85. Henry James to Frederick Macmillan, 28 Sept. [1879], *Henry James Letters,* II, 257.
86. Henry James to Frederick Macmillan, 19 Oct. [1879] (Macmillan Archive, British Library).
87. William Charvat notes that the half-profits arrangement "was the Harpers' favorite method with novelists in the 1830's, and Herman Melville was its victim for over thirty years." Melville owned the plates of his first book, *Typee,* but was on the half-profits system for all the others. The first 1190 copies of *Pierre* were also exempted from royalty. To make matters worse, Melville always borrowed in advance against a new book and was charged interest against these advances, so that he was in debt to the Harpers for almost his entire career. A closer contemporary of James, Mark Twain, was duped out of almost $50,000 by Elisha Bliss and the American Publishing Company on his half-profits contracts between 1869 and 1880. See William Charvat, *Literary Publishing in America, 1790–1850* (Philadelphia: Univ. of Pennsylvania Press, 1959), p. 44; and Hamlin Hill, *Mark Twain and Elisha Bliss* (Columbia: Univ. of Missouri Press, 1964), pp. 156–57. Equally revealing are *Mark Twain's Letters to His Publishers, 1867–1894,* ed. Hamlin Hill (Berkeley: Univ. of California Press, 1967), and Janet Ainsworth Rich's unpublished dissertation, "The Dream of Riches and the Dream of Art: The Relationship Between Business and Imagination in the Life and Major Fiction of Mark Twain," Diss. Harvard, 1980.
88. George Haven Putnam, *Authors and Publishers,* p. 22.
89. James Spedding, *Publishers and Authors* (London: J. R. Smith, 1867), pp. 18–19. Spedding had intended his essay for periodical publication, but it was refused by several editors who feared that it "would offend the Powers upon whom the sale of books depends, and might materially damage the value (as property) of the publication" that printed it (p. vi).
90. Richard Poirier's assessment—that the novel is "light to the point of vap-

idity"—is characteristic, though easily anticipated by James himself. *Confidence,* the novelist told a friend in 1914, "is a very poor thing—I wholly disowned it in the definitive [New York] Edition; I mean I kept it, with various other things, snubbingly out. So do I try to live down a shameful past—or at least one with shady episodes." See Poirier, *The Comic Sense of Henry James,* p. 155; and Henry James to Constance Gardner, 9 April 1914 (James Papers, Harvard).

91. Howells did encourage James to find other outlets besides the *Atlantic,* especially for nonfiction, but he harbored a special dislike for *Scribner's* editor, Dr. Josiah Holland. A letter to James from 1873 is typical: "By the way, I hope you wont [*sic*] send any of your stories to Scribner's. We have of course no claim upon you, but we have hitherto been able to print all the stories you have sent, and so it shall be hereafter. Scribner is trying to lure away all our contributors, with the syren [*sic*] song of Doctor Holland, and my professional pride is touched" (William Dean Howells to Henry James, 5 Dec. 1873, *Selected Letters,* II, 39).
92. James was not the only beneficiary of *Scribner's* generosity. From the beginning the magazine favored the American contributor, according to Clarence Gohdes, "encouraged writers from various regions to deal with their own sections, and forced the payment of authors to a higher level by competing for the work of the newer men—among them Eggleston, Howells, James, Harte, and later, Marion Crawford and S. Weir Mitchell." See "The Later Nineteenth Century: The Age of the Monthly Magazine," in *The Literature of the American People,* ed. Arthur Hobson Quinn (New York: Appleton-Century-Crofts, 1951), p. 594.
93. Henry James to Thomas Sergeant Perry, 28 Oct. 1864, *Henry James Letters,* I, 56.
94. Henry James to William Dean Howells, 24 Oct. [1876], *Henry James Letters,* II, 70.
95. By contrast, James received $100 a number for the twelve installments of *Roderick Hudson* (1875) and $1350 altogether for *The American* (1876), which was originally planned in nine installments at $150 each, but which the *Atlantic* published in twelve shorter segments.
96. Henry James to Alice James, 26 March [1879], *Henry James Letters,* II, 225–26.
97. Charles Scribner's Sons to Henry James, 5 Aug. [1879], Edward L. Burlingame Letter Books, I, 159 (Scribner Archive, Princeton).
98. Edward L. Burlingame to Charles Scribner, 29 Aug. 1879, Burlingame Letter Books, I, tipped in after p. 226 (Scribner Archive, Princeton).
99. Charles Scribner's Sons to Henry James, 3 Sept. [1879], Burlingame Letter Books, I, p. 226 (Scribner Archive, Princeton).
100. Henry James to Chatto & Windus, 27 Sept. [1879] (James Papers, Harvard).
101. Chatto & Windus to Henry James, 1 Oct. 1879, Chatto & Windus Letter Books, MS 2444/11, p. 471; Henry James to Chatto & Windus, 5 Oct. [1879], tipped into Chatto & Windus Letter Books, MS 2444/11, after p. 483 (Chatto & Windus Archive, Univ. of Reading).
102. Henry James to Chatto & Windus, 13 Oct. [1879], tipped into Chatto & Windus Letter Books, MS 2444/11, after p. 483; and Chatto & Windus to

James, 14 Oct. 1879, ibid., p. 484 (Chatto & Windus Archive, Univ. of Reading).

103. Henry James to Henry James, Sr., 11 Oct. [1879], *Henry James Letters,* II, 259–60.
104. In his biography of James, Leon Edel fails to distinguish between the different kinds of agreements that the novelist entered into with his publishers. In reference to the letter quoted here, for example, Edel writes, "[James] had had substantial advances against his royalties; nevertheless Macmillans now had six of his books in print, and the sum [James received from the firm] . . . seemed pitifully small. . . . If Macmillan could not do better, he would publish elsewhere." Edel's gloss masks the real source of James's disenchantment with Macmillan—his suspicion that the publisher was inflating production costs at the expense of their shared profits. By consistently referring to James's income from Macmillan as "royalties," Edel confuses a technical, but important, issue. See *Henry James: The Conquest of London,* pp. 402, 344.
105. Henry James to Henry James, Sr., 11 Oct. [1879], *Henry James Letters,* II, 260.
106. Henry James to Mrs. Henry James, Sr., 18 Nov. [1879] (James Papers, Harvard). For *Confidence* Houghton, Osgood paid James their standard royalty of 10 percent on all copies sold.
107. Frederick Macmillan to Henry James, 10 Nov. 1879, MLB, MS 55409, p. 940 (Macmillan Archive, British Library).
108. Frederick Macmillan to Henry James, 12 Nov. 1879, MLB, MS 55409, p. 959 (Macmillan Archive, British Library).
109. Frederick Macmillan to Henry James, 14 Nov. 1879, MLB, MS 55409, p. 976 (Macmillan Archive, British Library).
110. George Lillie Craik to Henry James, 17 Nov. 1879; Frederick Macmillan to James, 19 Nov. 1879, MLB, MS 55409, pp. 993, 1006 (Macmillan Archive, British Library).
111. Henry James to Mrs. Henry James, Sr., 18 Nov. [1879] (James Papers, Harvard).
112. Hans Schmoller, "The Paperback Revolution," in *Essays in the History of Publishing: In Celebration of the 250th Anniversary of the House of Longman, 1724–1974,* ed. Asa Briggs (London: Longman Group Ltd., 1974), p. 292; and Simon Nowell-Smith, *International Copyright Law and the Publisher,* p. 52.
113. Chatto & Windus to Freiherr von Tauchnitz, Jr., 3 Feb. 1880, Chatto & Windus Letter Books, MS 2444/12, p. 191 (Chatto & Windus Archive, Univ. of Reading).
114. James informed Thomas Sergeant Perry on 22 March 1878 that he had just received a visit from "the Freiherr v. Tauchnitz jr. . . . [who] is republishing my 'works'—having begun with *The American*" (Harlow, *Thomas Sergeant Perry,* p. 299).
115. Chatto & Windus to Henry James, 23 Feb. 1880, Chatto & Windus Letter Books, MS 2444/12, p. 228 (Chatto and Windus Archive, Univ. of Reading).
116. Henry James to Chatto & Windus, 26 Feb. [1880] (Collection of American Literature, Yale).

117. On 5 Oct. 1879 James informed Chatto & Windus that he was sending them five-sixths of the novel, "& the remaining sixth, the proofs of which have not yet been sent me from New York, will be forthcoming about a month hence"—a statement which suggests that James had the opportunity to revise proof before serial publication.
118. As usual, James was slightly ahead of his time. After the passage of international copyright legislation, American writers generally were advised to consider the English market when preparing their manuscripts. "[I]t is desirable for authors to avoid as far as possible, the use of words and phrases which are not common to both countries," one publisher suggested in 1899. "Many a book otherwise suitable . . . fails of wide acceptance in [England] because of what are looked upon as the 'Americanisms' in it, and the author who desires to avail himself of the increased circulation which the English market affords would do well to bear this in mind." James anticipated this problem by twenty years and revised proofs accordingly. See Charles Welsh, *Publishing a Book* (Boston: D. C. Heath & Co., 1899), pp. 37–38.
119. Henry James to Mrs. F. H. Hill, 21 March [1879], *Henry James Letters,* II, 219–20.
120. Most, but not all, of the variants between the manuscript and serial publication in *Scribner's* are available in Herbert Rhum's edition of *Confidence* (New York: Grosset & Dunlap, 1962), which can be supplemented by the recent Library of America volume of James's *Novels 1871–1880* (New York, 1983), pp. 1275–77, 1284–87.
121. Henry James to Alice James, 15 Sept. [1881] (James Papers, Harvard).
122. Henry James to William Dean Howells, 3 Jan. 1880 (Howells Papers, Harvard).

CHAPTER IV

1. James first had occasion to comment publicly on Hawthorne in his review of the posthumously published *French and Italian Notebooks* (*Nation,* 14 [14 March 1872], 172–73); the critical biography was published seven years later. Subsequent (and in some respects more genial) assessments appeared in 1897, as an introduction to a selection from Hawthorne's work (in volume XII of the *Library of the World's Best Literature,* ed. Charles Dudley Warner [New York: R. S. Peale and J. A. Hill]), and in 1904, the year of the Hawthorne centenary, in an open letter to the Essex Institute of Salem. The three briefer essays are conveniently collected in *The American Essays of Henry James,* pp. 3–31.
2. Henry James, *Hawthorne* (1879; rpt. New York: St. Martin's Press, 1967), p. 149. In the remainder of this chapter, references to this edition appear parenthetically in the text.
3. Robert Emmet Long, *The Great Succession: Henry James and the Legacy of Hawthorne* (Pittsburgh: Univ. of Pittsburgh Press, 1979), p. 12.
4. Lionel Trilling, "Our Hawthorne," in *Hawthorne Centenary Essays,* ed. Roy Harvey Pearce ([Columbus]: Ohio State Univ. Press, 1964), p. 433.
5. Henry James to Henry James, Sr., 11 Jan. 1880, *Henry James Letters,* II, 263.

6. Henry James to Thomas Sergeant Perry, 22 Feb. [1880], *Henry James Letters,* II, 274.
7. Henry James to Elizabeth Boott, 22 Feb. [1880] (James Papers, Harvard).
8. "The main impressions produced by [Hawthorne's] observations," James wrote in 1872, "is that of his simplicity. They spring not only from an unsophisticated, but from an excessively natural mind. Never, surely, was a man of literary genius less a man of letters" (*American Essays,* p. 6). In the biography James expanded on this peculiar aspect of Hawthorne's notebooks:

> They contain much that is too futile for things intended for publicity; whereas, on the other hand, as a receptacle of private impressions and opinions, they are curiously cold and empty. They widen, as I have said, our glimpse of Hawthorne's mind (I do not say that they elevate our estimate of it), but they do so by what they fail to contain, as much as by what we find in them. . . . He appears to have read a good deal, and that he must have been familiar with the sources of good English we see from his charming, expressive, slightly self-conscious, cultivated, but not too cultivated, style. Yet neither in these early volumes of his Note-Books, nor in the later, is there any mention of his reading. There are no literary judgments or impressions—there is almost no allusion to works or to authors. The allusions to individuals of any kind are indeed much less numerous than one might have expected; there is little psychology, little description of manners. (pp. 54, 57)

9. John Morley to Henry James, 9 Oct. [18]78 (James Papers, Harvard); James to Frederick Macmillan, 11 Oct. [1878] (Macmillan Archive, British Library); James to Henry James, Sr., 18 Oct. [1878] (James Papers, Harvard).
10. Frederick Macmillan to Henry James, 22 Jan. 1879, MLB, MS 55407, pp. 1216–17 (Macmillan Archive, British Library); Harper Contract Books, III, 95–96; James to Macmillan, 22 Jan. 1879, and James to Henry James, Sr., 17 Jan. [1880], both quoted in *A Bibliography of Henry James,* 3rd ed., p. 47.
11. Edwin and Virginia Price Barber, "A Description of Old Harper and Brothers Publishing Records Recently Come to Light," *Bulletin of Bibliography and Magazine Notes,* 25 (Sept.–Dec., 1966), 5; Harper Memorandum Books, V, 46.
12. Henry James to Alice James, 19 Aug. [1879] (James Papers, Harvard); James to Frederick Macmillan, 14 Sept. [1879] (Macmillan Archive, British Library); James to Grace Norton, 21 Dec. 1879, *Henry James Letters,* II, 262.
13. Ralph Thompson, *American Literary Annuals & Gift Books, 1825–1865* (New York: H. W. Wilson, 1936), p. 22.
14. Trilling, "Our Hawthorne," p. 448.
15. Nathaniel Hawthorne to James T. Fields, 6 Nov. 1861, quoted in James C. Austin, *Fields of the Atlantic Monthly: Letters to an Editor, 1861–1870* (San Marino, Calif.: The Huntington Library, 1953), p. 217.
16. James T. Fields to Mary Russell Mitford, 30 Sept. 1851, in Austin, *Fields of the Atlantic Monthly,* p. 209.
17. Nathaniel Hawthorne to William D. Ticknor, 24 July 1852, in *Letters of Hawthorne to William D. Ticknor, 1851–1864* (1910; rpt. 2 vols. in 1, Washington, D.C.: NCR/Microcard Editions, 1972), I, 4.
18. The peculiar intensity with which Hawthorne apparently criticized himself for attempting to live by his pen has long been a subject of debate, for the

writer left a multitude of clues to follow. With surprising regularity his fictional artists consign their manuscripts to the flames ("The Devil in Manuscript"), renounce their choice of vocation ("The Village Uncle"), or stand accused of isolating themselves from the "throb of humanity" *(The Blithedale Romance)*. The charge is made against Ethan Brand, who renounces his quest (to find The Unpardonable Sin) and ends by immolating himself, but whose "crime," as Marius Bewley once remarked, "sounds suspiciously as if he had become a novelist":

> [Brand's heart] had ceased to partake of the universal throb. He had lost his hold of the magnetic chain of humanity. He was no longer a brother-man, opening the chambers or the dungeons of our common nature by the key of holy sympathy, which gave him a right to share in all its secrets; he was now a cold observer, looking on mankind as the subject of his experiment, and, at length, converting man and woman to be his puppets, and pulling the wires that moved them to such degrees of crime as were demanded for his study.

Bewley's comment and the text from Hawthorne appear in *The Complex Fate: Hawthorne, Henry James and Some Other American Writers* (1952; rpt. New York: Gordian Press, 1967), p. 59. Also see Annette K. Baxter, "Independence vs. Isolation: Hawthorne and James on the Problem of the Artist," *Nineteenth-Century Fiction,* 10 (Dec. 1955), 225–31; Edwin Fussell, "Hawthorne, James, and 'The Common Doom,'" *American Quarterly,* 10 (1958), 438–55; Millicent Bell, *Hawthorne's View of the Artist* (New York: State Univ. of New York, 1962); and Neal F. Doubleday, "Hawthorne's Estimate of His Early Work," *American Literature,* 37 (Jan. 1966), 403–9.

19. Nathaniel Hawthorne, *The House of the Seven Gables,* Vol. II of the Centenary Edition of the Works of Nathaniel Hawthorne, pp. 28–29. For the next several pages, subsequent references to this edition of the novel appear parenthetically in the text.
20. R[ichard] H. Fogle, *Hawthorne's Fiction: The Light and the Dark* (Norman: Univ. of Oklahoma Press, 1952), pp. 165–66.
21. The editors of the Centenary Edition substitute *term* for the more vivid *throe* of the first and subsequent editions. Their decision is based on what seems to be an arbitrary reading of the poorly preserved holograph manuscript.
22. Nathaniel Hawthorne to James T. Fields, April 1860, quoted in Fields, *Yesterdays With Authors* (1871; rpt. Boston: Houghton, Mifflin, 1885), p. 89.
23. Nathaniel Hawthorne to James T. Fields, [20 Jan. 1850], quoted in Fields, *Yesterdays With Authors,* pp. 51–52.
24. James T. Fields to Nathaniel Hawthorne, 12 March 1851, quoted in Centenary Edition, XI, 388.
25. Nathaniel Hawthorne to James T. Fields, 25 Feb. 1864, quoted in Charvat, *Literary Publishing in America,* p. 60.
26. Charvat, *Literary Publishing in America,* p. 60.
27. Nathaniel Hawthorne to William D. Ticknor, 19 Jan. [18]55, *Letters of Hawthorne to William D. Ticknor,* I, 75.
28. James, *American Essays,* p. 3.
29. Randall Stewart, "Mrs. Hawthorne's Financial Difficulties: Selections from

Her Letters to James T. Fields, 1865–1868," *More Books: The Bulletin of the Boston Public Library,* 21 (1946), 52.

30. Stewart, "Mrs. Hawthorne's Financial Difficulties," p. 48.
31. Nathaniel Hawthorne to James T. Fields, 1 July 1863, quoted in Randall Stewart, "'Pestiferous Gail Hamilton,' James T. Fields, and the Hawthornes," *New England Quarterly,* 17 (1944), 418.
32. Mrs. Nathaniel Hawthorne to James T. Fields, 2 Aug. 1868, quoted by Randall Stewart, "Mrs. Hawthorne's Quarrel with James T. Fields: Selections from Letters to Fields by Mrs. Hawthorne and Elizabeth Peabody," *More Books: The Bulletin of the Boston Public Library,* 21 (1946), 255.
33. Ticknor & Fields to Mrs. Nathaniel Hawthorne, 28 Aug. 1868, quoted in Ellen B. Ballou, *The Building of the House: Houghton Mifflin's Formative Years* (Boston: Houghton Mifflin, 1970), p. 148. Depending on the context, "copyright," in nineteenth-century parlance, was often synonymous with "royalty." Fields neglected to remind Sophia that Hawthorne's "attorney" at this time was William D. Ticknor, who was also a member of the firm.
34. See Randall Stewart, "Mrs. Hawthorne's Quarrel with James T. Fields," p. 254; and William Charvat, *Literary Publishing in America,* p. 57.
35. Ballou, *Building of the House,* p. 156.
36. Ticknor & Fields to Mrs. Nathaniel Hawthorne, 28 Aug. 1868, Ticknor & Fields Letter Book (1866–78), p. 33 (Houghton Mifflin Archive, Harvard).
37. Elizabeth P. Peabody to James T. Fields, 20 Nov. 1868, quoted in Stewart, "Mrs. Hawthorne's Quarrel with James T. Fields," p. 259.
38. Sophia Hawthorne grudgingly abided by her sister's recommendations and gave Ticknor & Fields Hawthorne's unpublished manuscripts, but she took her own volume of *Notes in England and Italy* to G. P. Putnam of New York, who issued it in 1869. Julian Hawthrone's bitter memories of his mother's degrading quarrel with Fields led him to omit any reference to the publisher in his family memoirs, *Nathaniel Hawthorne and His Wife* (1885) and *Nathaniel Hawthorne and His Circle* (1903). James T. Fields died in 1881, and the ranks of the trade soon closed in defense of his memory. When Thomas Bailey Aldrich, editor of the *Atlantic,* got wind that Julian's 1885 volume was to leave out any mention of Fields, he advised his chief reviewer, Thomas Wentworth Higginson, to teach him a lesson:

> Give Julian a rap on the knuckles for his shabby treatment of Fields. It was he who discovered Nathaniel Hawthorne in his obscurity and despondency, and put hope into his heart. The literary history of Hawthorne that omits mention of J. T. Fields in connection with the publication of *The Scarlet Letter* & the later books, is no history at all. The whole thing is a little piece of small revenge, growing out of a needless quarrel brought about years ago by the pestiferous Gail Hamilton. It seems to me that it is only justice to Fields' memory that Julian Hawthorne's offence should not be overlooked.

Higginson's review dutifully took up the charge: "of all the pettinesses of Mr. Julian Hawthorne's book, there is nothing so petty as this omission. For the sake of what can only be a personal grievance, he has left a gap in his delineation; he has sacrificed the completeness of his work to what can be but an ungenerous whim." Both Aldrich's letter (of 24 Nov. 1884) and Higginson's review (from the Feb. 1885 *Atlantic*) are quoted in Stewart, "'Pestiferous Gail Hamilton,'" p. 422.

39. Mary Abigail Dodge [Gail Hamilton], *A Battle of the Books, Recorded by an Unknown Writer, for the Use of Authors and Publishers: To the First for Doctrine, to the Second for Reproof, to Both for Correction and for Instruction in Righteousness* (New York: Hurd & Houghton, 1870), p. 285.
40. Ballou, *Building of the House*, p. 153.
41. Mrs. Henry James, Sr. to Henry James, 5 April [1870] (James Papers, Harvard).
42. Mrs. James's letter of 5 April 1870 to Henry is the only document in the family papers that refers specifically to *A Battle of the Books*, but Mary Abigail Dodge was no stranger to the household. She conducted a vigorous correspondence with Henry James, Sr. in the 1860s, and her disputatious letters were often circulated at the family dinner table (see Henry James to Thomas Sergeant Perry, 25 March [1864], *Henry James Letters*, I, 50–51). Her presence was still felt after *A Battle of the Books* appeared, for, contrary to Mrs. James's expectations, she remained an active participant in literary circles. In 1872 Miss Dodge invited young Henry James to contribute a story to a new periodical she was publishing; he replied by sending a manuscript, but plans for the magazine eventually collapsed and the story ("The Sweetheart of M. Briseaux") was forwarded at Henry's request to the editor of the *Galaxy*. James met up with Miss Dodge again during his visit to Washington in 1882. "[A]ttired in pale blue satin, point lace and diamonds," she was the novelist's partner at a dinner where James was introduced to President Chester A. Arthur (James to Mrs. Henry James, Sr., 22 Jan. [1882], *Henry James Letters*, II, 370–71). Dodge was obviously a prosperous, if an ephemeral, writer.
43. Henry James to Mrs. Henry James, Sr., 13 Jan. [1878] (James Papers, Harvard). Lathrop's marital problems were no surprise: Hawthorne's son-in-law was a notorious alcoholic. Before his estrangement from Rose Hawthorne, Lathrop made use of the family's papers to write *A Study of Hawthorne* (Boston: J. R. Osgood & Co., 1876), upon which James relied heavily for biographical information when compiling his critical essay for the English Men of Letters series. When James's book appeared, Lathrop's predictably violent reaction to it (which echoed the almost universal charge that James suffered from a want of patriotism) led the novelist to suggest that he be "put to bed, and forbidden the use of pen and ink" (Henry James to Thomas Sergeant Perry, 22 Feb. [1880], *Henry James Letters*, II, 275). Richard Watson Gilder, soon to be editor of the *Century*, went even further:

> Lathrop's letter in the Tribune is the most astonishing thing I have seen lately! Who could have advised him to do such a thing to a fellow-biographer of Hawthorne and fellow-novelist—& what could have led him into such puerile talk[?] I have not read James's "Hawthorne," but I have his "International Episode" and a more *patriotic* book has not been written lately. We "Americans in England" appreciated that. Emerson, Lowell . . . & James have given English people such settings-down as no one else has, & James has in his works "carried the flag" through London Society as no other American has ever done. (Richard Watson Gilder to Robert Underwood Johnson, 3 March 1880 [R. U. Johnson Papers, New York Public Library])

George Monteiro reprints the text of Lathrop's hyperbolic response to James in "'The Items of High Civilization': Hawthorne, Henry James, and George Parsons Lathrop," *Nathaniel Hawthorne Journal 1975,* ed. C. E. Frazer Clark, Jr. (Englewood, Colo.: Microcard Edition Books, 1975), pp. 147–53.

44. This and other entries in Julian Hawthorne's journal are quoted in David W. Pancost, "Henry James and Julian Hawthorne," *American Literature,* 50 (Nov. 1978), 461ff.
45. Henry James to William James, 4 March 1879, *Henry James Letters,* II, 216.
46. Pancost, "Henry James and Julian Hawthorne," p. 463.
47. Pancost, "Henry James and Julian Hawthorne," p. 463.

CHAPTER V

1. James earned his way by writing at least until he was past fifty (in 1893), at which point he derived a comfortable increment to his income from rent and dividends paid on his share of the family's Syracuse, New York, properties, which were transferred to him the year before at the time of his sister's death. James received approximately $1500 a year from 1893 to 1906, at which point William James's eldest son, Harry, assumed responsibility for managing the family's properties and quickly made them much more profitable. After a year's surcease owing to renovations in Syracuse, James's income from the properties effectively doubled. As he wrote to his nephew in June 1907,

> Two precious letters from you have reached me within two or three days. . . . They advise me, to my dazzled stupefaction, of *two* Syracuse remittances (one of *£82* &c, the other of *£51* &c;) of the receipt of which Brown, Shipley & Co. have also notified me. Your munificence overwhelms me, & I'm not sure I'm wholly clear about the source of it. But I read over again your two so precious letters, & there seems to be no mistake. So I thank you devoutly for the whole proceeding—yet feeling as if I should try in vain to express to your blessed activity in this *whole* present Syracuse connection. I am only lost in admiration of your virtue, wisdom & power,—& must ask you to believe this without my multiplying words. (James to Henry James III, 21 June 1907 [James Papers, Harvard])

James diaries record payments of $3300 in 1909, $3150 in 1910, $2700 in 1911, $3850 each in 1912 and 1913, $1650 in 1914 (perhaps only partially recorded), and $3600 in 1915. See also Leon Edel, *Henry James: The Untried Years,* p. 16; *Henry James: The Middle Years,* p. 304; and his introduction to *The Selected Letters of Henry James,* pp. xviii–xx.

2. Rebecca West once recalled that it

> was interesting to note how often in the obituary notices of Mr. James it was said that he never attained popularity, for it shows how soon London forgets its gifts of fame. From 1875 to 1885 (to put it roughly) all England and America were as captivated by the clear beauty of Mr. James's work as in the nineties they were hypnotised by the bright-coloured beauty of Mr. Kipling's art. (*Henry James* [1916; rpt. New York: Haskell House, 1974], p. 46)

3. Henry James to Sir John Clark, 8 Jan. [1882], *Henry James Letters,* II, 367. A fortnight later James reported to Isabella Stuart Gardner with obvious rel-

ish that he had upstaged "the repulsive and fatuous Oscar Wilde" at another Washington gathering (ibid., II, 372). James may have loved London more than his vanity, but he clearly was not indifferent to a certain measure of literary lionizing.

4. Henry James to Frederick Macmillan, 20 Oct. [1881], *Henry James Letters,* II, 361.
5. Henry James to Frederick Macmillan, 27 Dec. [1881] (Macmillan Archive, British Library).
6. Henry James to Houghton, Mifflin & Co., 23 Nov. [1881] (Houghton Mifflin Archive, Harvard). Houghton, Mifflin & Company was formed in 1880 after James's original Boston publisher, James R. Osgood, dissolved his partnership with Henry Oscar Houghton. Under the terms of a special agreement, Houghton, Mifflin retained the rights to all of Osgood's earlier titles, including eight of James's: *A Passionate Pilgrim, Transatlantic Sketches, Roderick Hudson, The American, Watch and Ward, The Europeans, Confidence,* and *The Portrait of a Lady.* For most of these books James continued to receive the standard royalty of 10 percent of the retail price. The one exception was *Transatlantic Sketches,* which earned a 15 percent royalty since James owned the stereotype plates. See Ballou, *Building of the House,* pp. 276–79.
7. Henry James to Thomas Bailey Aldrich, 23 Nov. [1881] (Aldrich Papers, Harvard).
8. Entry for 11 Nov. [1882], *Notebooks,* pp. 44–45.
9. Carl Weber, *The Rise and Fall of James Ripley Osgood: A Biography* (Waterville, Maine: Colby College Press, 1959), p. 198.
10. Henry James to William Dean Howells, 27 Nov. [1882], *Henry James Letters,* II, 392. At the center of the dispute was Howells's assertion that

    > The art of fiction has, in fact, become a finer art in our day than it was with Dickens and Thackeray. We could not suffer the confidential attitude of the latter now, nor the mannerism of the former, any more than we could endure the prolixity of Richardson or the coarseness of Fielding. These great men are of the past—they and their methods and interests.

    See William Dean Howells, "Henry, James, Jr.," *Century,* 25 (Nov. 1882), 28.
11. Edmund Gosse to William Dean Howells, 8 Nov. 1882, *Transatlantic Dialogue: Selected Correspondence of Edmund Gosse,* ed. Paul F. Mattheisen and Michael Millgate (Austin: Univ. of Texas Press, 1965), p. 102. Also see Donald M. Murray, "The Critical Reception of Henry James in English Periodicals, 1875–1916," Diss. New York Univ., 1950, p. 91.
12. Henry James to James R. Osgood, 19 April 1883, *Henry James Letters,* II, 413; James to Frederick Macmillan, 11 June 1883 (Macmillan Archive, British Library). When some of the English sketches had first appeared in the late 1870s, James observed to a friend, "The thing is to hit the happy medium of irony—to be ironical enough without being too much so" (Henry James to Elizabeth Boott, 22 Aug. [1877?] [James Papers, Harvard]).
13. Donald D. Stone, *Novelists in a Changing World: Meredith, James, and the Transformation of English Fiction in the 1880's* (Cambridge, Mass.: Harvard Univ. Press, 1972), p. 231.

14. Henry James to William Dean Howells, 20 March [1883] (Howells Papers, Harvard).
15. See Harper Royalty Accounts, I, 31, 194, 369; II, 9–10. It could be argued that, especially after 1880 (when his last Harper book—until 1893—was published), James's sales did not merit more regular attention; but even during the height of "Daisy Miller"'s popularity the firm made payments to James only twice—in 1879 and 1881.
16. A space was also left blank in Osgood's and Houghton, Mifflin's contracts for exempting a certain number of copies from royalty; the Harpers' had a standing clause exempting the first thousand. A printed form, of course, did not preclude modification. Exemption clauses, for example, were frequently crossed out before a contract was signed. Rates of royalty, however, were seldom altered.
17. Memorandum of Agreement between Henry James and James R. Osgood & Co., 13 April 1883 (Houghton Mifflin Archive, Harvard).
18. Henry James to James R. Osgood, 8 April 1883 (Benjamin Ticknor Papers, Library of Congress). James copied substantial extracts from this letter—including plot outlines of *The Bostonians* and "Lady Barbarina"—into his *Notebooks* (pp. 46–49), and Caroline Ticknor reprinted much of it in *Glimpses of Authors* (Boston: Houghton Mifflin, 1922), pp. 246–49, but the full text, including all of James's language of negotiation, is available only in manuscript.
19. Henry James to Frederick Macmillan, 19 April 1883, *Henry James Letters,* II, 411; Macmillan & Co. to James R. Osgood, 3 & 10 July 1883, MLB, MS 55416, pp. 130, 194 (Macmillan Archive, British Library).
20. Henry James to James R. Osgood, 8 April 1883 (Benjamin Ticknor Papers, Library of Congress).
21. Edmund Wilson, "The Ambiguity of Henry James," in *The Triple Thinkers* (1952; rpt. Harmondsworth, England: Penguin Books, 1962), p. 122.
22. Henry James to Grace Norton, 19 Jan. [1884], *Henry James Letters,* III, 21.
23. Henry James to William James, 20 May [1884] (James Papers, Harvard).
24. James C. Derby, *Fifty Years Among Authors, Books and Publishers* (New York: G. W. Carleton & Co., 1884), p. 198; and Sidney Kobre, *Development of American Journalism* (Dubuque, Iowa: William C. Brown, 1969), p. 369.
25. Henry James to James R. Osgood, 29 Jan. 1884 (James Papers, Duke University).
26. Henry James to Thomas Sergeant Perry, 6 March [1884], in Harlow, *Thomas Sergeant Perry,* p. 316.
27. Henry James to Alice James, 5 Feb. [1884] (James Papers, Harvard). Some critics have suggested that James might have repented had he seen the garish headlines that accompanied his stories in the provincial papers. The Cincinnati *Enquirer* extended one title to read: "'Georgina's Reasons': Henry James's Latest Story; a Woman Who Commits Bigamy and Enforces Silence on Her Husband!" The additional subtitles, however, genuinely reflect the exaggerated melodrama of James's story (surely one of his weakest), which was deliberately calculated to appeal to a newspaper audience perpetually exposed to sensationalism. See Edward P. Mitchell, *Memoirs of an Editor:*

Fifty Years of American Journalism (New York: Charles Scribner's Sons, 1924), p. 280.

28. Henry James, *The Bostonians* (New York: Macmillan, 1886), pp. 122, 124. In the remainder of this chapter, references to this edition appear parenthetically in the text.
29. Henry James, "The Art of Fiction" [1884], in *Partial Portraits* (1888; rpt. Ann Arbor: Univ. of Michigan Press, 1970), p. 378.
30. James, "The Art of Fiction," p. 380.
31. James, "The Art of Fiction," p. 383.
32. Entry for 8 April 1883, *Notebooks,* p. 47.
33. Henry James to William James, 5 Oct. [1884] (James Papers, Harvard). The novelist's sense of the probable reception that awaited this book was absolutely correct. After half of the serial appeared in the *Century,* Francis Parkman (a thoroughly proper Bostonian) commended James for "a masterly analysis of a most vile and rotten stratum of our society," but he also reminded him, "You are hardly fair in calling it the Bostonians, since there is a good deal here, quite as representative as the other, that is as sound as a nut. I never knew Olive Chancellor, but I have had the ill-luck to know her component parts, and you have combined them with admirable felicity and truth" (Francis Parkman to Henry James, 15 Sept. 1885 [James Papers, Harvard]).
34. Henry James to Thomas Sergeant Perry, 6 March [1884], in Harlow, *Thomas Sergeant Perry,* p. 316.
35. Ransom's language, like Olive's, also reverberates in James's letters. In the months prior to writing *The Bostonians,* James complained to Howells of the phenomenal sales of F. Marion Crawford's latest novel, *To Leeward:*

    > What you tell me of the success of Crawford's last novel sickens and almost paralyses me. It seems to me (the book) so comtemptibly bad and ignoble that the idea of people reading it in such numbers makes one return upon one's self and ask what is the use of trying to write anything decent or serious for a public so absolutely idiotic. It must be totally wasted. I would rather have produced the basest experiment in the "naturalistic" that is being practised here [James was writing from Paris] than such a piece of sixpenny humbug. Work so shamelessly bad seems to me to dishonour the novelist's art to a degree that is absolutely not to be forgiven; just as its success dishonours the people for whom one supposes one's self to write. Excuse my ferocity, which (more discreetly and philosophically) I think you must share; and don't mention it, please, to any one, as it will be set down to green-eyed jealousy. (Henry James to William Dean Howells, 21 Feb. 1884, *Henry James Letters,* III, 27)

36. Henry James to Mrs. Humphrey Ward, 9 Dec. [1884], *Henry James Letters,* III, 59.
37. James returned to this theme with greater effectiveness when he wrote *The Tragic Muse* five years later. In a sense, that novel embodies James's suggested revisions of *Miss Bretherton.*
38. Paul John Eakin, *The New England Girl: Cultural Ideals in Hawthorne, Stowe, Howells, and James* (Athens: Univ. of Georgia Press, 1976), p. 213.
39. David Howard, *"The Bostonians,"* in *The Air of Reality: New Essays on Henry James,* ed. John Goode (London: Methuen, 1972), p. 67. Also useful,

though more general in scope, is Clinton Oliver's discussion of "Henry James as a Social Critic," *Antioch Review,* 7 (Summer 1947), 246–47.

40. James's venom is unmistakably present in his elaboration of Pardon's character:

> For this ingenuous son of his age all distinction between the person and the artist had ceased to exist; the writer was personal, the person food for newsboys, and everything and every one were every one's business. All things, with him, referred themselves to print, and print meant simply infinite reporting, a promptitude of announcement, abusive when necessary, or even when not, about his fellow-citizens. He poured contumely on their private life, on their personal appearance, with the best conscience in the world. His faith, again, was the faith of Selah Tarrant—that being in the newspapers is a condition of bliss, and that it would be fastidious to question the terms of the privilege. (pp. 122–23)

"[I]ndelicacy," James bluntly concludes, "was his profession" (p. 140). The novelist's lifelong contempt for "newspaper vulgarity & mendacity" is documented throughout his correspondence and is perhaps even more vividly embodied in such fictional characters as George P. Flack, who edits *The Reverberator* (1888), and the anonymous but thoroughly detestable "publishing scoundrel" of *The Aspern Papers* (1888). After Charles Scribner's Sons became James's publishers in the United States at the turn of the century, he pleaded with the firm not to send him any reviews or clippings from the American papers: "I have long since ceased even to be conscious of newspaper vulgarity & mendacity—it is too great an abyss of ineptitude & puerility—so I beg you kindly to think of me always as one for whom such things don't exist." Henry James to Charles Scribner's Sons, 12 Dec. 1904 (Scribner Archive, Princeton).

41. Henry James, "Emerson" [1887], in *Partial Portraits,* p. 9.
42. William Dean Howells to Edmund Gosse, 9 March 1885, *Selected Letters,* III, 118.
43. See, for example, F. O. Matthiessen, *The James Family* (New York: Knopf, 1947), pp. 325–29; and Edel, *Henry James: The Middle Years,* pp. 142–43.
44. Henry James to William James, 14 Feb. [1885], *Henry James Letters,* III, 70.
45. Henry James to Benjamin Ticknor, [1885] (Benjamin Ticknor Papers, Library of Congress).
46. George E. Brett to Frederick Macmillan, 23 April, 19 March, & 1 May 1886 (Macmillan Archive, British Library).
47. He even attributed a similarly urgent motive to Verena, who announces early in the book, "I want to do something great!" "You will, you will," Olive rapturously assures her, "we both will!" (pp. 85–86).
48. Even though he eventually inverted most of them into ironic parodies of popular stereotypes: see Marcia Jacobson, *Henry James and the Mass Market* (University: Univ. of Alabama Press, 1983), pp. 30–38.
49. Donald D. Stone, *Novelists in a Changing World,* p. 261.

CHAPTER VI

1. Henry James to William Dean Howells, 2 Jan. 1888, *Henry James Letters,* III, 209.

2. Henry James to William Dean Howells, 19 Oct. [1886] (Howells Papers, Harvard).
3. Henry James to Thomas Bailey Aldrich, 13 Feb. [1884], *Henry James Letters,* III, 25.
4. Henry James to Thomas Bailey Aldrich, 19 March 1884, *Henry James Letters,* III, 37–38. James's price was still rather high for a novel that would not be published in volume form by the *Atlantic*'s owners, Houghton, Mifflin & Co. Most publishing houses sought to profit from the marketing potential of their affiliated magazines by requiring contributors to issue their serials under the same firm's imprint. At the time the deal for *The Princess* was settled, however, the novel "as a republication" was "definitely promised to Osgood." James to Aldrich, 16 April [1884] (Aldrich Papers, Harvard).
5. Henry James to Thomas Bailey Aldrich, 30 Dec. [1884] (Aldrich Papers, Harvard)
6. Carl J. Weber, *The Rise and Fall of James Ripley Osgood,* pp. 137–38.
7. Henry James to Benjamin Ticknor, 26 Feb. [1885] (Collection of American Literature, Yale).
8. Henry James to James R. Osgood, 18 April [1885], *Henry James Letters,* III, 78.
9. Henry James to Frederick Macmillan, 5 May [1885], *Henry James Letters,* III, pp. 79–80.
10. Frederick Macmillan to Henry James, 6 May 1885, MLB, MS 55419, p. 1125 (Macmillan Archive, British Library).
11. Frederick Macmillan to Henry James, 13 & 20 May 1885, MLB, MS 55419, pp. 1160, 1193 (Macmillan Archive, British Library).
12. William James to Henry James, 21 May [1885] (James Papers, Harvard).
13. Henry James to William Dean Howells, 23 May [1885] (Howells Papers, Harvard).
14. Henry James to Frederick Macmillan, 2 June [1885] (Macmillan Archive, British Library).
15. George E. Brett to Frederick Macmillan, 2 June 1885 (Macmillan Archive, British Library).
16. In this and other important respects, the complicated history of *The Bostonians'* publishing career vividly illustrates the changing nature of the Anglo-American literary marketplace. As was the case in so many other industrial enterprises during the late nineteenth century, the transition to a recognizably modern form of organization in the book trade was not always rational or consistently legal. In extending its publishing operations to the United States, the Macmillan Company, for example, was handicapped by high tariffs on imported books and the absence of international copyright controls. The latter problem was eventually solved in 1891, when the United States and Great Britain adopted the first Anglo-American copyright convention. To circumvent the American duty on imports, however, the firm deliberately underestimated the declared value of its shipments to America. When copies of *The Bostonians* and one of F. Marion Crawford's novels arrived in New York harbor in March 1886, officers at the Custom House impounded Macmillan's shipment until George E. Brett arrived to settle the government's claims. The alternative, Brett explained to the London office, was simply unthinkable,

because the customs agents threatened to turn the matter over to a jury of American publishers who more knowingly could appraise the market value of Macmillan's books. "[Henry Oscar] Houghton is a very good fellow," Brett chuckled in Macmillan's ear, "but you will agree with me in thinking that there is no reason why we should be ready to let him see the details of our business." George E. Brett to Frederick Macmillan, 19 March 1886 (Macmillan Archive, British Library).

17. William James to Henry James, 6 June [18]85 (James Papers, Harvard).
18. Henry James to Benjamin Ticknor, 26 June [1885] (Benjamin Ticknor Papers, Library of Congress).
19. Macmillan & Co. to J. R. Osgood & Co., 6 July [18]85, MLB, MS 55420, p. 109 (Macmillan Archive, British Library).
20. Henry James to William James, 24 July [1885], *Henry James Letters,* III, 95; and 31 July [1885] (James Papers, Harvard).
21. Henry James to William James, 21 Aug. [1885] (James Papers, Harvard).
22. The novelist still came out ahead, however, because even if every copy that Macmillan printed had been sold, a 15 percent royalty (without the advance) would have yielded James only £395:

15 percent of 600 copies @ 31*s*./6*d*.	=	£142
15 percent of 2000 copies @ 6*s*./-	=	90
15 percent of 3000 copies @ $1.75	=	163 ($788)
Total	=	£395

The publisher learned his lesson in arithmetic and offered James a more realistic advance of £400 on *The Princess Casamassima.* For printing figures and prices of Macmillan's English and American editions of *The Bostonians,* see *A Bibliography of Henry James,* 3rd ed., pp. 73–75.

23. Henry James to William James, 9 Oct. 1885, *Henry James Letters,* III, 102.
24. The phrase is James's; see his preface to *The Princess Casamassima* in *The Art of the Novel,* p. 78.
25. Lionel Trilling, *"The Princess Casamassima,"* in *The Liberal Imagination: Essays on Literature and Society* (1950; rpt. Garden City, NY: Doubleday-Anchor Books, 1953), p. 64; W. H. Tilley, *The Background of "The Princess Casamassima,"* University of Florida Monographs in the Humanities, No. 5 (Gainesville: Univ. of Florida Press, 1960), p. 5 and passim; and Marcia Jacobson, *Henry James and the Mass Market,* pp. 41–61. As evidence of the working-class novel's popularity, Jacobson notes the publication of several works by Gissing (*Workers in the Dawn* [1880], *The Unclassed* [1884], and *Demos* [1886]) and Walter Besant (*All Sorts and Conditions of Men* [1882] and *Children of Gibeon* [1886]), which established the genre's conventions of plot and character: the socially conscious aristocrat, typically female, who goes to work in the slums; the lower-class stiff who, through luck and initiative, wins a place (often through marriage) in the middle class—neither of whom finally threatens the existing class structure in any fundamental way. While James's novel leans heavily on these precedents, it also stubbornly rejects "the usual sentimental and optimistic resolution of public fiction" (p. 59).
26. *Notebooks,* p. 68.

27. To the end of the crisis, William James failed to appreciate the magnitude of his brother's setback. In September 1885, when he asked Henry to repay a small loan ("now that you turn out not to be a loser by Osgood"), the novelist exploded, "What do you mean . . . by saying—'now that I am to lose nothing by Osgood!' I lose every penny—not a stiver shall I have had for the serial, for which he received a large sum from the *Century.*" William James to Henry James, 17 Sept. [18]85 (James Papers, Harvard); and Henry to William, 9 Oct. 1885, *Henry James Letters,* III, 102.
28. Writing from "the depths of anti-literary British Philistinism" at Bournemouth, James confessed his troubles to a more fortunate friend:

> You see I have turned away from Paris, instead of toward it. I shan't get there this summer, I greatly fear. There are *entassements* of obstacles—culminating a week ago in the failure of J. R. Osgood and Co. my Boston publishers by whom I have lost a largeish sum of money. That puts a spoke in my wheel for the present. And in fact I shall be all summer a kind of *garde-malade.* (Henry James to Theodore E. Child, 13 May [1885], *Henry James Letters,* III, 88)

29. Leon Edel, *Henry James: The Middle Years,* p. 190.
30. Henry James, *The Princess Casamassima* (New York: Macmillan, 1886), p. 120. Throughout the rest of this chapter, subsequent references to this edition appear parenthetically in the text.
31. Clinton Oliver, "Henry James as a Social Critic," p. 252.
32. "For James," Goode continues, "the audience is an impingement, and the extent to which he feels it as such is indicated by the force of the irony with which he describes the pragmatic attitude to the novel [in 'The Art of Fiction']":

> Literature should either be instructive or amusing, and there is in many minds an impression that . . . artistic preoccupations, the search for form, contribute to neither end, interfere indeed with both. They are too frivolous to be edifying, and too serious to be diverting; and they are moreover priggish and paradoxical and superfluous. That, I think, represents the manner in which the latent thought of many people who read novels as an exercise in skipping would explain itself if it were to become articulate. They would argue, of course, that a novel ought to be "good," but they would interpret this term in a fashion of their own, which indeed would vary considerably from one critic to another. One would say that being good means representing virtuous and aspiring characters, placed in prominent positions; another would say that it depends on a "happy ending," on a distribution at the last of prizes, pensions, husbands, wives, babies, millions, appended paragraphs, and cheerful remarks. Another still would say that it means being full of incident and movement, so that we shall wish to be one jump ahead, to see who was the mysterious stranger, and if the stolen will was ever found, and shall not be distracted from this pleasure by any tiresome analysis or "description." But they would all agree that the "artistic" idea would spoil some of their fun.

See John Goode, "The Art of Fiction: Walter Besant and Henry James," *Tradition and Tolerance in Nineteenth-Century Fiction: Critical Essays on Some English and American Novels,* ed. David Howard et al. (London: Routledge and Kegan Paul, 1966), pp. 251, 261–62.

33. James, "The Art of Fiction," pp. 395–96.
34. Henry James to Henry James, Sr., 16 April [1879] (James Papers, Harvard).

35. James, "The Art of Fiction," p. 389.
36. Although Pinnie and Mr. Vetch hope that Hyacinth's work will satisfy his instinctive appreciation of finer materials (and better literature) than he will ever find in Lomax Place, his choice of vocation, James notes, is "both a blessing and a drawback to him," because it educates his taste and "train[s] him in the finest discriminations, in the perception of beauty and hatred of ugliness" (p. 117). As Frederick Crews has suggested, the development of Hyacinth's artistic sensibility "amounts to the first step toward an aesthetically grounded disgust with the lower classes" (*The Tragedy of Manners: Moral Drama in the Later Novels of Henry James* [New Haven, Conn.: Yale Univ. Press, 1957], p. 22).
37. To some critics, Hyacinth's superior tone is frankly embarrassing. As Irving Howe has wittily remarked, James describes Hyacinth as "a youth . . . 'on whom nothing is lost,' and that is true: one fully credits his talent for registering every nuance of moral chivalry or coarseness. But he is also a youth on whom nothing rubs off; a bastard by birth, he behaves as if he were immaculate in conception" ("Henry James: The Political Vocation," in *Politics and the Novel* [New York: Horizon Press, 1957], p. 152). Even Hyacinth's defenders are obliged to confess that, for a novel purportedly dealing with the sordid conditons of the urban proletariat, the characters in *The Princess* spend less time in factories or workshops than they do on the fringes of Bohemia. Amanda Pynsent, the dressmaker who raises Hyacinth in Lomax Place, plies her needle in a dirty corner of London ("miles away from the West End"); nevertheless, in her window she hangs a sign advertising "*Modes et Robes* . . . Court Dresses, Mantles and Fashionable Bonnets" (pp. 125–26). Her neighbor Mr. Vetch is a failed gentleman "whose fate [has] condemned him . . . to play a fiddle at a second-rate theatre for a few shillings a week" (p. 18). Even Millicent Henning, the robust, cockneyfied incarnation of the People, considers herself a brilliant performer in the theatrical world of fashion. Pathetically, Millicent sustains this illusion to the end, even though in her last scene (when the vulgarly lascivious Captain Sholto lets his eyes travel "up and down the front of [her] person") her modeling becomes a ritual of prostitution. To Millicent, as J. A. Ward points out, such behavior is "an entrance into the sublimity of the upper classes" (*The Search for Form: Studies in the Structure of James Fiction* [Chapel Hill: Univ. of North Carolina Press, 1967], p. 129).
38. Joseph W. Rogers, "The Rise of American Edition Binding," in *Bookbinding in America: Three Essays,* ed. Hellmut Lehmann-Haupt (Portland, Maine: The Southworth-Anthoensen Press, 1941), pp. 145–58.
39. Indeed, if Hyacinth Robinson had kept a diary, one can easily imagine that it would read like Cobden-Sanderson's. An entry of 8 March 1887, for example, conveys the psychological dimension of his divided social and artistic sympathies:

> Depression and suicidal wickedness in my heart! Is it because I have immersed myself in bookbinding pure and simple, and in the life of the body and of its trappings, the last few weeks? No Greek, no Henry George, no wide horizon and hope of higher things, but plod, plod, plod, morning, noon and night, books, books,

> books, till the body, even, aches. Oh, come back the higher life, the aspiration and the hope of higher things, the self-sacrifice, the burden to be borne for others unhappier still, the agonizing till the light burst and flood the skies now dark! Strive, strive, strive.

Hyacinth also suffers pangs of guilt when he returns from a self-indulgently extended visit to the Princess Casamassima's country house to discover that his foster-mother has contracted a terminal illness during his absence. At the end of the novel, of course, Hyacinth's own depression and suicidal tendencies are tragically fulfilled. See Thomas James Cobden-Sanderson, *The Journals of Thomas James Cobden-Sanderson, 1879–1922,* 2 vols. (London: Richard Cobden-Sanderson, 1926), I, 289, 254–55.

40. T[homas] J[ames] Cobden-Sanderson, *The Ideal Book or Book Beautiful* [1900], in *Cobden-Sanderson and the Doves Press* (San Francisco: John Henry Nash, 1929), pp. xii, xvii; and Adeline R. Tintner, "Henry James and Fine Books," *AB Bookman's Weekly,* 61 (3 April 1978), 2410.
41. William Dean Howells, "The Man of Letters as a Man of Business," p. 35.
42. Edmund Gosse, "The Profession of Authorship," in *The Grievances Between Authors & Publishers, Being the Report of the Conferences of the Incorporated Society of Authors Held at Willis's Rooms, in March 1887: With Additional Matter and Summary* (London: Field & Tuer, 1887), pp. 63–64.
43. James Stanley Little [secretary of the Society of Authors] to Henry James, 30 Jan. & 3 Feb. 1888, Add. MS 37052, pp. 349, 368 (Society of Authors Deposit, British Library).
44. See Appendix A, "Henry James and the Movement for International Copyright," following Chapter VIII.
45. Henry James to Edmund Gosse, 18 April 1902 (Berg Collection, New York Public Library).
46. By the 1890s, James was utterly exasperated with "the robust & virtuous Besantry" and their incessant agitation "about the too-iterated money-question." If only they would stop chattering, James told Edmund Gosse,

    > some little sound may at last get a chance to be heard on some *other* aspect of authorship, which is no more mentioned, mostly than if it didn't exist. The fact is that authorship is guilty of a great mistake, a gross want of tact, in formulating & publishing its claim to be a "profession." Let other trades call it so—& let it take no notice. That's enough. It ought to have of the professions only a professional thoroughness. But *never* to have that, & to cry on the housetops instead that it *is* the grocer & the shoemaker is to bring on itself a ridicule of which it will simply die.

    Henry James to Edmund Gosse, [10 May 1895] (Brotherton Collection, Univ. of Leeds).
47. As J. A. Ward has noted, "James's major alteration in *The Princess Casamassima* and most of his novels of the next fifteen years is to diminish the stature of the hero. He is not only poor, but he is also powerless. Unlike the Americans who invade Europe with dynamic vigor and confidence, the heroes of the London novels are armed only with their sensibilities." See *The Imagination of Disaster: Evil in the Fiction of Henry James* (Lincoln: Univ. of Nebraska Press, 1961), p. 56.

48. Entry for 10 Aug. 1885, *Notebooks,* p. 68.
49. Irving Howe, "Henry James: The Political Vocation," p. 155.

CHAPTER VII

1. James, *The Art of the Novel,* p. 79.
2. Henry James to Frederick Macmillan, 22 Oct. [1886] (Macmillan Archive, British Library).
3. Henry James to Frederick Macmillan, 24 June 1886; Macmillan to James, 24 June [188]6, MLB, MS 55422, p. 349 (Macmillan Archive, British Library).
4. Frederick Macmillan to Henry James, 3 April, 2 & 29 May [188]8, MLB, MS 55426, pp. 209, 608, 620 (Macmillan Archive, British Library).
5. Henry James to William Dean Howells, 2 Jan. 1888, *Henry James Letters,* III, 209.
6. If editors were keeping James's manuscripts back, Edel observes, "it was not because they had rejected them, but because they wished all the more advantageously to publish them." Most literary magazines were now using line engravings to attract readers, and James's work (like that of other writers) was stuck at the bottleneck of the illustrator's drawing table. See Leon Edel, *Henry James: The Middle Years,* p. 243.
7. Robert Louis Stevenson to Henry James, 28 May 1888, in *Henry James and Robert Louis Stevenson: A Record of Their Friendship and Criticism,* ed. Janet Adam Smith (London: Rupert Hart-Davis, 1948), p. 172. In a collective appraisal of James's recently published work, Howells echoed Stevenson's judgment, but he also directed a salvo of scornful disbelief at the periodical reviewers who treated James so shabbily:

   > It is in a way discreditable to our time that a writer of such quality should ever have grudging welcome; the fact impeaches not only our intelligence, but our sense of the artistic. It will certainly amaze a future day that such things as [James's] could be done in ours and meet only a feeble and conditioned acceptance from the "best" criticism, with something little short of ribald insult from the commom cry of literary paragraphers.

   Happily, Howells continued, newspaper critics were not an author's only readers—and not even his judges. The editors of the magazines, which were now the real avenues to the public, played that role; and "their recent unanimity in presenting simultaneously some of the best work of Mr. James's life in the way of short stories indicates the existence of an interest in all he does, which is doubtless the true measure of his popularity." See William Dean Howells, "Editor's Study," *Harper's Monthly,* 77 (Oct. 1888), 800.
8. Henry James to Frederick Macmillan, 24 May 1888 (Macmillan Archive, British Library).
9. Frederick Macmillan to Henry James. 25 May [188]8, MLB, MS 55426, p. 608 (Macmillan Archive, British Library). Neither James nor Macmillan expected a noticeable return from *Partial Portraits;* collections of critical essays, of whatever merit, rarely sold in large numbers. For purposes of comparison, therefore, Macmillan's advance of £125 can be considered a measure of his expectations for *The Reverberator* alone.

10. Henry James to Frederick Macmillan, 5 July 1888, *Henry James Letters,* III, 237–38; Macmillan to James, 6 July [188]8, MLB, MS 55426, p. 940 (Macmillan Archive, British Library).
11. Henry James to Charles Eliot Norton, 6 Dec. [1886], *Henry James Letters,* III, 145.
12. Henry James to William Dean Howells, 25 Feb. [1887] (Howells Papers, Harvard).
13. Henry James to William Dean Howells, 29 Sept. 1888 (Howells Papers, Harvard); James to Frederick Macmillan, 13 Oct. [1888] (Macmillan Archive, British Library).
14. Exact sales records have not survived, but this inference is sustained by the printing history of each volume. Within two years of publication, 4500 copies of *The Reverberator* were in print, 4650 of *The Aspern Papers,* and 4500 of *A London Life,* representing both English and American issues. The first printing of *Partial Portraits* consisted of 2000 copies, divided between both countries; additonal printings of 500 copies each were made at roughly five-year intervals after publication. See *A Bibliography of Henry James,* 3rd ed., pp. 76–83; supplemental printing records are contained in Macmillan's Editions Book, pp. 266–67, which is kept in the company's offices at Basingstoke, England.
15. Roger Gard, *Henry James: The Critical Heritage,* p. 552; cf. Appendix B, "Henry James's Literary Income."
16. Henry James to Grace Norton, 23 July 1887, *Henry James Letters,* III, 198.
17. The germ of the story had been available to him since the preceding winter, according to Leon Edel, when a young American woman named May Marcy McClellan had scandalized Venetian society "by writing a gossipy letter to an American newspaper about the very society which had entertained her." The case struck James as yet another example of "the invasion, the impudence and shamelessness, of the newspaper and the interviewer, the devouring *publicity* of life, the extinction of all sense between public and private . . . the sinking of *manners,* in so many ways, which the democratization of the world brings with it." See Edel, *Henry James: The Middle Years,* p. 228; and James, *Notebooks,* p. 82.
18. Henry James to Robert Underwood Johnson, 16 Jan. 1888 (Johnson Papers, American Academy of Arts & Letters).
19. Henry James to Frederick Macmillan, 30 Nov. 1887 (Macmillan Archive, British Library).
20. Henry James to Thomas Bailey Aldrich, 3 March 1888, *Henry James Letters,* III, 223.
21. James, preface to *The Tragic Muse,* in *The Art of the Novel,* p. 90.
22. Henry James to Charles Scribner's Sons, 7 April 1886 (Scribner Archive, Princeton).
23. Henry James to Thomas Bailey Aldrich, 30 Sept., 24 & 28 Oct. [1888] (Aldrich Papers, Harvard); James to Houghton, Mifflin & Co., 30 Oct. 1888 (Houghton Mifflin Archive, Harvard).
24. Frederick Macmillan to Henry James, 22 March [18]90, MLB, MS 55430, p. 648 (Macmillan Archive, British Library).

25. Henry James to Houghton, Mifflin & Co., 25 Feb. 1890 (Houghton Mifflin Archive, Harvard).
26. It would, of course, fill an expensive triple-decker for the circulating libraries, but Macmillan's concern reveals the increasing importance of the market for less costly reprints. If, because of its length, the novel could not be reprinted in a single volume, its chances with book *buyers* would be hurt (two volumes naturally costing more than one). Despite the inordinate size of *The Tragic Muse,* Macmillan crammed it into a single volume with 492 pages of closely printed text, which sold for 3/6 ($0.85). Houghton, Mifflin preferred a more comfortable format, even though they invariably would sell fewer copies in two volumes (at $2.50 the set) than in one (at the usual price of $1.50). "I am sorry to learn that the [book] must make two volumes," James confessed, "& can only hope it will triumph over this disadvantage" (Henry James to Houghton, Mifflin & Co., 25 Feb. 1890 [Houghton Mifflin Archive, Harvard]).
27. Henry James to Frederick Macmillan, 24 March 1890, *Henry James Letters,* III, 274. The Harpers paid James £350 ($1700) for the translation of *Port Tarascon,* the signed receipt for which is deposited at the Morgan Library.
28. Frederick Macmillan to Henry James, 3 Jan. 1885 & 25 March [18]90, MLB, MS 55419, p. 55; MS 55430, p. 674 (Macmillan Archive, British Library).
29. Henry James to Houghton, Mifflin & Co., 25 March 1890 (Houghton Mifflin Archive, Harvard).
30. Henry James to Frederick Macmillan, 26 March 1890, *Henry James Letters,* III, 274–75.
31. Frederick Macmillan to Henry James, 26 March [18]90, MLB, MS 55430, p. 691 (Macmillan Archive, British Library). Simon Nowell-Smith prints an extract from this letter in *Letters to Macmillan,* p. 171.
32. Henry James to Frederick Macmillan, 28 March 1890, *Henry James Letters,* III, 275.
33. Leon Edel, *Henry James: The Middle Years,* p. 265.
34. Edmund Gosse, "The Profession of Authorship," in *The Grievances Between Authors and Publishers,* pp. 73–74.
35. Henry James to Edmund Gosse, 24 Dec. [1887] (Brotherton Collection, Univ. of Leeds).
36. George H. Doran, *Chronicles of Barabbas, 1884–1934* (New York: Harcourt, Brace, 1935), p. 92.
37. John Tebbel, *A History of Book Publishing in the United States,* II, 131–32.
38. Henry Holt, "The Commercialization of Literature," p. 583. Many other American publishers shared Holt's disparaging attitude, because the influence of the literary agent broke the shins of their favorite hobbyhorse: courtesy of the trade. Again and again the same anxieties surface in publishers' memoirs from this period. The agent subverted a publisher's traditional "personal" dealings with his authors and corrupted writers by enticing them with a "mirage of a new Eldorado in the literary world." By pitting one publisher against another in competiton for a manuscript, the agent comercialized the writer's sacred calling and vulgarized his efforts. Of course, no truly American author would suffer this dishonor. As George Haven Putnam proudly observed in 1897, agents were a foreign invention: "The agency system has

not yet taken any very considerable part in the publishing relations in the United States. American authors have, for the most part, found it to their advantage to select their own publishers, and after once establishing with a publisher satisfactory relations, they have also realized the advantage of preserving those relations." Publishers maintained this chauvinist fiction well into the twentieth century. In 1913 Robert Sterling Yard claimed that literary agents did "not thrive in America upon commissions from American authors. The American author is more of a business man than his English cousin and much prefers to manage his own publishing arrangements. Nor is he so changeable. As a rule he makes a partner of his publisher and works amicably with him year after year for their common good." This was more wish fulfillment than statement of fact, but the overwhelmingly nostalgic impulse that inspired Yard's treatise is characteristic of the genre. Only a few perceptive observers grudgingly recognized the agent's potential value in managing the increasingly complex market for literary property. "These 'Literary Agents' are a nuisance in many respects," Charles Scribner's scout in London reported in 1906, "but as they save the authors much trouble with details, they are likely still to be utilized, & now ours are making their appearance constantly." In time, as Donald Sheehan has written, "publishers were to discover that the agency system did not preclude the personal ties with authors upon which they placed such value. If the drawing of contracts became a contest between business men, the relation between editor and author remained relatively undisturbed."

See G[eorge] H[aven] P[utnam] and J. B[ishop], *Authors and Publishers: A Manual of Suggestions for Beginners in Literature,* 7th ed. (New York: G. P. Putnam's Sons, 1897), pp. 132–33; [Walter Hines Page], *A Publisher's Confession* (New York: Doubleday, Page & Co., 1905), pp. 65–67; Robert Sterling Yard, *The Publisher* (Boston: Houghton Mifflin, 1913), pp. 174–75; Lemuel Bangs to Charles Scribner, 9 Feb. [19]06 (Scribner Archive, Princeton); and Donald Sheehan, *This Was Publishing,* p. 78.

39. Henry James to Edmund Gosse, 3 Jan. 1888, *Henry James Letters,* III, 211.
40. Henry James to William James, 20 Feb. 1888 (James Papers, Harvard).
41. A recent query to A. P. Watt Ltd. (which is still very much in business) yielded only a bewildered response: "None of us here were ever aware that this firm had acted for Henry James" (A. P. Watt Ltd. to the author, 23 July 1982).
42. Frederick Macmillan to A. P. Watt, 2 April 1890; Henry James to A. P. Watt, 2 April 1890 (Berg Collection, New York Public Library). Even after paying Watt his 10 percent commission, James still made out rather well. The publisher, by comparison, was down more than £170 on the transaction at the time his lease expired. See Simon Nowell-Smith, *Letters to Macmillan,* p. 172.
43. Henry James, *The Tragic Muse,* 2 vols. (Boston: Houghton, Mifflin, 1890), I, 172. Since the two volumes are continuously paginated (dividing between p. 422 and p. 423), volume numbers are omitted in subsequent references to this editon, which appear parenthetically in the text throughout the rest of this chapter.
44. See James's letters to Hendrik Anderson, quoted in Chapter I, and one of 14

April 1912 to the same artist (in response to Andersen's plans for a "World City"), from *Henry James Letters,* IV, 611–12:

> Not another day do I delay to answer (with such difficulty!) your long and interesting letter. . . . Brace yourself . . . though I don't quite see why I need, having showed you in the past, so again and again, that your mania for the colossal, the swelling and the huge, the monotonously and repeatedly huge, breaks the heart of me for you . . . I have practically said these things to you before—though perhaps never in so dreadfully straight and sore a form as today; when this culmination of your madness, to the tune of five hundred million tons of weight, simply squeezes it out of me. For that, dearest boy, is the dread Delusion to warn you against—what is called in Medical Science MEGALOMANIA (look it up in the Dictionary!) in French *la folie des grandeurs,* the infatuation and disproportionate love and pursuit of, and attempt at, the Big, the Bigger, the Biggest, the Immensest Immensity, with all sense of proportion, application, relation and possibility madly *submerged.*

45. James, "The Lessson of Balzac," in *The Question of Our Speech,* p. 104. Kenneth Graham also notes the relevance of this passage in *Henry James: The Drama of Fulfillment* (Oxford: Oxford Univ. Press, 1975), p. 123n.
46. There is truth as well as humor in Alwyn Berland's charge that "the very end—the last fifty pages or so—seems a frantic packing of luggage into the groaning trunk, the whole banged shut with sleeves and snippets bulging out still, and the train gates closing" (*Culture and Conduct in the Novels of Henry James* [Cambridge: Cambridge Univ. Press, 1981], p. 176).
47. Kenneth Graham, *Henry James: The Drama of Fulfillment,* p. 125.
48. Henry James to Francis Boott, 20 May [1889] (James Papers, Harvard).
49. Henry James to Theodora Sedgwick, 9 Oct. 1890 (James Papers, Harvard).

CHAPTER VIII

1. Henry James to William Dean Howells, 10 Jan. 1891 (Howells Papers, Harvard).
2. After their sister's death in 1892, William warned Henry not to deplete the capital from her legacy: "You will need a good deal more than you are likely to have when your writing powers are cut short, as in the nature of things they must be some day if you live" (William James to Henry James, 22 March [18]92 [James Papers, Harvard]).
3. Henry James to Edith Wharton, 20 Dec. 1911, quoted in Millicent Bell, *Edith Wharton and Henry James: The Story of Their Friendship* (New York: George Braziller, 1965), p. 167.
4. Entry for 21 April 1894, *Notebooks,* p. 158.
5. [Curtis Brown], "'The Commercialization of Literature' and the Literary Agent: By One of Them," *Fortnightly Review,* 80 (Aug. 1906), 359.
6. Entry for 26 Jan. 1895, *Notebooks,* p. 180.
7. Anne T. Margolis offers a persuasive account of James's uncomfortable relation with the emerging avant garde in her recent study, *Henry James and the Problem of Audience: An International Act* (Ann Arbor, Mich.: UMI Research Press, 1985).

8. Henry James to William Dean Howells, 4 May 1898 (Howells Papers, Harvard).
9. Leon Edel, "The Architecture of Henry James's 'New York Edition,'" *New England Quarterly,* 24 (1951), p. 171. Edel repeats his argument in *Henry James: The Master,* pp. 321–39. In his new edition of James's tales, Maqbool Aziz asserts correctly that "the design of the New York Edition *evolved* as work progressed on it," but he accepts Edel's claim that James alone limited the edition to twenty-three volumes. See Aziz's introduction to *The Tales of Henry James,* 3 vols. to date (Oxford: Oxford University Press, 1973–), II, 1v.
10. Henry James to Hendrik Anderson, 25 Nov. 1906 (James Papers, Univ. of Virginia).
11. Henry James, "The Middle Years," *The Novels and Tales of Henry James,* 24 vols. (New York: Charles Scribner's Sons, 1907–9), XVI, 103.
12. Henry James to Charles Scribner's Sons, 30 July 1905, *Henry James Letters,* IV, 367.
13. Theodora Bosanquet, *Henry James at Work* (London: The Hogarth Press, 1924), p. 13.
14. Henry James to James B. Pinker, 6 June 1905 (Collection of American Literature, Yale). In 1921–23, the Macmillan Company issued a comprehensive edition of *The Novels and Stories of Henry James* in thirty-five volumes.
15. James B. Pinker to E. L. Burlingame, 3 Aug. 1904 (Scribner Archive, Princeton). Pinker and Burlingame had first discussed the possibility of a collected edition of James's work in April 1900, but the matter was dropped later in the year.
16. E. L. Burlingame to James B. Pinker, 16 Sept. 1904 (Collection of American Literature, Yale).
17. James B. Pinker to Macmillan & Co., 17 July 1905 (Macmillan Archive, British Library).
18. Henry James to LeRoy Phillips, 8 Sept. 1904, quoted in *A Bibliography of Henry James,* 3rd ed., p. 11.
19. Henry James to Robert Herrick, 7 Aug. 1907, *The Selected Letters of Henry James,* p. 159.
20. Henry James to James B. Pinker, 25 June 1905 (Collection of American Literature, Yale).
21. James B. Pinker to Col. George B. M. Harvey, 18 April 1904, Harper Contract Books, XI, 340.
22. Harper Royalty Ledgers (1905–9), VI, 937–38; Harper Brothers to Charles Scribner's Sons, 3 Aug. 1905, Harper Contract Books, XI, 372.
23. George P. Brett to James B. Pinker, 21 June 1905 (Scribner Archive, Princeton).
24. Memorandum of a letter from the Macmillan Company to Charles Scribner's Sons, 23 June 1905 (Macmillan Archive, New York Public Library). Charles Scribner to James B. Pinker, 15 June 1905, Charles Scribner Letterbooks, XXV, 181; Pinker to Scribner, 22 June 1905; Scribner to Pinker, 23 June 1905, Charles Scribner Letterbooks, XXV, 195; and Pinker to Charles Scribner's Sons, 7 Feb. 1907 (Scribner Archive, Princeton).

25. Houghton, Mifflin & Co. to Charles Scribner's Sons, 19 Sept. 1905 (Scribner Archive, Princeton).
26. Houghton, Mifflin & Co. to Charles Scribner's Sons, 25 Oct. 1905 (Scribner Archive, Princeton).
27. Charles Scribner to James B. Pinker, 31 Oct. 1905, Charles Scribner Letterbooks, XXV, 319 (Scribner Archive, Princeton).
28. Memorandum of Agreement between Charles Scribner's Sons and Houghton, Mifflin & Co., 5 April 1906 (Scribner Archive, Princeton); Charles Scribner to James B. Pinker, 6 Oct. 1908 (Collection of American Literature, Yale). This was roughly equivalent to the 12½ percent royalty James was to receive on the Macmillan titles, since he—not Scribner's—was debited for Macmillan's permissions fee. James received 10 percent on all other volumes.
29. Memorandum of Agreement, 5 April 1906 (Scribner Archive, Princeton).
30. *Roderick Hudson* does not appear on Houghton, Mifflin's list, because James had voluntarily relinquished his royalties from that work after 1881, when the original sheet stock of the 1877 American edition was exhausted. Preferring to put his 1879 revised English text before the American public, James instructed the firm to import sheets from Macmillan for binding and distribution in the United States. He gave up his royalty—10 percent of the retail price—to compensate Houghton, Mifflin for their lost investment in the original stereotype plates. Hence the firm could hardly ask for an additional royalty on the Edition *Roderick Hudson* when they had paid James nothing during its continuous twenty-five year sale. Henry James to Houghton, Mifflin & Co., 23 Nov. [1881] (Houghton Mifflin Archive, Harvard).
31. Henry James to James B. Pinker, 10 June 1906 (Collection of American Literature, Yale).
32. Henry James to Charles Scribner's Sons, 27 Jan. 1908 (Scribner Archive, Princeton).
33. At least part of Scribner's anxiety resulted from the purely technical problem of composing type from James's terrifically revised texts. When the first installment of the revised *Roderick Hudson* arrived, a mutiny in the pressroom seemed likely:

> The portion [of *Roderick Hudson*] received gives us considerable concern and perplexity. Mr. James's interlineations and emendations, though made with the greatest care evidently as to clearness, are nevertheless so numerous and, from the point of view of "copy," so intricate that it is simply out of the question, we fear, for us to furnish it as it stands to the printers. . . . We should, we may say frankly, fear the effect on the cordial cooperation of the printers if we began with such difficult "copy." (Charles Scribner's Sons to James B. Pinker, 27 March 1906 [Scribner Archive, Princeton])

More important, Scribner was also concerned "lest Mr. James should so transform his early books that those who had known and delighted in them for years should feel disappointed with the new edition, owing to loss of freshness." Thus Pinker paraphrased Mr. Scribner in his response to the firm dated 15 June 1906 (Scribner Archive, Princeton). When informed of Scribner's reservations about his textual emendations, James immediately responded:

> Also let me add, for more explicitness than I have yet used, that I have absolutely no doubt whatever of the benefit I shall have conferred on each of [the revised novels]—and I mean of course benefit not only for myself, but for the public at large. It is beyond any question with me, for instance, that what I have just been very attentively doing for the "Portrait" [*may* crossed out] must give it a new lease of such life as it may still generally aspire to. (Henry James to Charles Scribner's Sons, 12 June 1906 [Scribner Archive, Princeton])

34. Houghton, Mifflin & Co. to Charles Scribner's Sons, 25 Oct. 1905 (Scribner Archive, Princeton).
35. Henry James to William Dean Howells, 17 Aug. 1908, *Letters of Henry James,* II, 100; Edel, "The Architecture of Henry James's 'New York Edition,'" p. 173.
36. Edel, *Henry James: The Master,* p. 322; Henry James to Charles Scribner's Sons, 9 May 1906, quoted in Edel, *The Master,* pp. 321–22.
37. Robert Herrick, "A Visit to Henry James," *Yale Review,* 12 (July 1923), 731. The letter to Howells is quoted above.
38. Henry James to James B. Pinker, 29 Sept. 1905 (Collection of American Literature, Yale).
39. Charles Scribner's Sons to Henry James, 27 April 1906 (Scribner Archive, Princeton); emphasis added.
40. Henry James to Charles Scribner's Sons, 9 May 1906, *Henry James Letters,* IV, 403–4. In the biography Edel omits James's emphasis in his quotation from this letter, which subtly shifts its meaning.
41. Henry James to James B. Pinker, 12 June 1906 (Collection of American Literature, Yale).
42. Henry James to William Dean Howells, 17 Aug. 1908, *Letters of Henry James,* II, 100; Henry James to Charles Scribner's Sons, 9 May 1906, *Henry James Letters,* IV, 403.
43. Henry James to Edmund Gosse, 25 Aug. 1915, *Henry James Letters,* IV, 777. These reasons also help to explain the absence of *Washington Square* and, coupled with the prospect of a reduced royalty, *The Europeans.* At least with respect to James's American stories, such commercial considerations had a self-intensifying editorial effect: exclusion of one precipitated the exclusion of others, because none was substantial enough to stand by itself in a single volume.
44. Henry James to Charles Scribner's Sons, 31 Dec. 1907, *Henry James Letters,* IV, 484–85.
45. W. C. Brownell to Henry James, 29 Jan. 1908 (Scribner Archive, Princeton).
46. Henry James to James B. Pinker, 12 June 1906 (Collection of American Literature, Yale).
47. See, for example, James's preface to *The Golden Bowl* in *The Art of the Novel,* p. 334 and passim; Joseph J. Firebaugh, "Coburn: Henry James's Photographer," *American Quarterly,* 7 (1955), 215–33; Edel, *Henry James: The Master,* pp. 333–38; and Charles Higgins, "Photographic Aperture: Coburn's Frontispieces to James's New York Edition," *American Literature,* 53 (Jan. 1982), 661–75.
48. Henry James to Charles Scribner's Sons, 26 Feb. 1908 (Scribner Archive, Princeton).

49. Henry James to Charles Scribner's Sons, 20 July 1908 (Scribner Archive, Princeton).
50. This information was gathered from various letters to Scribner's, the dates of which are given in the text. All are deposited in the Scribner Archive at Princeton.
51. Henry James to Charles Scribner's Sons, 10 March 1908 (Scribner Archive, Princeton).
52. *The Art of the Novel,* p. 130.
53. Edel, "The Architecture of Henry James's 'New York Edition,'" p. 177.
54. Henry James to Charles Scribner's Sons, 14 Dec. 1908 (Scribner Archive, Princeton); cf. Edel, *Henry James: The Master,* p. 339.
55. James B. Pinker to Charles Scribner, 16 Sept. 1908 (Scribner Archive, Princeton).
56. Charles Scribner to James B. Pinker, 6 Oct. 1908 (Collection of American Literature, Yale).
57. Henry James to James B. Pinker, 20 Oct. 1908 (Collection of American Literature, Yale).
58. Henry James to James B. Pinker, 23 Oct. 1908, *Henry James Letters,* IV, 498–99.
59. Entry for 23 Jan. 1895, *Notebooks,* p. 179.
60. Henry James to William Dean Howells, [31 Dec.] 1908, *Letters of Henry James,* II, 119. James knew whereof he spoke: his literary income in 1908 was smaller than it had been in 25 years. See Appendix B.

APPENDIX A

1. Laurence Hutton, *Talks in a Library with Laurence Hutton,* ed. Isabel Moore (New York: G. P. Putnam's Sons, 1905), pp. 415–16.
2. Henry James to Benjamin Ticknor, 28 Sept. [1884] (Collection of American Literature, Yale).
3. Henry James to Robert Underwood Johnson, 19 & 22 Dec. 1887 (Johnson Papers, Harvard).
4. Henry James to the American Copyright League, 15 Nov. 1887, *Selected Letters of Henry James,* p. 87.
5. Senator Jonathan Chace to Robert Underwood Johnson, [20 Aug.] 1888 (Johnson Papers [Correspondence re Copyright, Box 1], New York Public Library).
6. Henry James to Edmund Gosse, 29 June 1888 (Gosse Papers, Duke).
7. Edmund Gosse to Walter Besant, 4 July 1888, Add. MS 56864, ff. 51–52 (Society of Authors Deposit, British Library).
8. Henry James to Edmund Gosse, 6 July [1888], in Rayburn S. Moore, "A 'Literary-Gossippy Friendship': Henry James's Letters to Edmund Gosse," *Southern Review,* 20 (1984), 574–75.
9. Henry James to Edmund Gosse & Walter Besant, 12 July [1888], *Selected Letters of Henry James,* p. 91.
10. Henry James to Robert Louis Stevenson, 31 July [1888], *Henry James Letters,* III, 240.
11. Henry James to Edmund Gosse, 29 June 1888 (Gosse Papers, Duke).

APPENDIX B

1. J. D. Fleeman, "The Revenue of a Writer: Samuel Johnson's Literary Earnings," *Studies in the Book Trade: In Honour of Graham Pollard* [Oxford Bibliographical Society Publications, n.s. 18] (Oxford: Oxford Bibliographical Society, 1975), p. 211.
2. Henry Nash Smith, *Democracy and the Novel,* p. 143.
3. See, for example, Thomas Whiteside, *The Blockbuster Complex: Conglomerates, Show Business and Book Publishing* (Middletown, Conn.: Wesleyan Univ. Press, 1981); and Leonard Shatzkin, *In Cold Type: Overcoming the Book Crisis* (Boston: Houghton Mifflin, 1982).
4. Constantly feeling the pressure of magazine deadlines (and often despairing of an opportunity to read proof of his monthly installments, so that their inevitable errors and roughly written passages went uncorrected), James himself advised his friends to await the publication of his stories and novels in volume form, when he would have a chance to revise and improve his work. "[H]ow little the habit of writing in the serial form encourages one to read in that odious way," he told Howells, immediately adding, "[the way] so many simple folk, thank heaven, think the best" (Henry James to William Dean Howells, 2 Jan. 1888, *Henry James Letters,* III, 208).
5. Unfortunately, even the most comprehensive analysis of James's sales (Roger Gard's appendix to his compendium of contemporary reviews, *Henry James: The Critical Heritage,* pp. 545–57) assumes just the reverse. Mr. Gard bases his interpretation on a predicted correlation between the novelist's sales and "the fluctuations of his reputation" (p. 545)—not necessarily bad logic—but the data upon which this argument depends are conspicuously incomplete. Mr. Gard's research among English publishers' archives was quite exhaustive, but for American sales he relied upon the printing figures provided by Edel and Laurence in the second edition of their *Bibliography of Henry James* (1961). The *Bibliography* usually gives the size of first editions only; the absence of further evidence led Mr. Gard erroneously to assume that the American career of James's books followed the pattern of his English sales: it seemed "unlikely that there would be important reprintings [in America] when there were none in England" (p. 546). Many errors of fact result. For *The American:* "Osgood's first printing (the only one recorded in B[ibliography of] H[enry] J[ames]) was 1000" (p. 549); another 5300 copies were actually in print by 1915. For *The Europeans:* "Houghton, Osgood & Co. published 1500 copies . . . in October 1878 (the only printing recorded)" (p. 549); 2320 were printed later. For *The Portrait of a Lady:* Gard reports a first printing of 1500 in 1881 and "five further impressions by August 1882, making a total of 6500" (p. 551); in fact, the *Portrait* went through many more printings by 1915, at which point 14,400 copies were in circulation. By no means do the revised figures elevate James to best-seller status, but they do suggest that the widely held impression of his unpopularity may be unduly pessimistic. Evidence of additional American printings of James's work was gathered from the Houghton Mifflin Archive at Harvard and from files at the company's headquarters in Boston. See the List of Sources which follows these Notes for a more complete description of this material.

6. This statement was offered by Daniel Estes, a partner in the Boston publishing firm of Estes, Lauriet & Co., and is quoted by Frank Luther Mott in his authoritative *History of American Magazines,* 5 vols. (Cambridge, Mass.: Harvard Univ. Press, 1938–68), IV, 41–42.
7. William Dean Howells, "The Man of Letters as a Man of Business" [1893], p. 7.
8. Henry James to James B. Pinker, 29 June 1904 (Collection of American Literature, Yale).
9. Henry James to James B. Pinker, 30 June & 27 July 1904 (Collection of American Literature, Yale).
10. Kermit Vanderbilt, *Charles Eliot Norton: Apostle of Culture in a Democracy* (Cambridge, Mass.: Belknap-Harvard Univ. Press, 1959), p. 87.
11. Thomas Bailey Aldrich to William Dean Howells, 10 May 1884 (Howells Papers, Harvard).
12. Mrs. Henry James, Sr. to Henry James, 28 Feb. [1873] (James Papers, Harvard).
13. Justus R. Pearson, Jr., "Story of a Magazine: New York's *Galaxy,* 1866–1878," *Bulletin of the New York Public Library,* 61 (1957), 295.
14. Henry James to Mr. & Mrs. Henry James, Sr., 4 May [18]73, *Henry James Letters,* I, 378.
15. See Frank Luther Mott, *History of American Magazines,* III, 14; and Henry James to Mrs. Henry James, Sr., 13 Jan. [1878] (James Papers, Harvard).
16. Frank Luther Mott, *History of American Magazines,* II, 21 and IV, 39; and "Confessions of a Literary Hack," *Forum,* 19 (July 1895), 638.
17. Harper Memorandum Book, V, 402.
18. Henry James to William James, 30 May [1894] (James Papers, Harvard).
19. Roger Gard, *Henry James: The Critical Heritage,* p. 554.
20. Roger Gard to the author, 15 Jan. 1983.
21. Alan B. Donovan offers a useful introduction to the correspondence in "My Dear Pinker: The Correspondence of Henry James with His Literary Agent," *Yale University Library Gazette,* 36 (Oct. 1961), 78–88.
22. See "Earnings in Selected Occupations: 1865 to 1970," in *Historical Statistics of the United States: Colonial Times to 1970,* 2 vols. (Washington, D.C.: Government Printing Office, 1975), I, 175–76; and "Average Annual Military Compensation Rates: 1870 to 1982," in the *Statistical Abstract of the United States, 1982–83* (Washington, D.C.: Government Printing Office, 1982), p. 363.

List of Sources

BIBLIOGRAPHY

Blanck, Jacob, comp. "Henry James," *Bibliography of American Literature.* 7 vols. to date. New Haven, Conn.: Yale University Press, 1962– . V, 117–181.

Brussel, I. R. *Anglo-American First Editions, Part Two: West to East, 1786–1930.* New York: R. R. Bowker, 1936.

Edel, Leon, and Laurence, Dan H., with Rambeau, James. *A Bibliography of Henry James,* rev. 3rd ed. New York: Oxford University Press, 1982.

MANUSCRIPT: HENRY JAMES PAPERS

While much of Henry James's correspondence has been published, thousands of his letters are available only in manuscript form. The bulk of the James family papers are deposited in the Houghton Library at Harvard University (bMS Am 1092.9+, 1093.1+, 1094+). Included here are James's letters to and from his parents, his brother William, and his sister Alice. The Houghton Library also holds important letters from James to William Dean Howells (bMS Am 1784 [253]) and other editors of the *Atlantic Monthly,* including Thomas Bailey Aldrich (bMS Am 1429 [2547–2622]), Horace E. Scudder (bMS Am 1094.1), and Bliss Perry (bMS Am 1343 [271–79]). James's holograph notebooks are at Harvard, together with six small pocket diaries for the years 1909–15 that contain records, not always exhaustive, of his literary income (MS Am 1094).

Other important collections of James material that I have examined include those at: Duke University (thirty-nine letters to Sir Edmund Gosse and several others to James R. Osgood, Benjamin Ticknor, Robert

McClure, and Richard Watson Gilder); the Library of Congress (six letters to Osgood and Ticknor, and one to Frederick Macmillan [LM 629K vols. 11–12], twenty-five to Gosse [MMC 1398], and ten to George B. M. Harvey [Ac.D.R.E. 1650]); the Berg Collection and Manuscript Division of the New York Public Library (letters to various New York literary figures and publishers); the Clifton Waller Barrett Collection (No. 6251+) at the University of Virginia (including James's remarkable letters to Hendrik C. Andersen and Alvin Langdon Coburn, the photographer who prepared the frontispieces for the New York Edition, as well as several miscellaneous letters to publishers); the Collection of American Literature of the Beinecke Rare Book and Manuscript Library at Yale University (nearly five hundred letters and telegrams to James B. Pinker, James's literary agent from 1898 until the novelist's death in 1916, and ten to James R. Osgood & Co.); and the Brotherton Collection at the University of Leeds (about two hundred fifty letters to Sir Edmund Gosse and nineteen to Clement Shorter, editor of the *Illustrated London News,* about the serial publication of *The Other House*).

MANUSCRIPT: PUBLISHERS' ARCHIVES

Most of the surviving records of James's English and American publishers have at last found their way into public archives.

The records of Houghton Mifflin Company and its predecessors (Ticknor & Fields; Fields, Osgood & Co.; Hurd & Houghton; Houghton, Osgood & Co.; and Ticknor & Co.) are mostly at Harvard (fMS Am 1185+). The collection includes letter books, production records, contract files, and surprisingly complete records of royalty payments. Much of this material remains uncatalogued. Also at Harvard are approximately eighty letters to and from James and his agent (bMS Am 1925).

The Archives of Harper and Brothers, 1817–1914, deposited at Columbia University Library, have recently been microfilmed by Chadwyck-Healey Ltd. (Cambridge and Teaneck, N.J., 1982), together with a printed index. The records include copies of contracts for all of James's books published by the Harpers, as well as royalty ledgers for the years 1884–1915 (virtually coterminous with James's affiliation with the firm). The Pierpont Morgan Library houses James's scenario for and correspondence relating to *The Ambassadors.*

The Scribner Archive at Princeton University holds James's voluminous correspondence wtih Charles Scribner's Sons (Author Files I, Boxes 80–82). The firm's responses can be traced in the letter books of Charles Scribner (26 vols., 1875–1906), Edward L. Burlingame (23 vols., 1879–1907), and William C. Brownell (10 vols., 1888–1910). Carbon flimsies of other letters are filed with James's letters to the firm. Unfortunately, the record of his sales and royalties is far less complete; the only surviving royalty ledger covers the years 1898–1903, although other payments are occasionally documented in the correspondence.

Records of the American branch of the Macmillan Company are deposited in the Manuscript Division of the New York Public Library. The bulk of these are files of correspondence with Macmillan authors. Seventeen letters from James or his agent are included. Other useful collections at the library are the Robert Underwood Johnson Papers (especially his correspondence relating to international copyright) and the account books for the *Nation* magazine, which record payments to James from 1873 through 1879.

The single most important source of information about James's publishing career in England is the Macmillan Archive at the British Library. James's correspondence with Frederick Macmillan is conveniently collected in one manuscript volume (Add. MS 54931), but responses from the firm must be traced through 133 volumes of press-copy letter books, covering the years 1877–1916, most of which have been meticulously restored and preserved (Add. MS 55403–55535). Other important records include the firm's correspondence with its American subsidiary (Add. MS 54797–54815, 55283–55292).

The records of Chatto & Windus have recently been transferred to the University of Reading. James's negotiations for the English rights to *Confidence* can be traced in the company's letter books (MS 2444/11–13), into which have also been tipped a number of James's holograph letters to the firm.

The archives of William Blackwood & Sons are deposited in the National Library of Scotland at Edinburgh. James's correspondence relating to the publication of *William Wetmore Story and His Friends* can be found here (MS 4660, ff. 145–47; MS 4702, ff. 27–30), although Blackwood's letter accepting James's terms for the book is deposited at Harvard (bMS Am 1095.2 [1a]).

The records of James's dealings with other English publishers are still in private hands. Many firms (such as Chapman & Hall and Martin Secker) lost their older files of correspondence during World War II, but considerable holdings have survived. Most important in James's case are the contracts and printing records for the books he published with Methuen (almost all the fiction after 1900); these can be found in the files of Associated Book Publishers at London and Andover. The contract for *The Wings of the Dove* is still on file at Constable & Co.; James's signed receipt for a seven-year lease of the rights to "In the Cage" is one of the earliest documents in the files of Gerald Duckworth & Co. Contracts for ten of James's books and a small number of the novelist's letters are still in the files of William Heinemann Ltd., but production and sales records have been destroyed.

One almost wishes that James had had more extensive dealings with John Murray, because this firm has made an extraordinary effort to preserve its historical archives, which can be examined by appointment at 50 Albemarle Street (an address associated with the house for almost two hundred years). A handful of letters from James to John Murray and George Prothero, editor of the *Quarterly Review,* is stored here, but they are more a record of failed opportunities to publish James than of anything else.

WORKS BY HENRY JAMES

The American Essays of Henry James. Ed. Leon Edel. New York: Vintage Books, 1956.

The Art of the Novel: Critical Prefaces. Ed. Richard P. Blackmur. New York: Charles Scribner's Sons, 1934.

Autobiography: A Small Boy and Others; Notes of a Son and Brother; The Middle Years. Ed. Frederick W. Dupee. New York: Criterion Books, 1956.

The Bostonians. London and New York: Macmillan, 1886.

The Complete Plays of Henry James. Ed. Leon Edel. Philadelphia: J. B. Lippincott, 1949.

The Complete Tales of Henry James. 12 vols. Ed. Leon Edel. Philadelphia: J. B. Lippincott, 1961–64.

Confidence. 1880; rpt. New York: Grosset & Dunlap, 1962.

Essays in London and Elsewhere. New York: Harper and Brothers, 1893.

French Poets and Novelists. 1878; rpt. London: Macmillan, 1908.

The Future of the Novel: Essays on the Art of Fiction. Ed. Leon Edel. New York: Vintage Books, 1956.

Hawthorne. 1879; rpt. New York: St. Martin's Press, 1967.

Henry James Letters. 4 vols. Ed. Leon Edel. Cambridge, Mass.: Belknap-Harvard University Press, 1972–84.

The Ivory Tower and *Notes for The Ivory Tower. The American Novels and Stories of Henry James.* Ed. F. O. Matthiessen. New York: Knopf, 1947.

The Letters of Henry James. 2 vols. Ed. Percy Lubbock. New York: Charles Scribners Sons, 1920.

Letters of Henry James to Walter Berry. Paris: The Black Sun Press, 1928.

Letters to A. C. Benson and Auguste Monod. Ed. E. F. Benson. New York: Charles Scribner's Sons, 1930.

Letters to an Editor. Ed. Clement Shorter. London: privately printed, 1916.

"A Most Unholy Trade," Being Letters on the Drama by Henry James. Cambridge, Mass.: Dunster House, 1923.

The Notebooks of Henry James. Ed. F. O. Matthiessen and Kenneth B. Murdock. New York: Oxford University Press, 1947.

Notes on Novelists with Some Other Notes. New York: Charles Scribner's Sons, 1914.

The Novels and Tales of Henry James. 24 vols. The New York Edition. New York: Charles Scribner's Sons, 1907–9.

Parisian Sketches: Letters to the New York Tribune, 1875–1876. Ed. Leon Edel and Ilse Dusoir Lind. New York: New York University Press, 1957.

Partial Portraits. 1888; rpt. Ann Arbor: University of Michigan Press, 1970.

The Portrait of a Lady. Boston: Houghton, Mifflin, [1881].

The Princess Casamassima. London and New York: Macmillan, 1886.

The Question of Our Speech, The Lesson of Balzac: Two Lectures. Boston: Houghton, Mifflin, 1905.

The Scenic Art: Notes on Acting & the Drama, 1872–1901. Ed. Allan Wade. New Brunswick, N.J.: Rutgers University Press, 1948.

The Selected Letters of Henry James. Ed. Leon Edel. New York: Farrar, Straus and Cudahy, 1955.

The Sense of the Past. London: W. Collins Sons, [1917].

The Tales of Henry James. 3 vols. to date. Ed. Maqbool Aziz. New York: Oxford University Press, 1973– .

The Tragic Muse. 2 vols. Boston: Houghton, Mifflin, 1890.

Index

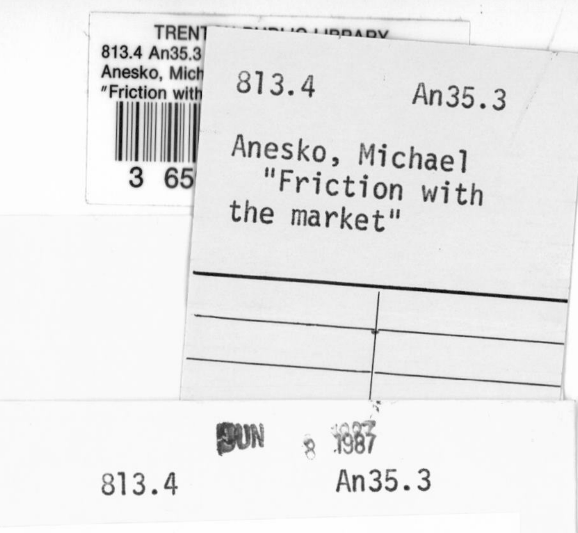